TRACKS ACROSS ALASKA

For Sheena and

Silver

Duran

Sensor

Alf

Nanook

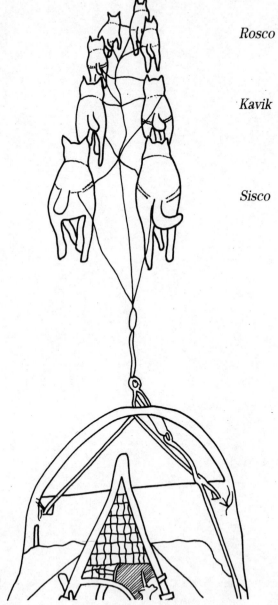

Rosco

Kavik

Sisco

TRACKS
Across
Alaska

A Dog Sled Journey

Alastair Scott

JOHN MURRAY

Other books by the author

SCOT FREE
A SCOT GOES SOUTH
A SCOT RETURNS

First published in 1990
by John Murray (Publishers) Ltd
50 Albemarle Street, London W1X 4BD

British Library Cataloguing in Publication Data
Scott, Alastair, *1954–*
   Alaska: a dog sled journey.
   1. Alaska. Description & travel
   I. Title
   917.98'045

   ISBN 0–7195–4773–3

Printed in Great Britain by
Butler & Tanner Ltd,
Frome and London

Acknowledgements

The dogs, of course.

The Bardarson family, for the loan of your cabin and the gift of your philosophy. You were part of the inspiration for this journey.

Gene Horning, for giving a hitchhiker a lift and taking him 1,200 miles out of your way.

Joee and Pam Redington, for your dogs, your generosity, for making a musher out of me. Without your support I could never have made the transition in time.

Eric Meffley, Linda Nelson, Linda O'Brian, Gwen Evans, and Carol and Tonya Schlentner, for dogs, dog advice, encouragement and home-cooking.

The inhabitants of Manley – especially: Damaris Mortvedt, Jim Catlin, Steve Fortelny, Cleo, Rose, the Hollingsworths, Pearsons, Zincks, Woods, Lees, Wrights, Darts, Kurt and Yvonne – for setting an extra place for winter and being my insurance against cabin fever.

Susan Butcher and David Monson, for dogs, meat, dog boxes, hours of talk, six punctures and the road to Minnesota. (My pullover is still shrunk.)

The many who assisted along the way, sharing your country, thoughts and homes. My debt of gratitude is large. I am overdrawn particularly to Bill and Kathy Fliris, Rod and Jan Kocsis, Victor and Judy Katongan, Jim Dory, Suz Burd, John Bryant and Peggy Kuropat. (Certain names have been changed and certain encounters relocated in order to preserve the anonymity and privacy of those for whom my route continues to provide a home.)

Macmillan London Ltd. for permission to quote from Barry Lopez, *Arctic Dreams*, pp. 310, 392, 298, 255, 258 and 345.

The publishers of *Pacific Northwest Quarterly* for permission to reproduce passages from Ed Jesson's account, 'From Dawson to Nome on a Bicycle', edited by Ruth Reat, in Vol. 47 (1956), pp. 65–74.

Hamish Hamilton Ltd. for permission to reprint an excerpt from John McPhee, *Coming into the Country*, p. 313.

The *Anchorage Daily News* for permission to quote from 'A People in Peril' (1988).

The passage on p. 206 is reproduced by permission of the Smithsonian Institution Press from *The Eskimo about Bering Strait*, Edward W. Nelson. © Smithsonian Institution, Washington, DC, 1983, p. 339. Originally published in 1899 as Part 1 of the Eighteenth Annual Report of the Bureau of American Ethnology. The legend on pp. 183–4 and the extract on p. 99 are reproduced by permission of the Smithsonian Institution Press from *inua: Spirit World of the Bering Sea Eskimo*, William W. Fitzhugh and Susan A. Kaplan. © Smithsonian Institution, Washington, DC, 1983, from the Introduction and p. 41 respectively.

Lastly, if obstructions must be thanked for this journey to rank as adventure, my appreciation goes to blizzards, cold, overflow, weak ice and Alaska's largest bank.

Illustrations

All photographs are the author's own.

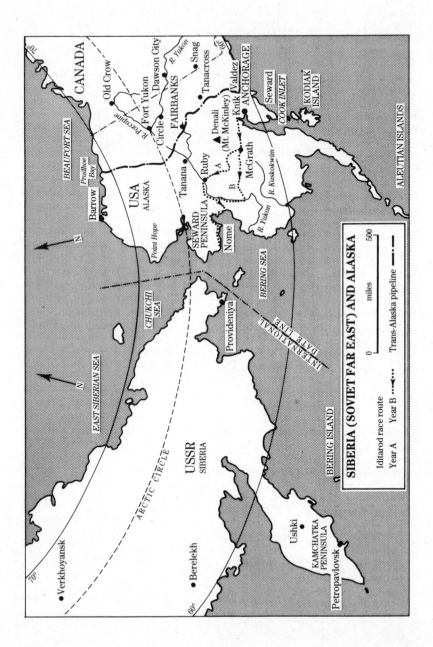

SIBERIA (SOVIET FAR EAST) AND ALASKA

Iditarod race route

Year A ··—··—··—

Year B ··········

━━━ Trans-Alaska pipeline

0   miles   500

1

THE IDEA OF making a journey with sledge dogs came out of a pot of simmering sheep heads. The pot had previously simmered skate wings, cods' heads, whales, pigs' hearts and a long litany of other horribles. What had not been horrible before became so as a result of my well-intentioned but incompetent interference. At the time I was pretending to be a cook because *Sudviking* needed a cook. *Sudviking* was a Danish freighter which worked the coasts of Greenland. I wanted to visit these coasts and so, naturally enough, I had signed on. My whale was tough, my pigs' hearts rubbery. My cods' heads fell to pieces. My sheep heads scowled. My captain scowled. The crew scowled. Each day the pot brought a new gallon of misery; and each day the galley porthole drew up the steam, drew my gaze to the land I had come to see, and framed a new dream of adventure.

The view thrilled me. It was unscrolled by the porthole, reversed and then repeated as *Sudviking* nudged aside icebergs and wove through a maze of sea channels. Below mountains sometimes scabrous and jagged, sometimes squashed and rounded, Greenland villages were sprinkles of bright colour in littoral boulder fields. Each was a habitation far removed from its neighbour in this land without roads, no more than a collection of small wooden houses, meat racks and strings of dogs. Ponderous wooden sledges lay on the beaches above high-water. They were harder to spot as they were the colour of driftwood and often used as supports for kayaks, the handlebars holding bow or stern proud.

My gaze always sought out dogs and sledges. It was spring then and Greenland was like a theatre out of season – ornate but empty, all grandeur but no action. I could only look on the dogs, chained in quagmires of neglect and running circles of boredom throughout the long snowless days, and transport them to winter in my mind. I borrowed the sledges as well and tried to piece the two images together and experience vicariously what I yearned should become reality. We never got far, my dogs and I. In the same way that I can never visualise enough well-behaved sheep leaping over fences to induce sleep, my sledge journeys always fell apart. They began and ended at the cooking pot. But ambition simmered on.

Nine years later my desire to travel with sledge dogs had become consuming. Anywhere in the snowlands of the north would do. I read every book I could find on the arctic and sub-arctic regions, from Greenland to Alaska. My quest for arcticabilia had me perusing Eskimo legends of genesis, frowning at ghoulish faces of *inua* – spirits – carved in ivory, and infiltrating the expeditions of explorers. I stuck with them even though they were superhuman and their suffering chilled me by the fireside. I followed the leaf-shaped tracks of Samuel Hearne on his epic two-year walk along the Coppermine River in the North West Territories, rubbed shoulders with Nansen on his Polar Expedition, and warmed my frostbitten skin which turned white out of sympathy for Rasmussen in Greenland. The redoubtable Amundsen left me breathless as he sailed, skied, sledded and ballooned the Arctic. He was a character much more to my liking than Cook or Peary, whom I abandoned, leaving them to blow their own trumpets to improbable conquests. There were many others. The Arctic had attracted its share of vainglorious fools, but also an uncommon number of quiet heroes.

I searched their writings for mention of dogs, how to handle and care for them. I searched for an understanding of the environment, why it attracted them, how to survive it. Victorian explorers were often discouraging. In their photographs they modelled self-sacrifice with sullen expressions and glaring, icicle-sharp eyes. For them, smiling was clearly incompatible with a heroic stance. The Arctic was to be endured, never enjoyed. They played on its reputation in order to enhance theirs. J. W. Tyrrell, for example, in his *Across the Sub-Arctic of Canada* (1895), refers to the natives as 'savages' despite their hospitality and assistance, and is unstintingly wordy on the privations he had to suffer while living among them. This is his disclosure on personal hygiene:

> With travellers in the north, particularly during the winter season, the practice of performing daily ablutions is quite unheard of. This is not due to neglect, but is rather an enforced custom due to the painful effects produced by the application of ice-cold water to the skin.

But Tyrrell did make me want to chew a genuine old Eskimo shoe.

> ... these boots or moccasins ... after having been wet and dried again, become
> very hard and the most convenient or effective – or possibly the most agreeable –
> way of softening them seems to be by mastication. ... nearly every morning
> the native women soften the shoes of the family most beautifully by chewing
> them. What to us would seem the disagreeable part of this operation cannot be
> thoroughly understood by one who has not some idea of the flavour of a
> genuine old Eskimo shoe.

Of all the travellers I came to know, Archbishop Hudson Stuck
was my favourite. I read and reread his *Ten Thousand Miles With a
Dogsled* until I could picture him in perfect detail, standing behind
the sacramental cloth which hung permanently from the sledge's
handlebars as he mushed across his parish – Alaska. He became my
mentor. I moulded myself on him. We became the closest of friends –
of a kind, for he died in 1921.

Frederick Schwatka, whose 1880 sledge journey remains one of
the longest ever recorded, taught me the essential dog commands.
AH-ROOT evidently turned the dogs to the left. WHY-AH-WAH-HA sent
them to the right. WHOA, as with horses, stopped them. To spur them
on you needed to let fly with AH-WAH-HAGH-OO-AR, even though it
sounded like a curse on hot soup.

Duncan Pryde, in *Nunaga* (1971), explained how to prepare a
sledge's runners.

> When it gets cold, the Eskimos flip the sled over upside-down and mix mud
> with water .... The mud is worked up and down the runner so that it is four or
> five inches deep, and is plastered right down around the edges to help it grip.
> ... The mud runner is allowed to freeze until it sets like concrete. Then an
> ordinary jackplane is used to plane the mud as smooth as possible ... then a
> pad of bear skin is dipped in water and brushed continuously along the mud
> runner ... until a layer of ice half an inch thick has been built up.

In the same way that I suspected igloos would be as alien to most
Eskimos as they were to me, I felt confident the use of mud runners
must have become outmoded by synthetic materials. But every bit
of knowledge might prove helpful in an emergency. I noted also that
'Cooked porridge can substitute for mud'. I felt cut out for this
lifestyle. I always travelled with porridge.

Barry Lopez's *Arctic Dreams* (1986) was far too precious to leave behind so I packed it along with Stuck's *Ten Thousand Miles*. Then I felt ready to go to the far north to find some dogs.

AH-WAH-HAGH-OO-AR!

2

The literature of arctic exploration is frequently offered as a record of resolute will before the menacing fortifications of the landscape. It is more profitable, I think, to disregard this notion – that the land is an adversary bent on human defeat, that the people who came and went were heroes or failures in this. It is better to contemplate the record of human longing to achieve something significant, to be free of some of the grim weight of life. That weight was ignorance, poverty of spirit, indolence, and the threat of anonymity and destitution.... In these arctic narratives, then, are the threads of dreams that serve us all.

Barry Lopez, *Arctic Dreams*

3

THE FIRST STAGE was by bus from Aberdeen to London. Aberdeen Coach station was surrounded by huge billboards with advertisements so clever no one knew what their products were. Its pavements were congested with passengers leading suitcases at heel like surrogate pets. On the bus I was seated next to an eighteen-year-old youth who had trained locally to be a chef. Malcolm Dermott, with a Roman nose and deep sunken eyes, was tall and gangling and capable of endless words unsupported by thought. He ran through an exhaustive explanation of his failings. He had found this 'module' too boring, that module too difficult, and had failed modules one, two and four for cleanliness. He had, however, passed cleaning module three, which covered the correct colour of scrubber appropriate to floor surfaces and the cleaning of lavatories.

Malcolm was unemployed. He had tried all the north-east hotels (including the Ambassador, seventeen times) and had been turned down. Now he was on his way to an interview at the London Hilton. He had applied to win a bet with a friend who had dared him to try 'one of the big ones'. He had done it as a joke but, to his surprise, had received an interview appointment by return.

It was a wretched journey. My non-smoker seat was in the lungs of the smoking section. The conductor simply snapped, 'You booked the last seat on the bus – take it or leave it.' The would-be chef kept me steeped in smoke. I imagined the ash he dribbled falling into his sauces and understood how modules one, two and four were lost. The bus broke down for two hours on the hard shoulder of the M6. When we reached London the chef and I shook hands and parted. He was going to the Hilton, I was going to the Arctic.

It was hard to feel invigorated as I tripped across Trafalgar Square with its fifty pigeons to a flagstone. This certainly wasn't the start one expected of a trek across Alaska. My only solace was the conviction that travelling with huskies had to be more comfortable than travelling with Scottish Citylink.

The second stage was by plane from London to Montreal – Montreal was the cheapest transatlantic destination at the time. The plane flew over Ireland. Through a scattering of cloud shavings those passengers with window seats glimpsed striking patterns on the land, minute rectangles and polygons in yellows and greens. Later we spied the coast of Labrador, a smattering of long islands like mud wind-sprayed over a blue floor. Then came the mottled browns and greys of tundra. Its emptiness excited me, and then, imagining myself alone down there in winter, I felt afraid. Mid September had not yet brought snow to this latitude, but it was only a matter of days away. I was beginning to understand Tyrrell's icicle-sharp eyes and sullen expressions when the plane landed in the bright lights and unabashed commercialism that are so many North American cities. They always seemed the same, concentrations of plastic colours and big letters shrilling for my attention. They suddenly made the tundra feel more like home.

The third stage was to travel 5,000 miles overland to a hamlet called Manley Hot Springs, Alaska, on the far side of the continent. This stage began with a forty-seven-hour bus journey to Wyoming – a slightly indirect route to Manley but I had a modest writing commission to undertake there. That was my last paid fare. Hitch-hiking took me the rest of the way faster than I could have driven in my own car.

An early travelling companion was Cin (or Sin, I didn't seek confirmation) Elders, a middle-aged woman with overgrazed hair. We met beside a stall which sold peaked caps sporting such slogans as 'If you feel I don't love you – feel again' and 'OLD FART'. Cin's small features swam in a pudgy face and all her movements battled with inertia. Her casual sports clothes were designed baggy but worn under tension. With motherly concern she hugged a grip and a bouquet of timetables. She consulted her leaflets and scribblings again and again, fussing and constantly confirming places and times until I felt sure travel for her was a paranoia of breathless dashes, wrong buses and missed connections. This was not the case. The worry was a crafted excuse to talk to strangers, to conquer, momentarily, loneliness. Aside from wanting to reach a destination, she travelled not to notice but to be noticed.

'Hi! Where you heading for? Chicago, I guess...'

'Yes, but passing straight through. I'm really heading for Alaska.'

'Your accent! Hey, don't tell me ... now let me see...' Thus preoccupied with my accent, she took some time to react to my destination. '*Alaska!*' she shrieked. 'Oh my, my!' Cin's face furrowed in sympathy. 'You have to, I suppose.'

Behind those furrows were the stereotyped images. Alaska was encased in permanent ice. Eskimos and draft-dodgers lived there. Soldiers, Okies, Texans, pipe-fitters, roughnecks, roustabouts, and *National Geographic* photographers were sent there to work: hardship postings. Alaska had oil, crab, salmon, and whales whose sticking-up tails made famous posters. Otherwise it was cold and useless. People went there out of necessity or desperation. 'You have to, I suppose.'

Cin's reaction was repeated by others, again and again, though interspersed with occasional expressions of envy. Alaska's name derives from the Aleutian Islanders' word 'Alaxsxaq', meaning the mainland or Great Land. It evokes only extreme responses, abhorrence or reverence, all compounded by misconception. When plans to go there are revealed, no intending visitor expects friends to exclaim 'Oh, how lovely!'; rather, the reaction one assumes Hannibal got when he confided to his mother his plans for elephants and the Alps. A trip to Alaska must not be casually mentioned, but proclaimed.

Justification is required, and if handled deftly wins admirers but seldom followers. You never simply 'go' to Alaska, you make an expedition there. Or so the popular myths run. Though for some it remains simply an economic destination, and for others a virgin state where the only laws are those of nature, The Last Frontier still in the recesses of southern minds. Ignored and grossly misunderstood, Alaska is an enduring mystery, continually teasing the imagination.

The mystery endures because of the intrinsic diversity of the land and the conflicting reports engendered; because the modern stampede of pioneers who career up the 1,500-mile Alaska–Canada (Alcan) Highway to bag the 49th state in mobile homes laden with boat, bicycle, windsurfer, everything but the garden gate, and car in tow – their bravado, 'Alaska or Bust!' plastered to the rear window – are confined to the relatively minute area where roads exist; and because there is a certain unwillingness to destroy a myth, to replace a fantasy of the unknown with knowledge.

How does one reconcile Alaska's diversity with the image of a single land? A land where, at one end, 4 inches of precipitation fall annually, and at the other, over 220 inches; where seventeen of the twenty highest mountains in the USA are to be found, and elsewhere regions so flat that topographic maps consist only of one or two lonely, meandering contours; where traffic jams are not infrequent yet where, beyond them, one Alaskan may not see another for months; where Eskimos hunt whales from walrus-hide boats and are directors of commercial corporations; where there is so much land and only 500,000 people, yet where it is forbidden, or beyond the means of most, to buy even a single acre; where the world's two great superpowers are separated, in summer, by two and a half miles of sea and joined, in winter, by a sheet of ice four feet thick (I dug a hole to check); where your weekly pay can be a couple of beaver pelts or 2,000 oily dollars; where, in comparison with the national average, *ten* times more native youths are likely to commit suicide than their white counterparts.

And why on earth was I going to Alaska if I didn't have to, Cin wanted to know? I found it hard to reply because it seemed that anyone who had to ask the question probably wouldn't understand the answer. Alaska would provide a sledge dog environment equal to Greenland, with fewer language problems, and two Alaskans had already offered me advice and assistance. The more I contemplated

7

Alaska, the tighter its fascination took hold. Its history was rife with characters and events so odd they bordered on the inconceivable, and in their own way they had also played a part in deciding my destination. It became obvious that Alaska was a world apart and had always attracted those outside convention – even long before Vitus Bering, the first white man associated with the Great Land, arrived to continue the tradition.

Cin would have understood Bering's motives for going there. He had had to.

4

THE EVENTS WHICH led to Russia's annexation of Alaska were set in motion with this intent by the six-and-a-half-foot Czar, Peter the Great. His chief instrument in the plan was a dumpy Dane, Vitus Johannes Bering. Their goal was eventually attained, but in a way neither had anticipated, and neither lived to see it.

By 1724 the fur trade had brought Russian interests to the eastern reaches of their empire. Knowledge of Siberia nevertheless remained sketchy, depending partly on the hearsay of traders and trappers and partly on the reports submitted by tax men exacting tithes of fur from the natives. The nearest known European colonies were Spanish Mexico and Peru, but Peter the Great could not be certain. It now seems probable that he knew Siberia and North America were *not* connected by land, as was previously thought, and feared European interest in finding a north-west passage to the Far East. If this passage around the north of Canada existed, foreign ships would arrive off Siberia, threatening his dominion. This was one concern, but his main preoccupation was with the state of affairs in North America. Bering was dispatched for the purposes of discovering a way to the new land and gathering information about it.

During his long tyranny, Peter the Great had brought about such a rapid expansion of Russia's navy that he had been forced to employ foreign captains. Bering had been invited to serve, changed his name to Ivan Ivanovich, fought with distinction on three seas and, when prospects of further promotion diminished, returned to Denmark as Captain (Second Class). Due to his exemplary record he was invited back in 1724, promoted to Captain (First Class) and, under oath of secrecy, sent on his first exploratory voyage.

It was no light assignment. From St Petersburg to the Kamchatka Peninsula and his port of departure, Petropavlosk, was a distance of 5,900 miles and it took his vast entourage four years to reach it. The resulting voyage achieved nothing. Bering sailed up to latitude 67°N and spotted the Diomede Islands but fog prevented him from seeing mainland America. On a clear day it would have been visible, just twenty-two miles away. Afraid of encroaching ice he turned back to Petropavlosk and then made the return journey overland to St Petersburg. Of the sixty months he had been away, only three had been spent at sea.

Bering was criticised for having aborted his voyage too soon and, at his own request, he was sent to undertake a second voyage to this *terra incognita*. Anxious that *something* beneficial to knowledge or empire should come out of this attempt, the authorities enlarged the project until it turned into an exploratory circus. Bering's voyage was to be just a part of the Second Kamchatka Expedition, and it took three years to gather the whole troupe together. Bering was fifty-three years old when he set off in 1733 with almost three thousand men, including dozens of cooks, astronomers, physicists, chemists, fourteen bodyguards, twelve doctors, seven priests, three bakers and two landscape painters; four thousand horses, a library containing hundreds of tomes, and a ludicrous assembly of fifteen-foot telescopes on wheels. Bering was required not only to honour the late Czar's instructions – in effect, to annex new lands on the American continent and exploit their animal and mineral resources – but, as he went, to Christianise the Siberian natives, build lighthouses along Russia's Pacific coast and establish a postal system along the way.

It took this second expedition five years to cross the desolate steppes and tundra. The cooks converted most of the horses into stew during the bitter winters. Bering had imprudently advised his superiors that the expedition would not cost the treasury more than 12,000 roubles. By then four years behind schedule and 300,000 roubles overdrawn, Bering learned through his new postal system

9

that his salary had been halved and his promotion to Admiral denied. He shrugged and persevered.

At Petropavlosk Bering had the *St Peter* (*Saviatoi Petr*) built for himself and a sister ship, *St Paul* (*Saviatoi Pavel*), for her captain, Aleksei Chirikov. The voyage began on 4 September 1740. Among Bering's company was a twenty-three-year old German of exceptional abilities. He had been signed on as a replacement mineralogist and to him fell the task of assaying the rock-borne wealth of the new territories. Georg Wilhelm Steller was a polymath, but a naturalist at heart. Through his diaries the world would learn of arctic foxes, sea cows and Vitus Bering's harrowing fate.

By mutual agreement Bering and Chirikov decided to make 'Juan da Gama' their first priority and wasted weeks which would later prove vital hunting for this mythical land. When they eventually abandoned the search and headed north, a storm blew up and separated the two ships. They never re-established contact. Chirikov reached the American shore near today's Sitka and sent a landing party of eleven men ashore. They rowed out of sight round a headland and were massacred by Tlingit Indians. When they failed to return after several days Chirikov unwittingly dispatched another four men to the same fate. After their disappearance he guessed the truth. The *St Paul* weighed anchor, unfurled her sails and headed back to Petropavlosk, losing a further seven men to scurvy on the way.

The *St Peter* happened to sail on a course almost parallel to that of the *St Paul*, only further north, and so likewise took one of the longest routes possible to the American coast. Bering saw and named Mount St Elias on the mainland before being enveloped in bad weather for three days. When he came across a small island (later named Kayak Island) he allowed Steller to go ashore for a short time to assay and record. In the ten years of Steller's life that this expedition occupied, only ten hours were spent on official duties. When he returned on board, the ship turned for home. By November 1741 the *St Peter* had lost twelve men to scurvy, out of her complement of eighty-two, and thirty-four were too weak to work. Bering himself was suffering from the disease. He beached the ship on a barren island a little over one hundred miles east of the Kamchatka Peninsula. Thus the discovery that would trigger the invasion of Alaska was made, *not* in Alaska, but in Russian Siberia.

The island provided so little shelter that the survivors dug pits in the sand. They transferred the remaining food from the ship to their wretched quarters and killed sea otters to lay in store against a shortfall. The abundance of sea otters was the island's only charity. The men ate the meat and used the pelts as blankets. Winds ravaged the region, temperatures plummeted, books had to be warmed with body heat before frozen pages could be turned, and scurvy continued its relentless rotting. And all the time there were arctic foxes, small, fearless and hungry. 'They crowded into our dwellings by day and by night,' Steller wrote, 'stole everything they could carry away, including articles that were of no use to them, like knives, sticks, bags, shoes, sacks, caps, etc.... While skinning [sea] animals, it often happened that we stabbed two or three foxes with our knives, because they wanted to tear the meat from our hands.... They observed all that we did and accompanied us on whatever project we undertook.' The foxes gnawed on the frozen bodies of sailors placed around the pits as windbreaks and they tried to gnaw on the dying. Vitus Bering died on the morning of 8 December, aged sixty, leaving his name to a sea he had no reason to love and to the island on which his expedition and his life foundered.

Steller struggled on. He concocted a palliative for scurvy out of wild grasses, and he discovered a strange sea mammal. Cracked and gnarled in appearance, it grew to between twenty-five and thirty feet in length and weighed over four tons. Two stumpy forelegs dragged its bulk through the shallows to which it was confined and here it grazed on seaweed, crushing the strands between two horny plates which served in the absence of teeth. The creatures lived in herds and, when resting, would roll over onto their backs and drift like logs. When one was harpooned, hunters reported, the others made pitiful attempts to free the victim. But they were easy game. Twenty-seven years after their discovery, the Northern or Steller's Sea Cow (*Hydrodamalis stelleri*) was extinct.

Forty-six men survived that hellish winter. Steller was one of them. They built a smaller *St Peter* from the timbers of the original, loaded it with their otter pelts and limped back to Petropavlosk.

They arrived on 27 August 1742. Up to that moment their expedition had lasted 9 years and 163 days, and cost 2 million roubles. They had nothing to show for it, nothing but a boatload of otter pelts. Yet it was enough. Siberia had become commercially trapped out and the fur trade had slumped. When traders and hunters heard about the boatload of rich pelts, eyes sparkled and boats were made ready. The hunt for the sea otter was on and it would lure unscrupulous men along the Aleutian archipelago to the great land beyond.

This was the first episode in the arrival of the white man in Alaska. If it was tragic, the next was far worse.

5

EVEN TO THIS day one of the most offensive insults a native of south-west Alaska can sling at a white man is 'Cossack'. The insult might be more apt, though less pronounceable, as *promyshlenniki*, for these were the first and most ruthless of the hunters who now used the Aleutian Islands as stepping stones. They were an ugly assortment of traders and thugs, mostly criminals who had opted for banishment to the east rather than execution, and for a century they terrorised their way across Siberia, trapping the sable (marten) to virtual extinction. Lusting now for the pelt of the sea otter they entered Alaska in hordes.

Article Four of the instructions given to Bering on his second voyage stated: 'If people are found there [America], they are to be treated kindly and in no way antagonised.... Should they wish of their own will to become our subjects, they are to be accepted as such. They should be treated especially with kindness and if necessary given protection and not burdened in any way.' Had the *promyshlenniki* been made aware of this, they still wouldn't have cared. They enslaved the Aleuts, worked them without food until they died, shot them for sport, and moved on. Among them, Feodor Solovief is recorded as having been curious to see how many men could be killed with a single shot from his musket. He had one dozen Aleuts lined up, tightly bunched chest to back, and he fired from point-blank range. Nine men toppled over dead, leaving three hysterical with fear.

By 1750 Russia had a firm hold on the edge of Alaska despite fiery opposition from the Tlingits. Explorers had made systematic landings along the coast and laid claim to the territory, marking each spot with the Romanov insignia of a two-headed eagle. Permanent trading posts were gradually established. The Russian-American Company came into being and Catherine the Great granted it a monopoly over the great blank on her globe, similar to the one the Hudson's Bay Company had received over the adjacent unknown. At the end of the first fifty years of Russian occupation the Aleut population had been reduced from an estimated 20,000 to 2,000 people, the sea otter had become rare and missionaries had arrived, carrying an invitation to the Good Life and the usual bag of white man's diseases. Sixty-five years later, the sea otter had all but vanished, half the Eskimo population had died through epidemics, and the Russians had danced Sitka's nights away at society balls, penetrated 500 miles up the Yukon River, and bumped into a little party of American telegraph engineers industriously unwinding a cable to Europe.

As attempts to lay a communication cable under the Atlantic met with continued failure, a subsidiary of the Western Union Telegraph Company negotiated an agreement with Britain and Russia for an overland route. This would involve crossing only the Bering Sea, an envisaged fifty-six-mile span from Alaskan St Michael to Siberian Plover Bay. The Russians were to build the trans-Siberian section while the Americans, whose nearest patch of home territory was 2,000 miles away in Seattle, were to fix the Alaskan side. With admirable enthusiasm the Americans started by building a hut and raising their flag on the Siberian side. Two years later their surveys were complete and work was progressing well. Twenty miles of wire had been strung and, even at the slowest rate in winter, half a mile of poles was still being erected each day. (In February 1867 a severe storm caught them by surprise and they were fortunate in reaching an Eskimo settlement before being overcome. One of the party weathered the blizzard in a hut, twelve feet by ten feet. He wriggled through the underground entrance and was cordially received by sixteen Eskimos and eleven dogs.) In June 1867 a ship from San Francisco brought sensational news: a successful transatlantic cable had been laid, their project had been abandoned and the ground they were standing on was now American. America had bought Russian Alaska.

Second only to the Louisiana Purchase, the Treaty of Cession which legally transferred Alaska to American ownership was the world's greatest act of property conveyance. Astonishingly, it could scarcely have evoked less interest on either side and the reasons behind it remain a mystery. Russia, due to limited resources, had confined its interest in Alaska to the fur trade. The home economy was stretched and still suffering the costs of the Crimean War against Great Britain. Possibly the enticement of hard cash, the realisation that their tenure of Alaska was marginal and the fear that America might simply annex Alaska without compensation (as she had with California), encouraged Russia to sell. But Russia and America were on good terms at this time (Russia had backed the Union during the Civil War). Perhaps Russia felt her choice was between transferring Alaska to friends or to their Canadian neighbours, the querulous British.

Yet the Russians had not been looking for a buyer. The proposal itself and the impetus behind it, feeble though this was, came from Secretary of State William Seward and a twilight character called Baron de Stoeckl. The latter suddenly rose to prominence and took it upon himself to act as mediator in the transaction. Through their efforts a treaty was formulated and ultimately ratified by a divided Senate; the motion was passed by a single vote. So keen was Seward to secure the purchase that when word of acceptance came from St Petersburg, he immediately rounded up the signatories and the Treaty of Cession was signed at four in the morning. Stoeckl vanished soon after, abandoning his false title and leaving unsolved the mystery of his true identity and whether the $125,000 unaccounted for in his expenditures really had been used to bribe senators to vote for the treaty. Alaska was bought for $7.2 million, the equivalent of $13 a square mile or just under 2¢ an acre. Seward's foresight went unrecognised and, worse, was ridiculed, for decades.

In Alaska nothing changed except a flag here and there. The Tlingit Indians disputed the right of either party to sell or buy their land but no one paid any attention to the views of 'uncivilized tribes'. The next wave of white men were whalers who harpooned and flensed at sea, and drank and debauched on land. Such was the havoc they caused among Eskimo communities that a new thrust of Good News was dispatched – not as one might expect to convert the whalers, but to dissuade the natives from copying them. Alaska was parcelled out among the missionising denominations. Military units were sent

14

as a deterrent against the assumed risk of native hostility, and intrepid prospectors went of their own accord to pan creeks for the colour that was known to exist.

Gold had been discovered in Alaska at least as early as 1865 but it had not been a priority at the time. The discoverers had been intent on preaching or digging post holes. It took the great Klondike gold rush of the Yukon Territory in 1897–8 to bring stampedes of miners into Alaska, and a concatenation of smaller strikes to send them walking, floating, mushing, skating and even cycling across the land to Nome. Tough as these prospectors were, the extreme cold of winter forced respect. In Circle City the jailhouse door bore the simple reminder 'Notice – All prisoners must report by 9 o'clock p.m. or they will be locked out for the night.' By the time Alaska was granted territorial status in 1912 the rushes were long over and many indigent prospectors had returned south.

The United States government maintained a comatose attitude towards Alaska for seventy years. The territory was simply too remote, too unproductive, too uninhabited. Access and communication were always problematical. Policy lagged behind the serious work of running the rest of the country. And for the most part this state of affairs suited Alaskans fine. Events ticked along quietly and Alaska's magnitude still dwarfed the minor contentions that arose.

Things changed suddenly when war appeared imminent in 1940. Until then Alaska had been defended by an antiquated post of a few hundred troops in the south-east. In 1942 the 1,520-mile Alcan Highway was cut through virgin forest and made serviceable within eight months: 140,000 troops were rushed north to counteract the Japanese advance, which came to nothing – fortunately, because only the Anchorage-Fairbanks coreland was considered essential for air supremacy and acknowledged to be defensible at the time. (Of the war's mini-theatres, Alaska had the highest mortality rate for fliers, due to the weather.) Militarisation, however, came too late to save two of the Aleutian Islands from Japanese invasion. On one of them, Attu Island, half the population lost their lives in a concentration camp.

Alaska's importance for defence strategy marked its rediscovery and placed it on the map in bolder outline, especially as the back door common to both the United States and the Soviet Union in the

15

Cold War. Until the late sixties military defence remained the largest industry. Gone were the old days of lackadaisical procrastination, replaced by burgeoning economic potential and a new sense of urgency to organise what became the 49th state of the Union in 1959 – almost a century after the Purchase.

Statehood introduced a welfare system which, despite its benevolence, devastated the natives' subsistence economy. For the Indian and Aleut peoples of the southern coastlines, its destructive effects combined with those of the 1964 earthquake. On 27 March 1964, Good Friday, an earthquake corresponding to a magnitude of 9.2 on the modern Richter scale struck out from Prince William Sound, caused a massive tidal wave which took most of the 131 lives lost, and detonated 12,000 subsequent tremors of lesser power. The damage to property was catastrophic; and to a culture, total. The coastal/Aleut way of life was dispersed through relocation, and its vestiges lost in a haze of re-education and alcohol.

The Statehood Act granted the state the right to select 103 million acres of public land for its own use but before it could do so, the oldest issue of all, the natives' claim to ownership, had to be settled. The matter came to a head in 1967, the pivotal year in a century of Alaskan history.

Otters, whales, gold, war and oil. The invasions of whites have always come in boom cycles. Each brought irrevocable changes to the indigenous inhabitants but, until the last, its impact on the land was minimal. Before Oil the land absorbed the influx, tolerated the exploitation and then reverted to very much how it had been before. It was still big enough and wild enough to drive away all except those who loved it for these very qualities. Its intrinsic value lay in its character, not in a superficial scattering of venal commodities. The discovery of oil in 1967 reversed that attitude instantly. The stakes were too high to ignore. Alaska was rich, rich beyond the wildest of dreams. Alaska shrank. Every acre became precious and contested.

In 1971, or 4 After Oil, the Alaska Native Claims Settlement Act was passed amid much confusion, praise and a fanfare that was to last ten years before being recognised as badly off-key. With the land issue settled, oil companies were able to press ahead with the construction of the celebrated 800-mile pipeline from the oilfields of the North Slope – the largest in North America and estimated to contain one-quarter of the USA's known reserves – to the ice-free port of Valdez in the south. When 1.5 million barrels a day began flowing on their month-long journey to Valdez, Alaska achieved commercial respectability. With ninety per cent of its revenue now coming crudely the state pays an annual dividend of about $800 to each Alaskan over the age of one year who has been resident for at least six months. These and other financial advantages have provided a small but significant degree of security.

An echo of Judas's shekels rings here: a modicum of economic stability bought at the risk of environmental cataclysm (such as the 1989 spill from the *Exxon Valdez* which befouled a thousand miles of coastline) and at a cost of accelerating the erosion of subsistence culture. The mid-1980s saw a drop in oil prices and an economic depression but proportionally fewer get-rich-quickers made the exodus to Outside than in the years when the slump was in gold or otters.

They were still leaving though, an estimated 18,000 from Anchorage alone, when I hitched up the Alcan in the autumn of 1987. With woolly long johns and woolly optimism I was going against the flow.

6

THE BUSH PLANE, a yellow Cessna Super Cub, was flying low over the forests of Interior Alaska. It changed colour wherever I met it. Sometimes it was blue, sometimes red, or white with red flashes, but always small and fitted with skis. I tried to identify the pilot but he too proved fickle, young and old and always local. In a state where one person in forty-two is registered as a pilot and where one person in fifty-eight owns a plane, it was not who he was but what happened that was cherished. His popularity depended on remaining anonymous. He was seen as being ordinary, representative of his type – if you like, the Unknown Soldier of the Last Frontier.

He was a trapper who used sledge dogs and lived out in the bush. Every two weeks he flew to Fairbanks for supplies and returned the same day, landing his plane on a frozen creek and parking it twenty yards from his cabin door. On this particular flight he was an hour into the wilds when he noticed his oil gauge showing a steady drop in pressure. He realised he was in trouble, without any means of calling for assistance and little hope of other aircraft happening by.

He managed to set the plane down safely on a small frozen lake. In cold climates a strange phenomenon called 'overflow' occurs and it is the curse of winter travellers. When cold is sufficient to penetrate the layer of ice covering rivers and lakes, it freezes more water underneath. Water expands when frozen, so pressure increases on both the remaining water below and the existing ice above. The ice cracks and water is forced up. The snow on this lake was saturated and beginning to freeze as the plane landed. Its skis sank deep into the slush. With the engine inoperative, the pilot could do nothing to prevent the plane from becoming frozen to the spot.

During winter most bush pilots strap snowshoes to the under-side of the wings, and using these he collected wood from the surrounding forest. He made a fire to keep himself warm, and set to work chipping the plane free from the ice. When he had finished he jacked the skis up alternately and left the plane perched on piles of wood just above the level of overflow. This took over four hours. Frequent trips had to be made for more firewood, and his snowshoes constantly needed de-icing.

The engine's fault was obvious, a leaking joint, but all the oil had been lost and he had no reserves. A jury-rigged repair mended the joint temporarily, but the engine remained useless without oil. With a shovel and an empty five-gallon fuel can he customarily used as a shopping basket, he set off to retrace his flight path, picking up dark spots in the snow wherever he found them. When darkness fell he built another fire and huddled by it through the night. His search resumed the next day. Whenever the can became too full he would stop, light a fire, melt the snow and boil off the water. By the end of the second day he believed he had recovered enough oil for a short flight.

By chance he had some stovepipes in the plane. He had bought them on his last visit to Fairbanks but they turned out to be the wrong size and he was going to change them. He used these to channel heat carefully from the fire to warm up the engine. He picked a time when overflow was not occurring. The engine sprang to life, and he made it to Fairbanks in several short hops. By then his dogs at his cabin had been a long time without food. He made his purchases, bought oil and the necessary spare part for the engine but had no time to fit it – on account of the dogs – and flew back on the jury-rigged repair.

The authenticity of the story is not, to my mind, in doubt. Both Alaska and Alaskans are highly unlikely, until you actually meet them.

Alaskans see themselves as custodians of the spirit of independence. Theirs is either a long tradition of mastering an environment that can be both bountiful and murderous, or a short history of pioneering a new life. To neither group is Alaska American. To the former, a nation of dispossessed aboriginals, the land is the Fourth World. To the latter it is a state of mind, an anachronistic bastion of enterprise and individuality hung over from last century, where your rights to fly a leaky plane and bulldoze a mountain through a sluice box are the stuff of life. Alaskans are part of a culturally rich legacy, a peaceful dream, the forces of exploitation.

They revel in their isolation and their tough image, and add inches to the snow of their stories. Each dash of blizzard augments personal prestige and, more importantly, tends to deter Outsiders from intruding. In everyday usage, the rest of America is 'Outside'. Washington DC is as alien as Sydney and – to the Alaskans of Attu Island – as distant. Even Juneau, the state capital, is so cut off it is a standing joke, and up until twenty years ago it was scarcely apparent who, if anyone, claimed or cared about these 550,000 square miles, these 500,000 people. A century and a quarter after its acquisition, Alaska still is American only in name.

Only by exploring Alaska's past can one begin to understand its present. The identity and attitudes of Alaskans today come fresh out of history's mould – more so than the people of any other land, even Australia whose situation bears the closest resemblance. The history of white occupation is remarkably short and its impact inversely great. It is still uncommon to come across an Alaska-born white, and third-generation white Alaskans are as rare as nuggets. The newcomers, though, stand in the majority – confident, progressive and well-off, at least by their own definitions. In general, the natives, the deedless denizens of Alaxsxaq, struggle to retain an identity, to manage their corporations, to carry on with the remnants of an old lifestyle amid the confusing values and addictions of a new one — profit-making, consumerism, fashion — and a frightening proportion fall under the incubus of alcoholism. Here is another world edge, an ideological distinction between a Last Frontier and a Lost Frontier.

'And why on earth are you going there?' Cin had wanted to know.

I wanted to make a journey that would draw together Alaska's past and present. I wanted to discover Alaska and Alaskans beyond the ends of the roads, and there to sort out for myself the facts from the myths. To place myself in the wilderness of which Alaska has so much, and on which, paradoxically, all its major contentions are centred. In its size, emptiness and contradictions lay its fascination. I had visited Alaska before but never in its most challenging season. And I wanted to travel with sledge dogs.

It means little to me when Alaska is uprooted, reshaped and thrown over other parts of the world. Statisticians delight in these catchy little distortions. They cast the 49th state over the main Lower 48 to demonstrate it covers one-fifth of the area. As a dust sheet, they assert, Alaska would protect one-fifth of Australia or smother six Great Britains. However it is equated, Alaska stretches the mind.

During a long affectionate look at the map of Alaska I detected the map looking back. Before me was the head of an old prospector, in profile, facing towards Siberia. His nose was bulbous, gnarled and slightly snub and it protruded from the sweeping indentation between jutting forehead and bushy beard. I took an instant liking to the man and plotted our relationship. I doodled a mite's crawl from where his ear would have been, the end of the road, to the tip of his nose, the end of the land.

Travelling on a map is one of the principal joys of confinement. Beside the comfort of a home fire, with pencil and steaming mug of chocolate in hand, you can inch your way effortlessly over hundreds of miles of unknown land. Delighted by the icy-blue of high mountain or the ring of a name, you can dismiss a month of hardship and strike out at a tangent to each new discovery, or float there on a crease you've mistaken for a river. At a mere touch you can push an HB trail where no human has gone before, come full circle and claim your place in history, all before the toast has burned.

Inspired by my modest line from ear to nose (Manley Hot Springs

20

to the Seward Peninsula), I backtracked a little and tattooed a continuation round the beard. This left me stranded at a point on his lower jaw (Anchorage) but from there it was just a dawdle back to the ear. The result was pleasing so I redrew my route in three colours and presented it to fifteen companies with the suggestion that, for a small contribution towards my expeditionary expenses, I would emblazon 'BAXTERS ROYAL GAME SOUP ... READ THE SUNDAY TIMES ... SCHHHHH! YOU KNOW WHO ... REST ASSURED BEDS' across the tundra. When Ballantine's Whisky expressed interest and then turned me down, I knew my life as a commercial traveller was not to be. Instead, I'd go without a grubstake; just me, some dogs and old man Alaska.

Friends had offered me the use of their summer cabin and Susan Butcher, a mushing legend, had invited me to visit for advice. Everything else was uncertain. I was afraid of the cold. I knew nothing about dogs. (I thought it would be nice to have nine.) I had no idea if it would be possible to acquire them, learn how to handle and care for them, and then travel over 800 miles with them – *all in one winter*.

Hopes and doubts are the essence of adventure. I hitched the length of the Alcan and arrived on foot, carrying a backpack and a dream of driving my own dog team across Alaska.

7

ONE EVENING, A week after my arrival in the village, Manley's old road-house was bustling. A yellow glow from the ground floor passed through shelves of antique bottles and lattice windows to cast bays of light upon footprints in the snow. These were the first flakes of winter, a modest dusting one inch deep. The sun had set at 4.36 that afternoon, but more important than this early closure was the one imminent at the road-house. The party being held there would end with the doors being locked until the following spring, thus marking the start of cabin fever season for Manley's eighty residents. I went along to meet my neighbours for the next four months.

The road-house was two-and-a-bit storeys high, a peaked roof

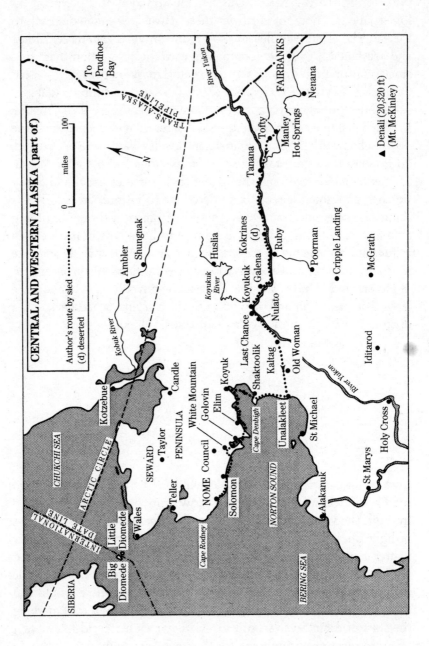

CENTRAL AND WESTERN ALASKA (part of)

Author's route by sled ·······
(d) deserted

0   miles   100

N

SIBERIA

CHUKCHI SEA

INTERNATIONAL DATE LINE

ARCTIC CIRCLE

Big Diomede
Little Diomede

Wales

Teller

Kotzebue

Kobuk River

SEWARD

Taylor

PENINSULA

White Mountain
Golovin

Candle

Ambler

Shungnak

NOME   Council

Solomon

Cape Rodney

Elim   Koyuk

Cape Denbigh

Shaktoolik

Last Chance

Kaltag

Old Woman

Unalakleet

NORTON SOUND

St Michael

Alakanuk

BERING SEA

St Marys

Holy Cross

Iditarod

River Yukon

McGrath

Cripple Landing

Poorman

Ruby

Galena   (d)

Kokrines

Koyukuk

Nulato

Huslia

Koyukuk River

River Yukon

Tanana

Tofty
Manley
Hot Springs

FAIRBANKS

Nenana

▲ Denali (20,320 ft)
(Mt. McKinley)

To Prudhoe Bay

TRANS-ALASKA PIPELINE

over a rectangular design, painted white and with a genuine 1920s exterior which promised simple comforts laced with woodworm. The external appearance suggested to the traveller that the interior would be cluttered with animal heads losing their stuffing, yellowing photographs, an archaic telephone exchange, rusty tools and other musty memorabilia. And, indeed, it was.

I negotiated a double barrier of flyscreen and door, passed through a deserted lounge where an enormous barrel stove raised the temperature to high summer, and entered the crowded bar at the rear of the building. I found a free stool just out of range of the jaws of a bear trap hanging against a wall. Above me, a paraffin lamp had been suspended from one tine of a moose rack which would have knocked five people senseless had it become detached. Other decorations were a pair of oversized bellows and a wooden pack frame for a mule, but the walls were mainly covered with illuminated beer names and mirrors advertising brands of spirits. Prominent were Johnnie Walker, White Horse and the inevitable obscure Scotch that few Scotsmen have ever heard of — Grand Macnish. The reflection in Grand Macnish showed a horseshoe bar extending into a ghoulish scene.

The stool next to mine was occupied by a witch. She wore a black shroud, black garbage bag drawn out into a tall pointed hat and plastic mask with a billhook nose set in a fiendish expression. Beyond her sat a bulky object whose head was a faceless mop of purple tassels crushed into a basket. Instead of eyes it carried a set of goggles with bulbs which periodically flashed. A man whose face was split black and white down the line of his nose was chatting to another plastered in a clownish assortment of red, green, white and blue. Each change of expression produced the entrancing effect of a kaleidoscope. My beer was brought by a monk. Enveloped in a khaki habit, she had a turquoise face speckled with sequins and ruptured by golden bolts of lightning. Her attention was caught by a frogman carping at his empty glass through a snorkel. 'Ich bin ein deutsches Mädchen' explained another girl at each introduction. With blonde hair braided into pigtails, in frock and pinafore, she lacked only a milk pail and a dozen Friesians. In the background a robust princess was shrieking with laughter and recalling a royal night when she had laid bar customers out on the counter and mixed Mexican cocktails in their mouths. Otherwise the apparitions were dominated by a remarkable number of beards. They were genuine, unlike the Hallowe'en guises of the others.

'Happy Hallowe'en!' I didn't know anyone in the room, and had no experience of chatting up witches.

'Heh-heh-heh-heh-heh-heh!' This was the only response she gave for ten minutes.

Festivities are played out to the full in northern climates. Each village has special days of madness. They celebrate the coming of spring and long summer days, they recharge morale in the great darkness of winter. The Hallowe'en fling in Manley did introduce me to my neighbours but it was weeks before I could fit real faces and personalities to the people I met that evening.

The witch remained anonymous. Mophead was a young artist, philosopher and woodcraftsman. The black and white face belonged to a trapper who had spent years up the remote Tozi River. The clown was a retired postman from California who carved diamond willow, nurtured a culture of sourdough which had been maintained for a century, and was reputed to be a wizard chef. The monk was the girl who cleaned the road-house, served in the bar, and was the postmistress. She also ran the store and rebuilt planes. She owned two planes, was a qualified flying instructor and a competent aircraft mechanic. The frogman drank a lot and appeared to do very little, but was said to write poetry that made old bushmen weep. The *deutsches Mädchen* had raised two children in the Bush with no more comforts than those she could fashion from the spot, and educated them to a level many grades above their age. Now she lived a life indistinguishable from the others, only in a semi-underground hut covered with turf. Someone had just come back from Antarctica. Those who had not felled trees, stripped the logs and built a luxurious cabin to an original design were rarities, and if ham radio operators, seamstresses and pilots had been auctioned they would have gone two for a cent. There was nothing special about the people of Manley, I was constantly told. They were just an ordinary bunch.

The witch sat hunched over a glass of yellow brew and prodded the end of the straw across her mask until she located the hole in the mouth. The level of yellow dropped slightly. Her mug of coffee alongside appeared to have been forgotten. A City Slicker with greased-back hair slithered up from behind and made her scream. He whispered 'Your coffee looks cold. Let me light a fire under it.'

Then, 'Hey! You must be the Scotsman ... we heard about you. You're going to mush cross country in a kilt.'

I knew it was pointless trying to kill a rumour by denying it. 'That's right. I'm a bit worried about frostbite.'

'No shit! Well, I reckon if you can survive the cold snap for the next three months, what's gonna get bit'll've been bit.'

'Very reassuring. What sort of temperatures can I expect? Minus twenty?'

'Minus twenty ... !'

'... heh-heh-heh-heh-heh ...!' The witch was listening in.

'... minus twenty's summer to us.' The Slicker turned and shouted 'Hey, barman! You'd better get this man another beer.' He held out his hand. 'My name's Dennis. I'm your nearest neighbour. If there's anything I can do for you, don't be a stranger.'

'Have you got sledge dogs?' I asked hopefully.

'Hell, no. I've just got Spike, and he's a mutt. If it's dogs you want, you should go and see the Redingtons. Yes, sir. The Redingtons have got dogs, lots and lotsa-dogs.'

The witch's yellow brew had begun working its spell and she offered some advice in a whinnying voice. She made me confess that I knew nothing about dogs, had never even seen a dog in harness, and she giggled horribly. She said I would need a strong pair of pants. It took me some time to work out that she was not referring to underpants, and when I continued to look blank, she explained that being dragged behind a sledge was tough on a dog driver's clothing.

'Does that happen often?' I asked. 'Being dragged?'

'YEAH, NO KIDDING,' she brayed enthusiastically. 'By the time you've learned what mushing's about, you'll have teethmarks all over the handlebars. Heh-heh-heh-heh-heh.'

I hated that laugh.

8

The *Fairbanks Daily News-Miner* announced my arrival with a few choice lines which did nothing to encourage me to take up a subscription. In a roundup of village news a local correspondent informed the nation that 'Snow is here and we have happy mushers. It seems that every winter we have an unusual musher ... and this year we have Alastair Scott. He arrived in Manley from Scotland with no dogs, no sled and no experience. As a matter of fact he's so green he calls a sled a sledge....'

The township of Manley Hot Springs, to give it its full title, was spread over several square miles of woodland at the base of rounded, 3,000-foot hills. Of the sixty-odd cabins within its precincts, approximately twenty were holiday homes which stood empty in winter. As late as the 1950s steamships had served the hamlet, leaving the Tanana River and coming up the six-mile stretch of slack water called Manley Slough. The slough hugged the base of the hills and divided the hamlet in half. The road-house, post office-store, Methodist church, school, medical centre, airstrip and main group of cabins were all on the flat side. Near the road-house a box-girder bridge spanned the steaming slough, which only froze over in the coldest weather on account of the famous hot springs which emerged from the ground 400 yards away.

On the hilly side of town were more homes and 'The Resort' – a log cabin bar and hotel with Las Vegas illuminations where you could swim in a small pool at four dollars a dip, take three-dollar showers and use a launderette. Further on was the wellhouse. There was no piped water supply in the village. Some cabins did have their own private wells and even full plumbing systems, but these were rarities. People collected their water in five-gallon containers, filling them from a hose kept thawed by an electrically-heated sheath.

Each evening the sounds of howling dogs reminded me of my greenness. Their choruses rose above the excited mumbling of the community generator and found echoes in every direction. *Canis familiaris* was in the majority here; over three hundred lived within a one-mile radius of my cabin. I longed to graduate from green to whatever colour accomplished mushers become, and to get my teeth stuck into the handlebars of a sled, but first there were all the chores to do to make my cabin habitable for the winter. After a hard day's work there was barely time to reset the mousetraps (eight mice, four shrews), let alone entertain thoughts of inviting nine dogs into my life.

My first task was to improve the insulation of the cabin. It had been built half a century earlier in the traditional style of interlocking spruce logs chinked with moss, and was now among the oldest in the community. It had one room down and one room up. The amenities comprised a wood stove at one end, a table, two beds, cupboards, an ancient radiogram, a gas cooker and a kitchen sink at the far end. It was almost a month before I felt the cold had been driven out of the old logs, and even then ice crystals grew and flowered on nailheads whose other ends were in touch with winter. I never managed to thaw a frozen puddle by the sink. It remained a sheet of ice inside my cabin until spring.

And the outhouse needed mending. It stood skew-whiff and alone, thirty measured paces behind the cabin. Apart from needing a new floor, for the seat stood as an island in a hole, this outhouse had a feature unusual in rural Alaska. It had a door. Alaska is the land of the open-plan john. Wherever a musher mushes across the land and seeks his relief at some wayside outhouse, with his strong pants down, he becomes part of the grand and general view. Doorless outhouses can be found facing the neighbours, main thoroughfares, even each other. If you have to bare your vitals to air at −50°F, perhaps the logic goes, you might as well have something interesting to take your mind off the nip.

The greatest fallacy held by romantics looking rosily on cabin life is that log-dwellers must have so much time. Time to read, time to write, time to keep cobwebs off violins, time to get bored. In reality the chores of the simple life expand into major events of the day. It can take an hour to collect or post your mail. An hour to make that essential phone call. A mechanical breakdown may require three hours of improvisation. There are always ashes to rake, water to haul, bread to bake, and logs to split; the latter, of course, is a privilege

27

earned only if you have worked like a beaver all summer and procured your share of the forest.

My beaver's work had yet to begin. I was able to buy a permit for subsistence woodcutting in an area two miles away. Sometimes I managed to hitch a lift but usually I had to walk there and back, lugging a chainsaw and cans of fuel and oil which gradually felt as if they were extending my arms to my knees. I wasn't an accomplished lumberjack, either. My trees defied the hinges I contrived at their bases and toppled the wrong way; they snagged on their neighbours and refused to come down to earth. One, whose trunk was completely severed, remained bolt upright as if McCulloch (the saw) and I were just bad dreams. Then, without warning, it lurched towards me and I had to drop McCulloch and run. Little on this planet is more treacherous than a disconnected tree.

I lost count of the number of trees I had to disconnect, but it was sufficient for the three cords recommended as the minimum to see me through to the end of February. Most households stashed away five cords for winter, and that was *dry* wood. I had no choice but to collect the much less efficient green wood but this, the *News-Miner* would have agreed, at least matched my colour scheme.

I trudged back from the woodcutting lot each day with long arms and in pensive mood. It was hard for one who, a month earlier, could have talked passionately about the senseless destruction of Amazonia, to reconcile such abduction of the boreal forest, even though it still wasn't clear whether I or the trees would eventually win. More than this, however, I was burdened by a feeling of inadequacy. From whatever angle, the early pioneers of this region rose to the stature of supreme adventurers, and made my efforts appear feeble.

The earliest pioneer to settle in the area arrived in 1902. In a photograph, 'Daddy' Karshner stands as a muscular, elderly man, moustached, smiling, and smart in a dress shirt as he hoes a farm out of the forest he has cut down with a handsaw. He was a farmer-turned-miner who reverted to farming when he came across the hot springs. He homesteaded 320 acres around these springs, which gush water at 135°F and allow only an inch of frost to penetrate the surrounding land. At the end of the 1906 season he had harvested watermelons, celery, tomatoes and, from three acres, a nineteen-ton crop of potatoes; then the eponymous Frank Manley arrived.

Manley was an enigmatic character who made and lost fortunes with faithful regularity and was seldom not involved in litigation over his mining claims. He was really Hilliard B. Knowles from Texas, where he had left behind a wife and an indictment for perjury in a case which accused him of having tied a mule to a railway line and successfully claimed damages after the train had passed. It is not known how much Mrs Manley, his Alaskan wife, knew of this, but they reached Karshner Hot Springs in 1906 after rich takings in the Fairbanks goldfields.

With one eye on the farming and recreational possibilities and the other on the nearby gold creeks of Tofty and Eureka, Manley bought out Karshner the same year. He at once felled what was known as 'the Balm of Gilead', reputed to be the finest grove of evergreen poplars in the land, and converted it into Alaska's first resort. His four-storey hotel was a creation of log-work gone Baroque and boasted forty-five bedrooms, steam heating, electric lights, fresh cows' milk, a dance floor, billiard room, a full-scale natatorium where vacationing miners could breaststroke a wake through winter, and a bar with 'the finest wet goods for those not interested in the water cure'.

Manley spent little time in the area, preferring to immerse himself in court cases and mine hunting elsewhere, but the resort prospered and a community developed. By 1908 the local newspaper whose banner head read variously *Hot Springs Echo, Hot Sprngs Echo* or *Hot Springs Egho* and whose editor obviously wasn't interested in the water cure, reported that many businesses had been established, including another bar, the Headquarters Saloon, run by Messrs Shipp & Stuck. It also reported on the return of the manager of the resort after a trip south. Manley, in order to boost the farming side of things somewhat, had dispatched the unfortunate man to fetch '2,000 thoroughbred Wyandotte hens, 100 roosters, two dozen each ducks, geese and guinea fowl, ten Jersey cows and a bull, and some pigs.'

For several years things went well. In summer tourists arrived from Fairbanks on one of the many steamboats plying the Tanana River and were met by the hotel launch which took them the remaining six miles up the slough. In winter they arrived by stagecoach, paying forty dollars a round trip. Horses pulled the coach along crude forest tracks and over frozen rivers, and if the snow became too deep specially designed snowshoes were fitted to their hooves. The trip took forty-eight hours each way.

By 1911 interest was rapidly waning in the local gold creeks, and with it went the resort's business. The place fell into disrepair and in April 1913 Manley's $100,000 investment caught fire and went up in smoke. He shrugged off the loss for he was in the new gold boom town of Iditarod, about to cash in on a $1.5 million dollar claim. He died in 1933 in California, still reaping millions from new investments in oil. Despite the disapproving verdict of the US Surveyor in 1910 – 'Frank G. Manley is not recognised by the government as having any interest in the homestead, so don't call it Manley farm or the Manley Hot Springs any more' – his name endured.

My walk to and from the woodcutting lot passed the site of Manley farm and the hot springs. One area of former fields was now the airstrip, which produced a crop of fifteen private planes and thrice-weekly letters from the flying mail service, and the rest of the land had reverted to forest. The hot springs remained privately owned by a family who occupied the most remarkable house in the community. For the last thirty years it had been kept toasted by underfloor geothermal heating, even though a wall on the longest side consisted of nothing more than three layers of plastic sheeting. Apart from this diversion of the springs, the hot water's route to the slough was intercepted by two immense greenhouses. The fattest tomatoes in Alaska grew here, but the cost of transporting produce to a market made a commercial venture unviable. Inside the second greenhouse reposed four concrete tubs which served as a public bath. Here you could step out of deep winter and enter a boudoir of tropical rain forest. Baths cost four dollars and could be had on monthly credit. Cleanliness was less a virtue in Manley, more the thrill of a day at the races or a night at the opera.

Manley never peaked to its 1908 level again. It dwindled to a population of two dozen in the fifties but experienced a revival with the building of a gravel road linking it to the state network in 1959. Until ten years ago Manley's denizens considered the road a mixed blessing and voted *not* to have it maintained during winter, in order to reclaim some peace and isolation. The vote changed with a slight demographic shift towards families with young children and now Manley was at the end of an all-weather road. Few of the population had full-time employment. There were several teachers and teachers' aides and two on road maintenance, but otherwise jobs came singly: one electrician, one postmistress, one medical aide, one cleaner, and so on. Seasonal workers found employment where they could, in the area or as far away as the Bering Sea, as fishermen, carpenters, firefighters, woodcutters, gold miners, trappers, and jacks-of-all-trades. Rural Alaska was, of necessity, full of these awesomely capable Jacks.

One of these owned an army truck, and I solicited his help to transport my logs from the cutting area to my cabin. I can't date trucks but this one might have fought the Japanese, and if so, had lost. It was a slow, noisy brute but an excellent workhorse, and we retrieved my wood in five loads. The arrival of my wood had one unexpected consequence. It earned me 'citizenship'. My jumble of wood was perceived as a serious declaration of intent. Even if I had *had* ten sacks of coal, it would have been worth sweating over fifty trees to make this symbolic gesture. Manley now knew for certain it was to have one extra for winter, and all its doors opened.

I had my wood supply. My outhouse was serviceable. My cabin was in order. Now I was ready for dogs. The Redingtons had dogs, lots and lotsa-dogs.

9

'WELL. WE'D BETTER get back to the office.'

'Where is it?'

'You're looking at it.'

I was looking at two acres of craters between Joee Redington's house and a sign which told visitors where to leave their vehicles: 'Whoa'. Some of the craters lay within fenced compounds but each contained a solitary post, a weatherproof wooden box lined with straw, and a member of staff on a five-foot chain. The office had a staff of 150 and of these only a handful conformed to my notion of a sled dog. The rest were smaller, lighter and less shaggy than I had expected, and their tails weren't curled. Every dog had its own colour scheme. Some came straight, others in patches, tints, stripes, masks. Some resembled dobermans, skinny Alsatians, spotless Dalmatians or shorn collies. There was no uniformity except that they were all fast.

'Alaskan huskies,' Joee remarked. 'They aren't recognised as a breed because they're all mongrels. But they're the fastest sled dogs in the world. These are sprint dogs. I'm not looking for strong pullers. I'm after fast dogs with good endurance, tough feet and thin coats. Some of these even have greyhound bred in – but overdo it and you get weak bones and bad feet. On a thirty-mile circuit these dogs will average sixteen miles per hour and hit bursts of twenty-three.'

He could be specific about the speeds because part of autumn training, before snow, involved hooking up sixteen-dog teams to a Honda four-wheel ATV (All Terrain Vehicle). With an ATV a musher had perfect control: brakes, accelerator, speedometer. To see a motorbike being dragged along frozen rivers by sixteen dogs was a glimpse of cultural integration, the meeting of Japanese engineering and Eskimo ingenuity.

'Twenty-three miles an hour, eh, Carlo?' He caught Carlo's front legs as the dog leapt up in response. Carlo was a leader and the most valuable dog in the lot. Joee had turned down an offer of $10,000 for him. 'Even when pulling me, and this...' He patted a slight bulge in his snowsuit to indicate his stomach. Below average height, sturdy and slightly overweight, Joee was one of the big-name racers in Alaska. Wherever there were races there were Redingtons. Joe, Joee, Ray. The generations varied but the first names stayed the same. Joee Ray was Joee's son; Joee had a brother Ray (who had sons Joe and Ray); they were sons of Joe, sen., 'The Father of the Iditarod' and a man of legendary proportions. I was to meet him later.

Through an oversight of his grandfather, Joee got drunk at the age of six and subsequently never touched alcohol. Now in his late forties, Joee liked to look on the funny side of life. He talked in a simple, frank manner and in short bursts, except when animated by the recollection of a dog story, of which he had an inexhaustible stock.

'Once, I remember, they changed the course of a race that had been the same for years. One guy came bowling along but had to stop as he took a wrong turn. Then his leaders caught the scent of a spectator's dog in heat and he lost control. WHAM! They were off, leading the team over a barrier and into the crowd. The female they were after was in a car with its rear window open, and a couple were

32

sprawled across the front seat necking.' He whooped. 'No shit! There were fourteen dogs in harness and three of them got through the window before the guy got his sled stopped.' Joee laughed for a long time, and 300 ears cocked at the sound of his voice.

We passed Teddy, Lucille, Hummer, Sly Girl, Racer, Tinker, Cougar, Mitch, Coke, Jasper, Missy, Trumper.... Not only could Joee recognise and name each dog instantly, he could recount its lineage. Spark had come out of Voodoo and Blaze. Voodoo had come out of Crackers and Rabbit and was a litter-mate of Snap. Crackers had been in so-and-so's winning Rondy team in such-and-such a year and was a son of Feisty.... He had a gift for remembering canine ancestry but ('What was your name again?') was not so hot when it came to humans. The gift was one shared by every kennel-owner I met, an ability to run off endless strings of blood lines. When two breeders met, this topic dominated their conversation. A dozen breeders, I was certain, would have had enough pooled knowledge to reveal who had run in lead for Adam and Eve.

'You think you've got all those names now...?' Joee asked, and he quizzed me thoroughly. I failed.

Radar, Spooky, Pistol, Lady, Goofy,...

The term 'husky' (early slang for an Eskimo) is applied to sled dogs in general, the descendants of three main breeds: the samoyed, which is one of the world's oldest breeds, named for the Samoyede people of the Siberian Arctic; the Alaskan malamute, named for the Malemut Eskimos of the Yukon estuary; and the Siberian husky, which has the lowest metabolism of any dog. Into this genealogy have been mixed, less successfully, elkhounds, wolfhounds, mastiffs and Great Danes; and, more successfully, Irish setters, Labradors, salukis, greyhounds, spaniels, Alsatians, akitas, Dalmatians and wolves. (Wolves *have* been trained to pull sleds, but they were found to lack endurance.) The Alaskan husky is the melting pot dog which results.... Fleet, Rush, Lightning, Blitz, Turbo, Cruiser.

'The quality of high performance dogs, racing dogs, has never been better. But the quality of work dogs has gone down. Forty years ago, every family in the Interior had at least five or six dogs. They used them for trapping, travelling, and hauling wood, game and water. Now they use snow machines. Working dogs have almost disappeared. It was racers and fun-mushers that saved the sled dog and sledding.'

'What sort of weights can they pull?'

'Depends on the dog. You can get small dogs that really pull and big dogs that only half-pull. They've done tests with a nine-dog team of average huskies and found their maximum pull was a force of 300 pounds. Pound for pound, that would get them into the Olympics. But a 300-pound pull on a sled will shift one hell of a load. It's on record that one mail-sled driver in the old days got six dogs to pull 2,000 pounds on three sleds. Every time he came to a hill he had to unhook two sleds and relay them up one at a time, but – the mail got through.' He explained that in general a dog should not be asked to pull more than twice its own weight. The average Alaskan husky weighs around 45 to 50 pounds, and so a load of up to 90 to 100 pounds per dog is a reasonable guide. Joee's dogs weighed only 30 to 35 pounds, but his sled was always empty, and with sixteen dogs pulling they could have towed eight Joees. With only one, they couldn't even feel if he was there.

I jotted down these statistics and tried to absorb them, but the flow of information was relentless. 'That's Snowy, Happy, Bean, Radish, Cabbage, Onion...' Good God! One hundred and fifty of them and, say, a turnover of forty a year. No wonder he was now on to vegetables.

When not driving his dogs in snow, Joee chauffeured them in style. His dog truck was a wooden box painted in gypsy colours and set on the bed of a new pickup. Each side was fitted with twelve mesh-covered doors leading into individual boxes. By doubling up, Joee could transport forty-eight dogs to a race and still have plenty of room for food, straw, harnesses and all the other paraphernalia. Three sleds could be clipped onto the roof rack. 'KOBUK', the name of a dog food manufacturer and Joee's sponsor, claimed the brightest paint.

'I get all my dried dog food free and this is what makes the scale of my operation feasible. It would cost fifty to sixty dollars a day to run this place if I had to pay for everything. Through sponsorship and selling trained dogs the kennel pays for itself, but not for me and the family.'

Only a few dog drivers in Alaska were fully professional. Most, like Joee, had to find a summer income to cover the year's expenses. Joee was a commercial fisherman in the Yukon delta. The number of licences in operation was fixed, a limited-entry system, and these were marketable commodities. Delta licences changed hands for $30,000. The Department of Fish and Game monitored fish movements each year and regulated the times when permits could be used, but these never exceeded forty-eight hours in any one week. In a summer's worth of two-day weeks Joee had to earn his year's income. But king salmon live up to their name and it was not rare to net fifty-pound specimens. On a 'best' day he could take $8,000 worth of fish. Factory ships anchored off the coast paid cash for his catch.

While Joee netted fish and his pockets bulged with greenbacks, his wife looked after the 'office' single-handed. One could find no better model for graft than Pam. Only a touch over five feet in height and of slight build, she was endlessly busy. Ruby, Fox, Dart, Nelly ... Pam knew them all, too.

'What about "king dogs"?' I asked. 'I've read that there's a boss dog in every team.'

'Used to be. Not now. You'll always get weak and strong personalities but no one can afford to have a boss dog. If you have a fighter, you get rid of it. Fighters cost time, dogs and money. They spook the whole team. No, the bad ones have been culled out over the years. Your dogs have got to learn that *you* are the boss dog. But of course you always need lead dogs. Without them, you don't go anywhere. Come over here, I'll show you how things work.'

10

HE LED ME over to a sled, ready to go, only no dogs were attached.

'What are you smiling at?' he asked.

'No mud. No porridge.' The runners were strips of tough, near-frictionless polyethylene plastic. The sled was a lightweight basket-type, a skeleton of lashed hickory. A pair of rubber footprints on the rear of the runners showed where the driver stood while holding the bowed frame of the handlebars. Between the runners and the driver's toes, held poised above the snow by a spring, was a steel claw which acted as a brake when depressed. The only other brake was a snow hook, a double-pronged anchor for securing the sled when parked.

A gangline was fastened to the front of the sled and this was the main line on which, indirectly, the dogs pulled. A nylon rope of hollow weave, half an inch in diameter, it was made up in sections so that by adding or subtracting lengths any number of dogs could be accommodated. Branching out of the gangline were tuglines, short lengths of quarter-inch rope, one to be clipped to the harness of each dog; and necklines, even shorter lengths of one-sixteenth inch rope. Necklines took no pulling strain but prevented the dog from running wide and tangling with obstacles. The most popular method of hooking up dogs was the double-tandem hitch. Dogs ran in pairs, one on either side of the gangline. A padded harness was slipped over each dog's head and the front legs eased through side loops. Designed to put the strain of pulling on shoulders and chest, harnesses came in different sizes and had to be selected for a comfortable fit. Too tight, they caused rubbing and restricted movement; too loose, they were inefficient and awkward.

Dog drivers no longer use whips, and reins have never played a part in sledding. Control depends entirely on vocal commands and the obedience of the dogs. Lead dogs are the vital element; they make life heaven or hell for the driver; they win races, save lives and make possible this co-operative form of transport. Good leaders are as effective as mechanical accelerators and steering wheels, are never distracted by other dogs or by surprises, learn to act without commands but never fail to respond to them, are able to turn a sled through 180° without allowing the team to tangle, can break trail through fresh snow, and hold the team in an orderly line when left unattended. Their attitude affects the morale of every other dog. It is rare to find a leader who excels in all these disciplines but all lead dogs possess these capabilities in varying degrees.

It is one thing to have a leader who will take the correct turn where a trail forks, another to have one who will hold a precise course into the wind on a flat landscape. What sets leaders apart within their own ranks is their extra-sensory powers. Top leaders can remember for years trails their drivers have travelled once and forgotten. By feeling for hard-packed snow they can find trails that have blown over and disappeared. They can sense weak ice, open water and the direction of shelter. Tales of lost mushers being led to safety by dogs they couldn't even see, so dense were the whiteouts, are legion. Such experiences bring man into preternaturally deep communion with this creature.

At the heart of the deepest man–dog friendships is loyalty. In the 1979 Iditarod Race, with about 400 miles down and 700 still remaining, one particular racer was riding through the night. Days of skimping on sleep had left him exhausted and he had tied himself to the handlebars. If he dozed off, there was no danger of him falling from the sled and losing his entire outfit. Inevitably, he fell asleep and collapsed over the handlebars. He woke some time later with the realisation that something was wrong. The absence of movement: the sled had stopped. He rubbed away the ice which had frozen his eyelashes together and found himself looking into the face of Rabbit, his main lead dog, who was standing only a foot away. When Rabbit saw him stir, without a single command he turned the team back again and resumed the race. No word was spoken and not a line was tangled. Rabbit had just been checking.

Although the qualities of a leader can be taught, the best leaders are endowed from birth. Supernormal abilities usually manifest themselves at an early age, but many a great leader has started its career late as a result of a driver not realising the dog's potential. Some dogs love to run up-front, others have neither the confidence nor the inclination to do so and will refuse. Leading can be stressful and tiring – always setting the pace and direction – and so most drivers have several leaders to share the task.

Under demanding circumstances the best leader is put up-front on his or her own. (Male and female sled dogs enjoy complete equality. Sex has no bearing on strength, speed or aptitude.) And while some prefer running alone, usually leaders run in pairs. One leader will commonly be the key command dog and the other a 'stringer', one who maintains a fast pace and strings the team out. The next pair occupies the position known as 'swing'. They also have an understanding of commands and their role is to follow the leaders and swing the team round accordingly. Good leaders achieve nothing if the swing dogs go their own way. The other important pair of dogs are the ones nearest the sled, the 'wheel' dogs. Usually the biggest and toughest dogs, they are often pushed about by the gangline on tight turns. When these turns take place on slow, difficult terrain, most of the sled's weight falls to their tuglines. When a sled is slipping off a trail or siding into an obstruction, an exceptional

37

wheel dog leaps over the gangline *and* its companion to lend its pull on the side that will correct the situation. The pair or pairs of dogs between wheel and swing are called simply 'team' dogs. The terminology differs in Canada, but I was trying to become an Alaskan musher.

There was much more to all this than I had expected. I tried to visualise what it was like to look out over sixteen dogs: two in wheel, ten in team, two in swing and two in lead – thirty yards of dogs and trappings.

'Are you ready, then?' Joee asked, his smile lying slightly askew.

'For what?'

'Your début. If you're going to mush across the country you'd better get mushing.'

11

FRANTIC TO BE off, the dogs were straining at the traces, yipping and cavorting so high they almost flipped. With my feet on the runners, one hand tight on the handlebars, I bent down and pulled up the snowhook. Before I could shout 'AH-WAH-HAGH-OO-AR!' the sled jolted with a violence that surprised me, and we were off.

Joee had impressed on me not to use the claw brake unless in an emergency, as it dug up the trail and ruined the surface. My senses might have been partially numbed by shock but one thing was obvious: I had embarked on one long emergency. I was standing on this brake with all my weight as we descended Joee's steep drive.

Hard-packed snow covered the drive. The claw achieved nothing. Out of control, or rather, never having achieved it, I was accelerated towards a 90° right turn. The sled whiplashed around. I was squatting low, leaning into the curve and thinking I had survived when the runners, careening sideways, were stopped dead by a rock. My body, however, continued its previous momentum, heading at a tangent towards a snowdrift. Only my jacket catching on the prongs of the snowhook stopped me momentarily, but long enough to find a handhold on the sled.

We continued downhill. The dogs had flattened to their task. Low elastic shapes, each trying to leap forward faster than the others. Their power was unbelievable but I was not in a position to admire it. On my knees, my arms wrapped round the handlebars, I watched multiple explosions of fur. The brake had had no effect, but all at once I had a brainwave.

'WHOA!' I yelled, 'WHOA! ... WHOA! ....' This startled the dogs so much they actually increased their efforts.

The trail became bumpy. Half the time we seemed to be airborne. The dogs were on their own, I was merely useless ballast waiting to be ejected. Down a bank, up a bank, over a bridge, across a road, through a wood: they went as they pleased. As they twisted this way and that I was wrenched from side to side, clinging on only because falling off appeared marginally more painful. Three, four or five times I was almost pitched into trailside shrubs, until at last we reached the frozen slough.

The trail here was flat and straight. The dogs had worked off their initial burst of enthusiasm and lapsed into a steady lope. I managed to stand up for the first time. For the first time, I felt the appeal of being a chef at the Hilton. After a mile we swung round a loop and returned. I delivered the team back safely – at least, they delivered me back, with only two cuts, a torn jacket and a large assortment of bruises.

And yet, I hadn't let go. I had stayed on. There were no teethmarks on the handlebars – though perhaps this was where I had gone wrong.

Joee had followed me on the ATV, watching from a distance. He was waiting for me when I got back.

'No shit! You did great. I'm *real* proud of you.'

I beamed. I felt pretty proud of myself too.

'*Great!*' he enthused. 'Maybe next week we'll try it with more than three dogs, OK?'

12

'AH-WAH-HAGH-OO-AR!' is actually an obsolete term which was last used in a different region a century ago. 'MUSH!', the most celebrated command, may mean something to film directors but it means nothing to sled dogs. It is a corruption of *'marche!'* and was borrowed from French-Canadian dog-drivers, who used it as their starting shout. Archbishop Hudson Stuck was still shouting 'MUSH!' at the turn of the century but it must have disappeared shortly after this, only to be revived as a name for the sport and its practitioners: mushing and mushers.

North American dog commands have been standardised because a common jargon makes exchanging dogs easier. There are variations but the basic commands are: ALL RIGHT or LET'S GO (to start), HIKE or GET UP (faster), HAW (left), GEE (right), ON BY or STRAIGHT AHEAD, EASY (slow down), and WHOA (stop). Tone of voice is important: sharp, short, excited sounds to encourage action, and long, soothing ones to reduce the level of action. 'WHOA!' yelled urgently can, as I had discovered, produce the same effect as 'HIKE!'

A sled has no form of steering. It is not particularly manoeuvrable but by adjusting one's weight, using the handlebars to lever a runner off the snow or, in desperation, jumping off and hauling the sled over while on the run, small changes of direction can be achieved and obstacles which the dogs side-step can be avoided. The more I learned, the more I realised how little I knew, and how much knowledge was needed.

I had no idea what, how much, or how often to feed a sled dog. I had little notion of how mushing worked, so could barely guess at the amounts and methods of training my dogs and I would need. I didn't even have any dogs yet and hadn't heard of any on offer. My funds were running low. Furthermore, it was perfectly obvious that the route I had doodled around Alaska in three cheerful colours, which had failed to impress Schweppes, Rest Assured Beds and thirteen others, was wildly ambitious. The logistics of organising such a trip, or any trip, became too awful to contemplate. My ignorance weighed heavily enough without adding these.

One evening I sat down to approach the problems methodically, starting with the easiest. I would shorten my proposed journey from the original 2,500 miles to one of 800 miles, and my destination would be Nome. I had been reading about a diphtheria epidemic which struck this town in 1925, and about a relay of dog teams which rushed serum there. I now intended to follow their route. The next problem, the difficulty of learning how to handle and care for sled dogs, had no quick solution. It was a matter of application, and I could do no more than sink all my time and energy into being among dogs. Finding a team of my own remained my chief anxiety. I had come to Manley because of the offer of a cabin. Now it seemed that Manley's dogs were sprint racers, too light and thin-coated for my purposes.

Before leaving Scotland I had written to Alaskan newspapers asking if an enclosed request for information about dogs could be forwarded to local dog clubs or enthusiasts. I had received only one reply and this, remarkably, from one of the best-known distance-racers in North America. Susan Butcher had offered to help me, and she happened to live only twenty miles from Manley. I had not been able to contact her since my arrival, but I knew that her dogs were much in demand, and priced accordingly. Puppies and novices were out because I had neither the time nor the know-how to train dogs from scratch. I needed dogs who could teach me. To find a trained dog which was inexpensive *and* good was a matter of rare luck. Cheap dogs were usually problem dogs. My best hope lay in becoming the 'caretaker' of a reasonable team for someone who wanted a season off from mushing.

The first two weeks of November were spent working with Joee and Pam. I started each day at the very bottom, as every dog owner starts each day, cleaning the 'office'. The daylight hours were used for running teams, the evenings were taken up with feeding, and the odd moments throughout were filled with clipping nails, trimming paw fur, pouring drinking water and playing the goat with all the staff. Mushing, however serious, must always include fun.

Little by little my understanding increased and brought ever deepening respect for these animals. We shared up to twelve hours

41

a day together, and I never tired of their company. They won me over. I was completely hooked.

Then one day (it was 16 November) Joee shouted from the woods beyond his dog lot. 'Come over here. I want to show you something.'

He led me to three dogs I had not noticed before, the excess from the craterland. They were chained to trees and had trodden their own craters. The first was a female, as large as any of the other dogs in the lot, weighing about fifty pounds. Her coat was flecked with silver but she was predominantly golden with a black-tinted saddle and dark muzzle. Her broad head was beautifully proportioned. She looked alert and intelligent but her eyes expressed resignation, a sense of hopelessness.

'That's Silver. See how she likes you.' He meant it as no test, for he knew Silver liked everyone. She sprang into a half-curvet, confidently expecting me to catch her front legs. She was gentle and licking and yet a wedge of caution remained, as if she read into me another of life's false promises.

'She's a leader, only six years old. She was never fast enough for my team so we used her as a puppy trainer. Then she got bored having to take out noisy pups twice a day round the same circuit, and at the end of the season having to run like hell to keep ahead of them. She just sat down on us and refused to go. We haven't run her since last season. She's sort of retired now.'

The next dog was a cream-coloured male of average size. Sensor had a pink blotch on his black nose and was nervously bouncy. He demonstrated three fast circuits of his domain, barked excitedly, and in an instant had disappeared into his house. He was not used to an audience.

The third dog was the strangest creature in sight. Alf was black except for a white muzzle, white chest, white socks and a white tip to his tail. The others *looked* like sled dogs but Alf, part terrier, was simply a scruff. He had a droopy moustache. His long hair, exceptionally fine, was tousled and stuck out in a manner suggesting a state of permanent shock. (Except for the colour, an acquaintance was to point out later, Alf and I at least had something in common.)

'He's a bit shy,' Joee cautioned. A single glance at Alf and he slunk away to the extremity of his chain. He let me stroke him at arm's length, but it was an ordeal to be endured. He sat stiffly, looking at me through the corners of his eyes, his lower jaw pulled to one side in a grimace.

'Why is he so afraid?'

'He never got enough attention as a puppy.' Joee explained that a critical period in a puppy's development occurs between its fourth and sixth weeks. It never forgets what it learns in this period. If it is played with and given lots of handling at this stage, it learns to trust people. If this is neglected, months or years of hard work may be needed to win its confidence. Alf had been raised by another breeder and given to Joee. 'Alf and Sensor are only two-year-olds but they aren't shaping up for my purposes. Why don't you borrow these dogs and maybe I can dig out an old sled for you. That way you can at least goof around here, see what it's all about and make the mistakes we all have to make.'

His generosity did not stop there. Joee lent me doghouses, harnesses, bowls and enough food to tide me over until I could arrange transport to Fairbanks to buy my own supplies. I sited the doghouses among trees close to my cabin and cleared an access trail. That evening, with a sled parked outside my cabin door, a bucket of warm feed to hand and six neon-bright eyes catching the light of my headlamp, I felt I had arrived. I believed I was almost halfway to Nome.

Optimism's stultifying effect on our perception is its major virtue. In reality my problems were only beginning.

13

OPTIMISM AND LUCK abounded in this hard country, though, as in the story of Fairbanks' founding. In 1901 Captain E. T. Barnette hired the skipper of the flat-bottomed *Isabelle* to ferry a cargo of supplies up the Tanana River into little-known territory. Captain Barnette had been a placer miner in Washington. He had no boat of his own and knew nothing about boats, for he had adopted the rank of captain during a five-year jail sentence for stealing his partner's share of gold.

His intention was to build a trading post at what is now Tanacross, to intercept the traffic of miners between Valdez and the Klondike where their route crossed the Tanana River. He had promised an acquaintance to name the post for Senator Fairbanks of Indiana.

Laden with the post's considerable inventory the *Isabelle* was unable to negotiate shallows far downstream from Barnette's goal. In an effort to get round the obstruction, the skipper entered Chena Slough, proceeded a few miles and hit bottom once again. Notwithstanding that he was still 175 miles from his potential clients and in an area containing only a handful of prospectors, Barnette refused to turn back. He unloaded his outfit onto the bank. The *Isabelle* steamed off downstream to escape the approach of winter, leaving two figures alone in the wilderness. Beside the tall heap of his belongings Barnette watched the boat go. His wife sobbed on his shoulder. The following summer a prospector called Felix Pedro made a rich strike a few miles away, and the Barnettes could not have been better placed for Alaska's penultimate gold-rush.

The pickings were difficult, however, and Fairbanks was slow to develop, but it was to prove the richest goldfield in Alaska. Within nine years the town had five churches, two hospitals and twenty-three saloons. Ladies left visiting cards, with their preferred day for receiving visitors printed in a lower corner, on trays provided for the purpose by cabin doors. By 1912 Captain Barnette had made a fortune, started a bank, embezzled its money – it took Fairbanks three years to recover – been in and out of jail, and left in a state of personal ruin. Fairbanks might have similarly fizzled out with the decreasing revenues from the mines, had it not been for its importance as a military base in the Second World War and as a construction centre for the pipeline.

Today Fairbanks is a city of 50,000 people. It looks as though the number of churches and hospitals has stayed the same, and the saloons trebled. Its central grid of streets might belong to any city and crossing it is just as testing, for Fairbanks has more cars per head than Los Angeles. Yet no other downtown offers the chance of watching a dog team bowl past rush-hour traffic. The city straggles over a large area to include a university, a military base, industrial estates, satellite suburbs and car parks equipped with electric sockets so engines can be plugged in and kept warm during winter. Fairbanks is a major trading post for the Interior. Its sales of alcohol, like those of Anchorage, are phenomenal. Inhabitants of dry villages across the north flock to it like pilgrims. It suited my interests admirably: easy to enter, easy to leave, well stocked with mushers' needs.

Passing through Fairbanks on my way to Manley several weeks earlier, I had gone to one of the state's largest banks and enquired about the fastest means of having money sent out from Scotland. It was best to arrange for a bank draft, I was told, to be sent by post. The clerk wrote down the bank's address, incorrectly. As a consequence, the first draft was returned to Scotland stamped 'Address unknown', my funds disappeared for two months, I fell into debt to Manley, and eventually travelled a total of 1,300 miles in efforts to claim my money.

However, the full drama was yet to play itself out. This was only the second of four visits to Fairbanks. Another Manley musher, Eric Meffley, had given me a lift in his empty dog truck. I phoned the bank on arrival and was delighted to hear two drafts had arrived. They would be ready for collection that afternoon. During the morning I used the last of my travellers' cheques to purchase enough supplies for my immediate needs. Our last call was at a dog-feed company and on a notice-board there the following message was posted:

> SLED DOGS FOR SALE. Six dogs including two leaders, $900.
> R. Roberts, North Pole. Tel. ---.'

'Eric, could we...?'

North Pole was twelve miles away. We drove there at once. R. Roberts was about to become a father for the second time and needed the money to pay maternity bills. Having only a novice's sentimentality to go on, I asked Eric to examine the dogs and assess their worth. We decided on four: Rosco, a black Siberian leader with white muzzle and clownish eyebrows; his sons, all-white Sisco, and Nanook, grey with a handsome mask; and Kavik, a tough wheel dog whose white woolly coat was patched with what appeared to be coyote. All were males; I wanted, as far as possible, to avoid a mixed team and the complications of females coming into season. We settled on a price of $650, to be paid when I returned later that afternoon with the money. I hadn't suspected that the bank would arrange my appointment for an afternoon on which they were closed; and, the following day, I could never have anticipated Bob Cranhoff.

45

Bob Cranhoff was a lanky streak of misery. Gaunt and balding, he did not directly state that it was the likes of myself who had caused his baldness, but his manner made it clear that at the very least I was ruining his day.

'What *appears* to be the problem?' Bob Cranhoff, the manager, asked. His words sounded on their last legs.

I handed him my two drafts, totalling $2,000, which had just been passed along a line of his tellers and rejected.

'Ahh, bank drafts. I really can't understand why you don't have your money cabled. Only takes twenty-four hours.'

I explained that one of his staff had advised bank drafts, *and* she had got the bank's address wrong.

He ignored this. 'The problem now is that these drafts can only be drawn on, respectively, a bank in Los Angeles and a bank in New York. They will take at least two weeks to clear.'

I told him about my journey and about the dogs. I explained that I only needed $650. It was a unique chance to buy these dogs. I was living 160 miles away without any means of transport. By next week the dogs might be sold, and after today I would no longer have the means of transporting them back to Manley. 'Will you give me an advance on my drafts?'

He was shaking his head. 'I admit it's ninety-nine per cent certain that the banks will pay up, but I am not at liberty to give advances where there is *any* chance of risk. You are, in effect, asking for a loan.'

'Then will you give me a loan? Maybe the dog-seller will accept a deposit at this stage. Please — will you lend me something? Just two hundred dollars?'

He refused. My collateral was unacceptable. He excused himself and said he had already given me more of his time than he could spare. I presented my plea once more but he suddenly interrupted and stood up. Bob Cranhoff tensed and flushed. His forehead was puckered, his shoulders hunched. He held out his arms at quarter-mast and said in a thin, high-pitched voice: 'Why ... why did you choose my bank?'

I phoned R. Roberts to apologise and let him know my funds had not come through. The deal was off. I returned despondently to Eric's truck with $1.60 in my pockets. Eric listened to my story and shrugged. 'Don't worry. There'll be plenty more opportunities. You'll see.' He stared at me for a moment, then took out his wallet and checked the contents.

'C'mon,' he said, 'let's go and get those dogs.'

14

SILVER, SENSOR, ALF, Rosco, Nanook, Sisco and Kavik. My new family.

Joee then added Duran, a powerful male with wolf markings and a superb physique. Of all 'my' dogs, Duran would always catch the attention of experienced mushers first. Eric lent me two of his dogs who needed more attention than he could spare, and so from having had no dogs I suddenly found myself with ten. I ran them in two teams and longed for the day when my expertise would enable me to take them out as one. My education suddenly began in earnest. I had first to get to know the personalities and temperaments of my dogs, and learn to read their body language. Each had its peculiarities. The gait, the angle of the ears, the level of the tail, the height of the head: these varied to suit an individual's style and any break in habit signified an unhappy dog. Dogs are like people. They have good days and off days. They can get bored, lazy and mischievous. They catch bugs, go off their food, pull muscles and fall in love.

I began keeping a record of my doings and observations. Each evening I would take several dogs into the cabin for a few hours so we could get to know each other more quickly. I would repair harnesses, make up ganglines, read books on sledding, and make entries in my log-book.

Some extracts from the dog log.

You don't get much sleep with dogs. Every day brings new anxieties and old ones linger on. Sensor has diarrhoea, but is eating. Duran's a bit dehydrated. A simple test. Pull up a handful of fur and skin above the shoulders and let go. If the skin instantly snaps back, all is well. If it slowly returns or stays up in a crease, the dog's dehydrated. The longer it takes the more serious it is. Two per cent dehydration reduces performance by twenty per cent. Dogs lose most fluid in *warm* and *very cold* conditions, and a dehydrated dog often refuses to drink.

You have to dribble fluid into the back of its mouth (along its cheek) with a syringe. Joee says dehydration will be the biggest problem on my trip. Sled dogs won't drink pure water — it needs to be flavoured. They'll snap up snow while running but this is not enough. Each dog may need as much as a gallon of water a day.

Minus 30°F today. Can't use bowls for feeding as dogs' tongues will freeze to the metal. They eat their food off the snow. Every evening I spend 20 minutes rubbing ointment into dogs' feet as they lie in their houses. Have to do it in bursts as cold on the hands, though their toes are lovely and warm.

Silver can do everything expected of a leader but she's crafty. She has perfected the art of keeping a taut tugline without actually contributing to the movement of the sled. I tread a delicate line between being friendly and being taken advantage of. Leaders can be forgiven for not consistently pulling hard, but is she losing interest in the whole business? I need to know before we end up in a blizzard.

Now I've raved about every dog and had doubts about every dog. Sensor always lopes. The rest will be trotting but he always lopes. Alf was useless — didn't pull, kept on tangling. Nanook got easily distracted and gave up. Yesterday he was the best of the lot. Duran only runs well on the left. Kavik is a grafter but I'm worried he has an aggressive side to him. I feel he's spoiling for a fight.

Rosco stops dead when I shout 'whoa' and the swing dogs run into him. Must remember to brake first, shout second. Silver needs it the other way round!

Problems, problems — all with Rosco. He suddenly began ignoring 'haw'. Refused to acknowledge the possibility of left turns. Five times I had to stop and haul him round to the left. Is it the way I say it? Is he just stubborn?

They say you aren't a real musher until you've repaired a chewed harness and lost your team. Today I became a real musher. During one run I dropped a mitten. Stopped to retrieve it. Stamped the snowhook into the trail and walked back. The next moment the dogs had taken off, ripping out the hook. 'Whoa' had no effect. What a terrifying feeling, seeing your dogs and sled heading off into the distance. As a last hope I yelled 'haw', anything to try and stop them. Silver turned 'gee'. Perhaps it was easier for her. What a dog! She led them into deep snow and they stopped. I was lucky. Must *always* secure my sled before leaving it. My life may depend on it. Also, a loose team invariably ends up tangled, and then fights may break out. Dogs have often been injured or killed in this way.

I've had enough of Alf. He just messes around. He chewed through two necklines today and ate a glove. Has the worst feet of all, so hairy they always gather iceballs. I'm forever having to stop to remove them. Leave them too long and they'll rub the skin raw between his toes. He also has web splits, as do several others. Am told their feet will toughen as the season progresses. So now have to use bootees on the bad feet – a big hassle but the only solution. Alf is as shy as ever – all my hours spent with him have done nothing. A waste of time. Am going to return him to Joee.

The Rosco saga continues. It *is* stubbornness. He only accepts left turns when he knows they are shortcuts to home. He'll never knowingly take a longer 'left' route. (Why then does he accept a longer 'right' route?) He's fine in areas he doesn't know – this gives me hope. But today he pulled Silver away from a correct turn. On Joee's advice I fell on him, held his muzzle and bit his ear (very sensitive). Hated doing it. He didn't like it either, but immediately refused the next left. I took him out of lead and put him in wheel. Meant to be degrading for a lead dog but unfortunately he seemed to like it. He's as stubborn as hell and yet I'm so fond of him. In the cabin he never leaves my side. Can I find a 'right-turns-only' route to Nome?!

I think I've got it. I think Rosco *only* likes leading on his own. He's not totally cured, but what an improvement. I just tried it as an experiment, and he couldn't wag his tail hard enough. Funny business, this. Often it's not the dogs who are the slow learners.

I'm not going to hand Alf back. Can't do it. Though he's always been the renegade, I'm determined to win him over. I want to hand him back as a *real* sled dog. That's in the spirit of this whole thing. It wouldn't be right to walk into a ready-made team. Yet I can't afford to let the emotional side sway me. It's a question of finding dogs who won't give up when the going turns nasty. Things don't look too good at the moment; half the team in bootees, Rosco unreliable, Alf devouring my equipment, Sensor not drinking, Duran not eating, Sisco with soft stools. I wonder how much snow machines cost!?

In order to try to understand Rosco's behaviour I hunted out all the available literature on Siberian huskies. I didn't come across a great deal, and that little was of no help.

'The master of a sled team is revered by the Siberian Husky, who is by nature a loyal, affectionate dog. The commands of the master are followed eagerly by the team while out on the trail.'

One book devoted pages to telling me how to give my husky a bath, which only made me envious. Another was obviously aimed at those who wanted the basics: a fantasy and a relaxing pre-dinner mush across the deep-pile carpet.

'The dog will wait expectantly each evening for the master's return from work, and will be overjoyed when he hears the jingle of keys at the door.'

I threw the book away. My attention turned to the Iditarod. And it was about this time that I met Susan Butcher.

15

'THE LAST GREAT RACE ON EARTH' — A race over 1,049 miles of the roughest, most beautiful terrain Mother Nature has to offer. She throws jagged mountain ranges, frozen rivers, dense forests, desolate tundra and miles of windswept coast at the mushers and their dog teams. Add to that the temperatures far below freezing, winds that can cause complete loss of visibility, the hazards of overflow, long hours of darkness and treacherous climbs and side hills, and you have the IDITAROD.

Each year the Iditarod brings a rush of excitement and media hype. And though the writer of the official press release above has Mother Nature throwing frozen rivers around as daunting obstacles (he clearly hasn't visualised how many mushers and dogs would be lost if the rivers weren't frozen), the essentials of his description stand. It is the longest sled dog race in existence and there is nothing quite like it.

The Anchorage authorities spend most of winter either grateful for not having any snow or laying out considerable sums on getting rid of the stuff, but come Iditarod time, they pay handsomely to have truckloads of snow hauled in and spread about the streets. The race starts in downtown Anchorage on the first Saturday of March and ends in Nome eleven days, two hours, five minutes and six seconds later, if the best-ever time is equalled. The race stop-watch is activated as each musher leaves the line on Fourth Avenue, but it stops twenty miles later at Eagle River. The racers then climb into vehicles and transport their outfits thirty-five miles to Settlers Bay where the real snowlands begin. A second staggered start takes place here, the stop-watch continues where it left off, and the race proper is under way. Time adjustments are made later at a compulsory rest stop so that no advantage accrues from the starting order. After this, it is the first to reach Nome who wins.

The route has a choice of two loops in its middle section, each being used in alternate years. The northern loop, considered slightly tougher, passes through Ruby, and the southern route goes via the ghost town of Iditarod. The route is flagged along its length and a convoy of snow machines breaks trail days ahead of the leaders, but neither measure is a guarantee against poor visibility or sudden dumps of snow. (Twenty inches have been known to fall in as many hours.) The total distance covered by either route is close to 1,150 miles, though the symbolic figure of 1,049 miles is more commonly touted. One hundred miles here or there don't mean much to promoters; much more sponsor-friendly is the fact that the race extends over approximately one thousand miles and takes place in the forty-ninth state.

There are twenty-two checkpoints between Anchorage and Nome, on average sixty miles apart. Automatic disqualification results if any item of mandatory equipment − axe, sleeping bag, snowshoes − is missing on arrival at a checkpoint. Weeks before the race mushers must send out sacks of food and supplies for distribution along the route and these may only be collected at checkpoints. The average racer will require 2,500 pounds of dog food and at least 1,000 bootees for the race. Most checkpoints are in villages where hospitality is available, a few are just crude shelters, but each has a vet who casts an eye over the dogs, offers free advice, medicines, vitamin injections, and can, if necessary, order a dog to be retired.

The rules of the Iditarod have been formulated largely to promote the welfare of the dogs. No team may contain more than eighteen. Each dog receives an identifying splotch of dye before leaving the starting line, and thereafter no dog may be substituted. Unfit dogs may be dropped off only at checkpoints, and are flown back to Anchorage. Teams are forced to withdraw if the number of active dogs in harness falls below five. Racers must take a twenty-four-hour rest sometime during the race at a checkpoint of their choice, and a compulsory six-hour layover at the last checkpoint, White Mountain, before the seventy-seven-mile dash for home.

Racers take part for fun, fame and the usual 'Everest' sort of reasons, but few hold expectations of making money. The first three or four finishers can expect to profit, largely through the indirect revenues of success — sponsorship, advertising, increased demand for their dogs — rather than from the actual prize money. The purse varies from year to year according to the level of sponsorship but is generally around $250,000. This is shared out proportionately among the first twenty finishers, with the winner taking $30,000–50,000. If this seems extravagant, the costs of taking part are equally so. The entry fee is $1,249. The budget-conscious entrant will have little change from $11,000 by the time he or she has trained a team for the season, purchased equipment and food, trucked the dogs to Anchorage, flown them back from Nome and trucked them back home again. To run the race on the scale of those who have a chance of winning can easily cost $25,000.

The Iditarod is one of two ultra-distance dog races, the other being the Yukon Quest which is several hundred miles shorter but with fewer checkpoints and considerably greater distances between them. It runs between Whitehorse in Canada's Yukon Territory and Fairbanks, the direction changing each year. Critics of the Iditarod assert that it has moved away from the spirit and tradition of the sport. It is theoretically possible for an Iditarod musher to complete the race in a series of sprints, sleeping each night under a roof and carrying no more than a light load of about a hundred pounds. The Quest, first run in 1984, was designed to test self-sufficiency and outdoorsmanship as much as dog driving ability. Competitors are restricted to smaller teams and, because of the distances between certain checkpoints, are obliged to camp out and carry loads of around 300 pounds. The Iditarod is long-distance Formula One, the Quest is long-distance Rally. Both are gruelling races but it is the Iditarod, the brainchild of Joe Redington, sen., which steals the limelight. Iditarod's gold-rush, which had lured F. G. Manley to new heights of fortune at the cost of his hotel, peaked between 1910 and 1912 and was Alaska's last major stampede. During this period a trail was cut from the port of Seward to the mining camps of Iditarod, and then on to the Yukon River where it connected with the existing trail to Nome. By the time Old Joe, Joee's father, came to Alaska in 1948 and homesteaded near Knik on the old trail to Iditarod, the trail had fallen into disuse and grown over.

Joe Redington owned a husky within ten minutes of his arrival in

Alaska and his life became centred on these animals. He was saddened to see the decline of sled dogs over the years and felt a marathon dog race, something sensational, might revive interest in them, especially if the purse were rich enough. In 1967, when Joe and some supporters first put forward the idea of reopening the Iditarod Trail and racing the length of it, the proposal was ridiculed. Then in 1972 the US Army agreed to clear and mark the trail, and the project finally became feasible. The first race was held the following year and attracted twenty-two teams. Since then it has, even through sporadic bouts of insolvency, remained an annual event, and achieved everything Joe had hoped. A record field of seventy-six mushers and over a thousand dogs took part in 1986. Other sports have found inspiration in the event and a racing lexicon has been born: Iditaski, Iditaskate, Iditashoe...

In 1985 Libby Riddles became the first woman to win. Within a week sweatshirts were proclaiming 'ALASKA — where men are men and women win the Iditarod'. When another woman won it the following year, the theme stayed the same. 'THE IDITAROD — where men hitch sleds to dogs and chase women across Alaska'. When the same woman won it again, men grudgingly had to give more ground but they didn't give it all. 'ALASKA — land of beautiful dogs and fast women.'

The back-to-back woman winner was Susan Butcher. Each win had produced a new record time. This year she was going for a hat trick.

16

'WELL? WHAT YOU think?' Susan asked as I came in.

She didn't care for telephones. Her cabin at Eureka had only an emergency phone whose battery drained quickly. She and her husband, David Monson, usually stayed at Eureka to look after their kennel but once a week they took it in turn to have a day off. The day off was for a chore. Feeding, exercising and cleaning up after their 250 dogs, six days a week, were the good things in life; talking on the phone was the chore. The Redingtons had a phone and so Susan and David travelled twenty miles to visit their friends and use it.

I had met Susan a week earlier when she was fully dressed. I had thought she was on the plump side but now it was apparent that I had been fooled by Yetification — the transformation through clothes and snow machine suits of any person into something large and lumbering. It happens to everyone in cold climates. She came as a jolt to my system, tired and damp as I was after a day's acrobatics behind a sled. It was hard to know what to think.

'To be honest,' I replied, 'the tie doesn't match, and I think the wind will get in the gaps. Is this your new Iditarod outfit?'

She stood before me wearing a bra, white boxer shorts patterned with an army of green frogs, a red necktie, a peaked cap with fixed headlamp, and a pig's head around each foot. Their mouths gagged on Susan, their eyes looked up at the frogs, and it took a moment for me to fight down a feeling of revulsion and realise they were only pink fluff. Converted to statistics Susan Butcher was thirty-three, five feet six inches, just under ten stone, and had a body temperature, she affirmed, of 96.6°F — that is, two degrees lower than normal. She was extremely pretty. Her straight black hair, one-and-a-half dogs' tails long, fell down her back as a single braid. Her eyes were a very pale blue and vital, but it was her smile which really enhanced her features. Framed, it would have found a place on the wall of any dental surgery. Susan was loud and bubbling, and if she had sufficient natural padding against the cold, one could imagine it being the minimum required of a champion musher. Delighted with my vacant expression, she chuckled noisily and left the room without enlightening me.

'Christmas presents for David,' explained Pam. 'They've just arrived by mail order. She couldn't resist trying them on.'

'The bra was her own,' Joee added, unnecessarily.

Susan's world is dogs. Her favourites receive wrapped presents at Christmas. All are legally retained outside the terms of common ownership that marriage confers. Just as dogs often display two personalities — one in the doghouse, a very different one in harness — Susan's personality changes behind a sled. Her vision narrows to trail width, the tomfoolery vanishes, she turns serious and wills herself into her dogs. In an interview she once tried to explain this to the inhabitants of Manhattan. 'You have to understand, this is all I care about, and this is all I think about. I'm with the dogs twelve hours a day. They're my friends and my family and my livelihood.'

Eureka is a gold mining area worked by barely a shovelful of other residents. Forested hills and a river-filled gulch surround Susan's Trailbreaker Kennels. The centre is a 'village' of dog houses of which two are converted barrel stoves, Granite's still complete with smoke stack. He lies inside with his nose and front paws protruding through the fire door, as if in charge of Stevenson's Rocket. The largest wooden building is devoted to dog care and the others are single-roomed log cabins. The one used by David and Susan as a kitchen and office is the darkest. The previous owner had found the interior so blackened by decades of smoke he had dismantled the cabin, swivelled each log about and rebuilt it inside-out.

One day I visited them at this cabin. David sat at a desk in one corner. A former South Dakotan, attorney, dog food salesman and Iditarod racer, he was always good-humoured and ready to parry and thrust with his sharp wit. His trimmed beard and gold-rimmed spectacles gave him an academic look as he scribbled notes in preparation for the Yukon Quest (two months later, he won its $20,000 first prize with Trailbreaker's second-best team). Beside him Meaty the cat lay Swiss-rolled on top of a carpeted cat tower. A sick dog lay on the sofa while Susan yelled his symptoms into a microphone and a boxful of crackles. Above her, a sturdy shelf supported a complete set of *Encyclopaedia Britannica*. Opposite and far from conspicuous on another shelf stood a pair of tall silver cups. Both were engraved 'The Last Great Race'. One held a pot plant.

Born in a place she never liked and raised in an unsettled family, Susan looked back on her childhood in Cambridge, Massachusetts with little fondness except for two loves which developed during this period: of the outdoors, and of animals. She left home at the age of fifteen and was lured to Colorado by the go-west catchphrase. Here she discovered dog-sledding, the ideal combination of her loves. She worked with dog mushers and as a veterinary technician for four years, all the while realising the west was no better than the east. 'I came to Alaska for the same reason as David, though we hadn't met then. To find a place where you are judged by your performance, not your pedigree.'

For two years she lived in a remote cabin in the Wrangell Mountains, doing nothing but mushing. Her tutor was Tekla, her first leader. Susan recalled an incident: crossing a frozen river, Tekla refused to 'haw' and led the team away to the right. Seconds later, with a sharp report, the section of ice Susan had tried to cross caved in and was sucked under. She and the team were left on the edge, two sled-lengths from open water. This, the cold, the blizzards and the Big Lonesome 'were the times when I learnt Mother Nature was bigger than me.'

The Iditarod was her goal right from the start. She developed a strong friendship with Joe Redington, sen., and he helped put together her first Iditarod team in 1978; in a joint venture the following year the two became the first to drive a dog team to the 20,320-foot summit of Denali (Mt McKinley). She was placed nineteenth in her first race. By 1984 she had finished twice in ninth place, twice in fifth and twice in second. Always just ahead of her was a man called Rick Swenson.

On the first night of the 1985 race Susan found her way blocked by a pregnant moose which charged, ran into the middle of her team and struck out in a frenzy of kicking and stomping. Twice Susan tried to frighten it away with her parka and an axe but was forced to retreat. She had no gun and could only watch helplessly as her prize dogs, still clipped to their lines, were knocked down and trampled. By the time another racer came along and killed the moose with four shots of a .44 revolver, one dog was dead, one was fatally injured and fifteen had injuries, from which they eventually recovered. Susan scratched from the race and watched an honour she coveted fall to someone else. That year the first to pass through the wooden arch in Nome was Libby Riddles.

The following year, in her ninth race, Susan at last saw her leaders, Granite and Mattie, presented with the garlands of victory — matching strings of plastic yellow roses (real ones would wilt too quickly in the cold). With her second win in 1987, Susan confirmed her celebrity status. The chores of telephoning increased. Fan letters arrived at a rate of one hundred a month and a secretary had to be employed to answer them. They came addressed as vaguely as 'Susan Butcher, Alaska' and 'Granite, Iditarod'; and they were delivered. Now she was winning every race she entered and was the measure of every musher.

'Will you tell me your secret?' I asked.

'Sure,' she replied. Her grin was almost as big as the banana *flambé* she was now cooking. 'I've always had a way with animals. It was birth-given. I know the power of a dog's mind and can harness that power. I know how to shape a dog's attitude. I take my dogs running and swimming with me in summer. They come into the cabin, we play a lot, we have fun and I reckon we've developed a special bond. All my dogs love to race.' She went on to explain that she had always made a dog's welfare and fitness her main concern and over the years this policy was showing its rewards. She had a good eye for a dog, bred them wisely and culled those with bad feet, thin coats and low stamina. Some of her dogs were seventh-generation Iditarod runners. She had thirty-one command leaders. Of her likely Iditarod team for that year, fourteen out of eighteen would be command leaders. An average musher would have felt blessed with four.

'You asked for my secret,' she added, 'but it won't bring instant success. More *flambé?'*

The papers and sweatshirts had made much of Libby Riddles' and Susan Butcher's wins. Susan was irritated by the gender preoccupation. She saw no distinction between a female and a male dog driver. Her goal was simply to be best in her chosen field: the world's best distance musher, the world's best dog person. The one who stood in her way was Rick Swenson.

No one had pulled in more Iditarod prize money than Rick Swenson. He had won the race four times and, until Susan's 1987 win, that was three times more often than any other victor. Rick was acclaimed as the master tactician. In addition to breeding and training top dogs, he raced them with skill and employed the full arsenal of psychological warfare. Those who knew him well said he could be either the perfect charmer or, euphemistically, 'real mean'. He had lived in Eureka before Susan moved there, and they had become friends as well as neighbours.

Recently the friendship had soured. Rick left Eureka and moved his entire kennel close to Fairbanks, supposedly because the area's trails were better for training, but it was rumoured he could no longer bear to be in Susan's shadow. His last win had been in 1982. Gossip columns lengthened on the affair. 'To say there is bad blood between these two mushers is an understatement. A river of red runs here,' wrote one monger. Earlier in his racing career Rick was variously referred to as the Mohammed Ali or the John McEnroe of dog-sledding. When he failed to win he was lampooned, even though he seldom slipped lower than second or third place. His abusive comments were seized by the media and further demeaned his image. Some comments were inexcusable, others were simply ill-considered, made under duress: thoughts uttered under harassment by reporters, after days without sleep, and when a year's income was about to be halved, quartered or lost.

It was hard to know the extent to which the animosity was genuine or just kept hot by the press. It was not a question I cared to put to Susan, or an issue I was particularly interested in – except for one strange fact. In 1985, the year of the moose, Susan Butcher married David Monson. The wedding was unusual. The ring-bearers were Tekla and Granite. The best man was a woman, and one of the bridesmaids was Rick Swenson.

As this year's Iditarod drew closer, the media eagerly awaited the red river with sharpened pencils. I took no part in the dispute. Susan and David befriended me and my cause. Invigorated by their enthusiasm (and too much *flambéed* brandy) I visualised myself passing under Nome's burly arch, and Silver and Rosco in hooplas of plastic yellow roses.

That night I mushed my ten dogs under moonlight, and almost believed it possible.

17

'WHOOOOAAA!'

It was almost a groan, slightly swollen at first and fading with our fall in speed. I braked as the team drew to a halt. As the final component it was my job to prevent the whole outfit from compacting like a concertina. We stopped, still strung out in line. A little sniffing, some location-marking; this was the usual form. Ten dogs in harness made a grand sight.

Silver and Rosco then turned upside-down. Rolling was not a trait confined to leaders, but these two were addicts. Silver combined her antics with direction and squirmed ecstatically into snowbanks. Rosco preferred to stay on one spot, raking his paws in the air as his body contorted through a ritual of U-bends. Silver righted herself and scooped up a facepack of snow. She looked abominable. A white mound to the height of her ears perched on her forehead, and a ridge of white ran along her snout. Rosco rolled on, and on. At any pause along a trail he always managed to hit upon an epicentre of pleasure.

The trail cleaved a passage through a forest of black spruce with scatterings of birch and aspen. Three months earlier leaves had wilted in their ephemeral blaze of yellow, fallen and been covered by three feet of snow, all that winter would drop on this region of the Interior. The Fairbanks Trail had once witnessed the passage of miners bent on grubbing for gold in the creeks of Tofty and Eureka, society tourists bound for the waters of Manley, 300,000 units of antitoxin on a mercy dash to Nome, and mail-carriers whose simple acts of delivery belied hardships of epic proportions. Now the trail was trampled by a few teams of dog-racers, snow machine-riders, fun mushers – and myself: somewhere between fun and L-plates.

A three-quarter moon broke free of the highest branches and sidled out into the night sky above the trail. Its corona formed a diffuse, smoky-amber band around its brightness. No more delicate or exquisite quality of light exists than that of the moon in polar regions. Snow crystals sparkle on the ground and in the air. The great expanse of white assumes a satin texture alive with these impish coruscations. Moonlight is a subtle, artful light, so unlike the brutal purge of the sun. I could clearly make out shapes two hundred yards away and discern bolder objects at a distance of half a mile. The view was rendered in monochrome; halftones disappeared. Beyond fifty yards, perspective evaporated. The land's shapes were all there but they might have been ink impressions of a woodcut. Sliding through page after page of imprinted flatness, the dogs ahead just shadows, I would wait in suspense for the impact of the last page, the somersault, the skid, the jumble of arms, legs and tails.

I pulled back my parka hood. From the distance came the falsetto warble of howling dogs. Sixteen ears pricked at the sound. Indistinguishable from the call of wolves, this haunting evocation is the voice of the Arctic. Though not beautiful, it strikes a deep chord in man and has done for tens of thousands of years. It touches something primeval within us, the hunter's edge where respect ends and fear of being hunted begins. Alf threw back his head, closed his eyes and let out a long note with his mouth half-open. He could never resist a song. When he finished he felt no embarrassment at his performance, no sheepishness at having been the only one to lose control. No, to Alf this was duty done, and his sole doubt was whether or not the message had got through.

'All right. HIKE!' Sled and driver were ripped into motion. After the initial surge of excitement the dogs settled into a comfortable trot. Eight miles per hour wouldn't win us any races but would one day, I hoped, get us to Nome. '*Sssssssssssss-schlissssh*'. The sled runners made susurrant protest. They were never happy. On crusty snow they crunched and rattled and groaned. On glare ice they grated. On a hard trail covered with a layer of fresh snow, such as we had now, they cut tracks with muffled abuse.

I felt myself scudding through the pages of winter. The bouncing silhouettes in front exhaled cloudy plumes of vapour which reached back to their tails and mysteriously disappeared before the next dog's approach. The trail occasionally left the woods and crossed open tundra meadows, only to enter another brake of timber. The straight before Dead Dog Corner, crisscrossed by a grid of forest shadows, was long and corrugated and made the sled rear and crash like a boat on a choppy sea.

Dead Dog Corner, Little Salt Creek, Rude River, Rockpile Pass, Groundhog Mountain, Bullfrog Island, Asses Ears, Frigid Crags, Stink River, Frozen Feet Creek. Alaska was littered with names that immortalised unusual encounters, whimsical impressions, hardship and the near-emptiness of a salt cellar.

'GEE!' It was the moment I loved above all others. A successful turn never failed to thrill me. I inflated grossly until my parka bulged with the first of the Deadly Sins. My elation was bounded only by the narrowness of the runners supporting me and my stature shot up to contain the burst of admiration for my dogs, their loyalty and intelligence. One word delivered with the ease of spitting and the whole team had changed direction. Unaware of the grotesque trans-formation they had brought about in their driver, pair by pair swung round and disappeared through a hole in some bushes, a hole in which their driver suddenly feared he would become wedged like a cork.

Whittled down to normal size by protruding branches, I squatted low behind the handlebars to protect my head and eyes. The trail through the osier-bed was no wider than the sled. I shifted my weight onto the right-hand runner, gripped tightly and leaned out into the bushes as the sled was wrenched around a sharp bend which had once caught me out before. From then on the brush withdrew a respectful distance and we glided along the snow-filled course of a creek. Lefts and rights, ups and downs, lean this way, now that, duck under a branch, a long glissade through brilliant night. *This* was my calling in life, *this* was what I was born to do. At that moment there was nowhere else in the world I would rather have been and no one who could have persuaded me to swap lives. For a while, at least, my world was reduced to the simplicity of the present and the primitive joy of being. In the cosiness of our bond it was perfectly obvious why DOG should be the inversion of GOD. I was on the plane of the sublime. But I fell off it when we reached the Tanana River.

When a river is frozen and covered in snow it takes some imagination to believe a river is there at all. Rivers in winter might be tundra meadows to look at, only no grassy tussocks or lone willows poke through, they are sunk below parallel banks and their incision through the scene is forthright. We joined the great Tanana where it was half a mile wide, and turned upstream. For a while Rosco was content to assist in leading but then, for no apparent reason, he pulled Silver over and struck out into deep snow.

'HAW! ROSCO! HAW!' Silver tried to pull him round but Rosco refused to be turned.

'HAW! ROSCO! GET UP, DAMN YOU!' The entire team and sled were now off the old trail, and floundering. I tried to set the snowhook but the snow was too soft and below was glare ice. It took a while to chip two notches to secure the hook and then I waded through thigh-deep snow to lead Rosco back to the trail. I had no sooner reached him than we were engulfed by the rest of the team. Delighted at having pulled the snowhook free, they were now leaping in and out and over each other, tying a glorious knot.

Then began the task of unravelling twenty yards of excited nylon rope. The solution could only come about if the sled stayed firm and the lead dogs advanced to take up the slack each time I untangled a pair. Rosco wouldn't oblige, and the tangle reformed. I unclipped him and led him aside. Five minutes later I was making progress when the snowhook was again pulled out. Another delay. Another knot. By now some tuglines were so tightly interwoven that the dogs had

61

to be unclipped and allowed to go loose before any headway could be made. Alf then chewed through his neckline. Kavik raised his hackles and snarled at Sensor. Duran, whom I had just set loose, began showing his affections to a female coming into season. I silenced Kavik with a word, thwarted Duran's amorous intent, and discovered Nanook's harness had broken. The tangle, if anything, had got worse.

It took what seemed an eternity to create a plausible impression of a dog team out of the canine chaos. We advanced fifty yards and then it all happened again. I have always considered myself to be retarded when it comes to feeling anger, but when Rosco bloody-mindedly headed off-course a third time and Alf bit through a second neckline, I saw red. I stormed up to the front to make a show of discipline, ranting threats of violence I could never have performed. And then realised what I was doing.

I turned and walked away to sit in the snow, ashamed of my loss of control. In one wild moment you can destroy the good work of weeks. Above all other creatures dogs display deep trust and con-fidence in humans. But until these attributes have been allowed to develop they are fragile commodities. Misbehaviour certainly requires correction, but in the right way and in calmly controlled measures. A rational mind is also needed to identify that other cause, the most common one: the *driver's* failure to convey to the dog what is required of it. Self-control in the face of persistent problems is the hardest part of learning to be a dog driver.

After calming myself for a while I sorted out the mess for the third time. When the lines were straightened out I went along and jollied each dog in turn. Their morales were as important as mine. I rubbed their faces in my one-gallon fleecy mittens and babied them with cheery gobbledegook. I put snow on Silver's face until she jumped up and licked me and I polished Rosco's stomach until his rolling bored a hole to Tanana ice. Then I returned to my drift and lay back in thought.

We'd taken forty minutes to cover 400 yards, and this on *familiar* trails with the sled one-quarter loaded. In exactly one month I wanted to fill the sled and leave for Nome. It was seven or eight hundred miles away across unknown terrain. My goal seemed so distant and my means of transport so temperamental, Nome might as well have been the moon. Except for one letter, it almost was.

They could be wonderful, these creatures; but, dear God, they could be exasperating. Had it always been like this for a beginner? Had it been like this for Hudson Stuck and the serum runners? Should I perhaps forget dogs and travel like Ed Jesson? These were the people whose tracks I would be following.

18

Archbishop Hudson Stuck had his share of problems with dogs, and without them. One summer the great man ran aground in his boat, the *Pelican*, on the Tanana River. Unable to refloat his missionary vessel he waited for one of the regular steamboats to pass. The first was in the command of a hard-of-hearing captain who kept his distance and bellowed through a megaphone, asking the Archbishop to identify himself. Twice he asked and each time moved the megaphone to his best ear and caught the one word 'stuck'. Irritated by this, he shouted, 'ANY DAMN FOOL CAN SEE YOU'RE STUCK, BUT WHAT'S YOUR NAME?' On hearing it for the third time he threw down his megaphone and steamed off, leaving the stranded Archbishop on his mudbank.

Between the years 1904 and 1920 Stuck travelled over 50,000 miles by boat and dog sled. The 'Archbishop of the Yukon and Tanana Valleys and the Arctic Regions to the North of the Same' had a parish of 300,000 square miles. He loved the land and his work and was addicted to dogs, tobacco, quoting Shakespeare and reading India-paper books. His sled library was never without Boswell's *Life of Johnson* and Gibbon's *Decline and Fall of the Roman Empire*. Puffing on his pipe whenever it did not interfere with mushing or preaching, he crossed Alaska behind a recalcitrant lead dog called Jimmy. Often unwashed — 'Intolerance of dirt is largely an acquired habit anyway' — but always dapper in well-tailored clothes and furs, this former maverick cowboy and schoolteacher would step off the sled and into village pulpits after days of rigour on the trail. Despite spending most of his life in America he remained essentially British and refused to relinquish his citizenship.

Born in London in 1863 and christened Hudson to preserve his mother's maiden name, the infant Stuck was brought up under the gaze of a green parrot and the influence of illustrated quartos on arctic exploration. The bird and the books were presents from his father's cousin, a sailor, subsequently lost at sea on a voyage from Australia. They proved sparks to a boy with a 'highly inflammable imagination'. Public school and King's College, London, provided him with a formal education and did nothing to dampen his yearning for parrots, icebergs and anything exotic. In 1885 he took steerage passage to New Orleans and retched through incessant storms. He spent the next few years working around Texas as a cowpuncher at the going rate of ten dollars a month, and as a part-time teacher. Regular attendance at church brought him into contact with a bishop who noticed the diligence with which Stuck swept the aisles after the services, and recognised his active mind craving for knowledge. The bishop arranged a scholarship for Stuck to study for Holy Orders.

After being ordained an Episcopalian priest in 1892, the Reverend Stuck served as a pastor in Texas for twelve years. Here his reputation as a defender of the weak was born. His cassock trailing in the humid Texan air, Stuck strode into crusades for social reform, particularly where children were involved. His strength of character and halo-raising achievements caught the attention of the Bishop of Alaska, Peter T. Rowe, who realised he had found just the man for the Arctic around and above the Yukon. The choice was perfect. To a man of energy who for forty-one years had nurtured such a craving for travel that even to read a travel book left him feeling utterly miserable, the offer of a 300,000 square-mile frontier parish could not have been more attractive.

Five feet ten inches tall and weighing 140 pounds, Stuck is usually pictured in a tailed fur hat and a knee-length parka whose hood has fallen and rings his neck with ruff. His chin invariably merges into the dark tones of the photographs so that it is impossible to be sure whether his moustache extends into a light beard, or just shadow. His eyes are well-spaced, and he has pronounced cheek furrows which run parallel to the fall of his moustache and deepen with the breadth of expressed humour. Few arctic cameras have found a face which displays so consistently an enjoyment of the far north, even if the camera was his own. He looks extremely approachable but possessed of the steadfastness one would expect of a man who took photographs (three-minute exposures) at minus 50°F.

Archbishop Hudson Stuck caught bronchial pneumonia in 1921, aged fifty-seven, and died at his home in Fort Yukon. If the low point in his life was being too poor to afford tobacco in 1888, the high point was 20,320 feet above sea level in 1913. In that year he became the first to climb Denali (the original Indian name – he vehemently refused to call it Mount McKinley), having relayed one and a half tons of supplies up the mountain using sled dogs, resting on Sundays.

But among the many religious pedagogues to descend on Alaska, he stands proud for his empathy with the indigenous peoples and their ways of life, his outspokenness in their defence, and for his perceptive vision of the future. 'The time threatens,' he wrote, 'when all the world will speak two or three great languages, when all little tongues will be extinct and all little peoples swallowed up, when all costume will be reduced to a dead level of blue jeans and shoddy and all strange customs abolished. The world will be a much less interesting world then: the spice and savour of the ends of the earth will be gone. Nor does it always appear unquestionable that the world will be the better or the happier. The advance of civilisation would be a great thing to work for if we were quite sure what we meant by it and what its goal is.'

While the other missionaries and teachers were forcing soap into the mouths of native children to punish them for using their 'filthy' languages, Stuck was campaigning for these languages to be officially recognised and preserved. Whereas other missionaries instilled godliness through threats of a vague Devil, Stuck was sensible enough to be more specific. His ecclesiastical thrust was directed at protecting the natives from the evils of white men. Perhaps because he was so outspoken and made enemies, probably because the truth he championed was later recognised and found painful, Stuck's name remains prominent only for his conquest of Denali. It is etched less deeply in Alaskan history than above the grave of a white man in the native cemetery of Fort Yukon.

Of all the winter travellers who had made the journey to Nome before me, undoubtedly the most unusual was Edward R. Jesson. A photograph shows him standing outside a canvas road-house. Across the foreground stretches a dog team, four dogs in single tandem hitch. Three other men share the scene and they are wrapped in fur, fit for the severest blast of winter. Ed Jesson wears a three-piece suit, white shirt with starched collar, tie, and what appears to be either a woolly beret pulled taut or an ill-fitting hairpiece. His hands grip the handlebars of the bicycle he pedalled 1,250 miles from Dawson City to Nome in February and March of 1900. It is a white bicycle with broad tyres. It lacks mudguards, but in style it is no different from bicycles today, ninety years later. They sold for $85 in Boston at the time, but Jesson bought this one second-hand in Dawson for $150.

Adventure and gold fever lured Ed Jesson to Alaska in 1896, three years ahead of the mad Klondike rush. He followed the smaller strikes without success and made nothing out of the big one, and when 'Nome' became the new cry of fabulous wealth he was running a store, post office and wood camp 120 miles downriver from Dawson. The sight of the mass exodus (which totalled 8,000 men that winter) passing his doorstep was too much. He hitched up four dogs and went against the human flow to Dawson to sell his property and business prior to joining the stampede.

Dawson was abuzz with world news, for a bundle of San Francisco and Seattle newspapers had just been delivered by a young man riding a bicycle from the coast. Jesson learned this from the first person he met. Within three minutes of his arrival he had tracked down the bicycle to the Alaska Commercial Co. store and bought it with a just measure of gold dust. In his diary he referred to it as 'a wheel' though it actually had two.

For the next eight days he was the laughing stock of Dawson as he fought the wheel's unwillingness to stay upright; then, after moderate success, he practised cycling within the eighteen-inch trails left by sleds. On the ninth day he felt ready for the journey. Shortly before leaving he had a brainwave which was to ensure him a heroic reception in Nome. He managed to obtain seven of the latest newspapers. They included the Dawson *Daily News*, Dawson *Nugget*, San Francisco *Examiner* and Seattle *Post-Intelligencer*, and all carried headlines in red ink. The only other luggage he took was a pack of food which contained 'a pound of butter, two cans of milk, a piece of bacon, some crackers and a little eggfrypan'. He refilled it where possible on the way. At the most it weighed twenty-five pounds, but for much of the journey it was empty.

66

He took to the frozen highway, the Yukon River, on 22 February. A friend followed close behind for the first 120 miles, driving Jesson's sled and four dogs. Jesson later recalled: 'I went ahead on the wheel and the dogs tried to keep up with me and they did. I took about twenty-five headers into the snow and the dogs would jump on top of me and almost smothered me. I could not break the dogs from piling on top of me without whipping them unmercifully which would break their spirit and this was the only fun they had had all winter so I played the rabit and tryed to keep ahead of them.'

One of his newspapers displayed an advertisement which pronounced 'Whether Your Nose Is Long or Short, Wide or Narrow, Inclined to Be Roman or Retroussé – "IT CUTS NO ICE" when covered with a REED'S "BLIZZARD DEFIER" FACE PROTECTOR. This device affords Perfect Protection... The wearer can See, Hear, Breath, Talk, Smoke, Swear, Chew or Expectorate just as well with it on as off....' But Jesson did not have a Blizzard Defier, and he must have regretted it the next morning when the temperature tumbled to − 48°F.

'The rubber tires on my wheel were frozen hard and stiff as gass pipe. The oil in the bearings was frozen and I could scarcely ride it and my nose was freezing and I had to hold the handlebars with both hands not being able to ride yet with one hand and rub my nose with the other.' He threw the machine in the dogsled. It was beginning to look like a white elephant, as he remarked, but at least it didn't eat anything and he didn't have to cook dogfeed for it. The following day was warmer. The wheel worked. Off he went, following eighteen-inch sled tracks, constantly overtaking dog teams and astonishing everyone with his speed. His was the first bicycle natives had seen and once they had overcome their awe, they chanted 'Mush! Mush! Mush!' to spur him on. He was a sensation. 'Geasus Crist!' exclaimed one Athabascan. 'What you call 'em? White man he sit down, walk like hell!'

Wherever the trail was smooth cycling was easy. Even on the slopes scraped by sleds running askew the tyres gripped the surface, for snow and ice are *less* slippery in extreme cold. The wheel frequently made thirty-five miles before lunch and sixty miles for the day's total. On 3 March Jesson covered seventy-five miles which included the worst surface of the trip, twelve to fifteen miles of icejam which he had to walk carrying the wheel on his back.

It was a week of great surprises for the largely Indian population of Fort Yukon. They had just seen their first horse, a little white mare which they referred to as a 'big white man dog', being driven by a Scottish stampeder called Archie Burns. (He had run out of fodder for the mare. The Indians were mystified why she would not eat the salmon they brought for her. A mile below the village she collapsed from starvation and died.) And they were only a few days from seeing a strapping Norwegian pass through on ice skates, also heading for Nome and averaging forty miles a day at first but rather less after his confidence was shaken by a fall through weak ice. Ed Jesson, his wheel and newspapers came in between. Two hundred villagers watched him resume his journey after only one night's rest.

Two days later he came upon 'a comical sight. It was a red short-haired dog frozen as hard as stone and someone had stood him on his nose on a little snow mound near the trail his tail strait up and feet in a trotting position. He looked like a circus clown doing his trick.' By this time he was pedalling through the Yukon Flats and strong winds knocked him about as they pleased. One gust tossed him head-over-heels on to jumbled ice and almost broke his knee. He lay beside his bicycle trying to collect the pieces of broken handlebar as the wind sent him and the wreckage sliding across the river. He managed to limp away with the salvage and used the disabled wheel as a crutch. His knee remained painful for days but he continued his journey after makeshift repairs to his machine. Two spruce boughs were lashed to the front forks and a sturdy branch fixed crossways effected handlebars. This improvisation enabled him to reach Tanana, where a blacksmith reassembled the original parts.

Another spell of cold snaps forced him to sit out the mornings until tyres and bearings thawed. Once under way the cold was less of a problem. He had to carry the wheel on another occasion when he lost the trail and tramped through knee-deep snow for seven miles, but otherwise he made remarkable progress. The Eskimos of Unalakleet were so impressed with this new contraption that Jesson was besieged with offers of $150 to part with it.

He cruised into Nome at 4 p.m. on 29 March. He was bruised, stiff and suffering from mild snowblindness but otherwise in good health, and he had used enough sapodilla seeds to rid himself of fleas. ('Sapidella seed powdered will sure keep the seam squirrels on the run.') His arrival was the social highlight of Nome's first winter, not because of his means of transport but because of his newspapers. The dance-hall was taken over, and filled for public readings of what had been announced to the rest of the world three months earlier. Throughout the night cheers were raised, hats were tossed and drinks were downed for the victorious end to the Spanish–American war in the Philippines, for Admiral Dewey, for the battleship *Oregon* and for Edward R. Jesson and his wheel.

His cycle run had taken thirty-five days. On six of them he had rested, on the remainder he had pedalled an average of almost forty-five miles a day. The following winter over 250 stampeders followed his example and rode wheels along the Yukon and over the mountains. Gold eluded Ed Jesson at Nome as at all the other places, until years later he bought rich claims in the Fairbanks area. Yet his fame rests not in gold but in being the first to cross Alaska by bicycle, and in the relief he brought Nomers starved of news during six icebound months.

Twenty-five years later the most celebrated journey to Nome took place, but it was relief of a very different kind.

An influenza epidemic ravaged the Seward Peninsula in 1918, leaving ninety-one orphans in Nome alone and many more in outlying villages. One January day seven years later Nome's only doctor, Curtis Welch, was called to examine two children of a visiting Eskimo family. When he found they had sore throats, high temperatures and shallow breathing, he suspected a recurrence of influenza. The children died that evening. Several days later, 21 January 1925, another boy developed the same symptoms: rapid pulse, bloodshot eyes and, at the back of the throat, spots of grubby white membrane which led to a single frightening diagnosis. Before nightfall emergency quarantine laws were in force and Nome's third diphtheria victim had died.

Diphtheria has an incubation period of less than a week and is highly infectious. Within days the symptoms broke out across the town and Dr Welch realised he had an epidemic on his hands. It was the first outbreak of the disease in Alaska for twenty years. The doctor had asked the US Health Service for fresh antitoxin a matter of months earlier, but none had arrived and now the town was frozen in for the winter. Nome's total stock of antitoxin amounted to a meagre 75,000 units and these were already five years old. One to three thousand units usually sufficed to overcome early infection but

30,000 units were required to combat each case of fully-developed diphtheria. At the time Nome had a population of 1,429 (974 whites, 455 Eskimos and mixed-bloods) and was a service point for another 8,000 transients.

The US Army Signal Corps had completed the construction of the WAMCATS (Washington-Alaska Military Communications and Telegraph System) line to Nome in 1903 and it was into this wire that an urgent request for serum was tapped. The plea caught the attention of the media and Nome suddenly became a focus of interest across greater America. A million units of serum were located in Seattle and sent to Seward by ship, the SS *Alameida*, but they would take over a month to arrive. Then 300,000 fresh units were discovered by chance in a hospital warehouse in Anchorage, and it was on these that Nome's hope rested. They were put on the first train north and locomotive Sixty-Six pulled them towards Fairbanks, 298 miles away.

It then had to be decided whether to send the serum by plane – incomparably faster but, equally, riskier – or by slow reliable dog team. Aviation was still in an experimental stage in Alaska at this time, and largely restricted to the summer months. The only two planes in Fairbanks – Hisso-powered Standard biplanes with open cockpits – had been dismantled and put into storage. It was decided to send the serum by dog teams along the mail route.

Nome's mail was thrown off the train at Nenana, a station sixty miles west of Fairbanks. The Northern Commercial Company held the contract and employed dog teams to travel continually back and forth between depots sited at intervals of approximately 100 to 125 miles, or three normal days' travel. Each driver collected mail sacks at one depot, delivered them to the end of his leg, collected the sacks travelling in the opposite direction, and retraced his route. This system enabled weekly collections and deliveries to be made in both Nome and Nenana. The route was Nenana, Manley Hot Springs, Tanana, Nulato, Kaltag, Unalakleet, Golovin and Nome, with various other stations in between. This amounted to a distance of 674 miles and, travelling at about thirty miles a day with an allowance for bad weather, a letter generally made the journey in thirty days. The NCC was now asked to set up a relay of the fastest dog teams along their mail route, each team to cover a section of between twenty and fifty miles, in the hope of getting the serum to its destination in fifteen days. Nome would send out a man whose dog-racing prowess had achieved legendary acclaim, Leonhard Seppala, to collect the serum at Nulato.

Seppala was then forty-eight years old, a Norwegian who had never driven a dog team until his late twenties. Small in stature with bunched, sharp features below a bulging forehead, he had husky-blue eyes and an intense expression. Yet another former gold-rush hopeful, he had lost interest in gold and taken to dogs, and was among the first to specialise in the newly imported Siberian husky. He worked as a 'dog-puncher' for Hammon Consolidated Gold Fields, freighting supplies and equipment to the company mines. He entered his first sled dog race at the age of thirty-six and subsequently built up a formidable team. With his favourite lead dog, Togo, Seppala had won every major race in Alaska, and many of them several times. In 1916 he was invited to compete in the Ruby Derby, a race of fifty-eight miles. He mushed his team 400 miles, won the race by slicing eight minutes off the previous record, and mushed 400 miles home. His time of nine days from Nenana to Nome stood unbeaten. He was the obvious choice to collect the serum at Nulato. Besides, Seppala knew all about diphtheria. His daughter Siegrid had been struck by the disease as a child but had been fortunate enough to recover.

Togo was a little grey dog, named for a doughty Japanese admiral who had trounced the Russian navy in 1904. His puppyhood had caused his owners nothing but consternation. Seppala received him as an unwanted present from a colleague fed up with his antics, and then gave him to a woman who wanted a pet. She let him run riot until he became impossible to handle, and returned him to Seppala. Togo was then eight months old, spoilt and fat. He had never been in harness. One day Seppala departed on a long trip with his best dogs and left instructions for Togo to be kept fenced in. That evening his custodian heard frantic yelping in the dog lot. Togo had tried to leap the fence and caught a leg. He dangled helplessly from the uppermost strands. The dog was released and eased to the ground, whereupon he struggled free and bolted into the darkness.

Seppala had travelled thirty miles when Togo caught up with him. He cursed the intrusion but had no choice but take him along. Togo ran loose until he led the team on a reindeer chase and so infuriated Seppala that a harness was thrown over him and he was placed in wheel. In that instant Togo was transformed. He was instinctively

71

responsive. Seppala later remarked that it was as if the dog had been waiting all his life for a chance to run in a team. He had never seen a dog pull with such determination, or a dog so eager to please. He moved Togo in stages towards the front of the team, and by the end of the day he knew he had found that rarest of dogs, a once-in-a-lifetime leader.

The glass phials containing the 300,000 units of serum were packed into a cylindrical container insulated against the cold. It weighed twenty pounds. Accompanying instructions requested each musher to warm the package beside a stove prior to setting forth to prevent the contents from freezing. At 11 p.m. on 27 January the temperature at Nenana was − 40°F when the serum was placed in the sled of one Wild Bill Shannon, and the dash began. Meanwhile, in Nome, Dr Welch had used up his last antitoxin and recorded five diphtheria deaths, twenty-two confirmed cases, thirty suspected cases and fifty probable infections. Seppala set out for Nulato, 254 miles away, on 28 January. With twelve-year-old Togo in lead he took twenty dogs, with the intention of dropping twelve along the way as fresh substitutes for the return journey. He left behind a dog called Balto, who was to become the most famous dog of this entire episode, but did not rank in Seppala's chosen twenty.

The twenty teams which eventually took part made excellent time. The serum was carried eighty-five miles past the intended handover point of Nulato and met a surprised Seppala near the hamlet of Shaktoolik. It was transferred to Seppala's sled. He about-turned and headed back to Nome, having already travelled 169 miles to make this rendezvous.

Unknown to Seppala, the Health Board in Nome had decided to send out three more dog teams, driven by Olson, Kaasen and Rohn, who were to space themselves over the last eighty miles and relieve Seppala. Olson was waiting at Golovin. Seppala had carried the serum ninety miles − a distance almost double that allowed any other musher. Olson endured the most hazardous conditions of the run as the weather deteriorated during his twenty-five mile leg. At Bluff he handed over to Gunnar Kaasen, who was running thirteen dogs led by Balto.

Because Seppala had such a low opinion of this sturdy black dog, named after a Lapp, Baltow, who had been on Nansen's 1882 expedition to Greenland, Kaasen was allowed the use of him. Kaasen

72

maintained that Seppala underestimated Balto, who had saved his life on several occasions. He did again on this night, as the storm continued. The Health Board began fearing for the runners' safety and wired a message to Solomon, thirty miles distant, to tell Kaasen to wait there until conditions improved. Shortly after this the line went down.

From Solomon it was ten miles to Port Safety where Ed Rohn was waiting to take over for the last twenty-two miles to Nome. The Rohn brothers' dogs hadn't lost a race that season. Kaasen struggled through the blizzard and realised too late that he had passed Solomon. When he reached Safety at 2 a.m. the road-house was in darkness and he saw no sign of life. Rohn had gone to bed, believing Kaasen would have received the Health Board's message and be laid up at Solomon. Kaasen swithered over what to do. He decided to press on. His dogs were going well, the worst was behind him, and it would take precious time for Rohn to hitch up his team and make ready. This hasty decision was to have certain bitter consequences.

On 2 February 1925 Kaasen roused Dr Welch at 5.30 a.m. and handed him the package, five days and seven and a half hours after its departure from Nenana. He carefully unwrapped the furs and canvas, opened the container and withdrew the glass phials. The serum was frozen solid.

It was gently thawed, and found to be still vital. The epidemic was soon checked, and nineteen days later the quarantine was lifted. News of the 'Great Race of Mercy' had electrified the country and the runners and their dogs were fêted across the states. The Territory of Alaska awarded the men who took part $25 for each day of their involvement. Public subscription raised an additional payment, $18.66 for each individual, and wordy citations were presented. The manufacturers of the serum, H. K. Mulford & Co., donated inscribed medals and a special payment of $1,000 to Kaasen for being the one who actually brought the serum into Nome. This sickened Seppala, and fuelled an enmity which he nursed till his death in 1967, aged ninety.

To add insult to injury, as Seppala saw it, Kaasen, Balto and *their* team were offered roles in a Hollywood film and lecture tours of the lower states. Newspapers heralded Balto as the all-time wonder dog and attributed all Togo's racing achievements to him. And it was a bronze Balto which the city of New York decided to erect in Central Park.

The courageous serum run – and courageous it was – fizzled into a bitching session of personal recrimination. The contributions of the eighteen other dog drivers and their teams were overshadowed by the controversy centring on Kaasen. He had covered 106 miles in collecting and carrying the serum. Seppala, who in comparison had covered 260 miles, and Rohn, who had been missed out, were the most outspoken in accusing Kaasen of having bypassed Port Safety road-house on purpose in order to claim the honour of bringing the serum into Nome. It was alleged that there had been scarcely any wind that evening at Solomon; that visibility had been good; that Port Safety road-house had displayed the agreed light signal indicating a relief musher was ready inside; and, most remarkably of all, that the diphtheria epidemic had been blown up out of all proportion. Eighteen months later Nurse Gertrude Ferguson wrote: 'Nome people laughed at the whole thing, and said that most of the scare was good newspaper work.'

Seppala went on using Togo in his team until this favourite dog was retired at the age of sixteen. He could hardly bring himself to talk about the 'newspaper dog', Balto. Seppala continued racing, toured extensively in the Outside states, and finally moved his home to Seattle. His renowned kindness towards dogs is commemorated each year in the Iditarod Race when the Leonhard Seppala Humanitarian Award is presented to the racer who displays the highest concern for the welfare of his or her team.

Balto, a great leader but perhaps not *the* greatest, was bought with 200,000 one-cent coins by the children of Cleveland and he lived out his natural life in pampered indolence. Then a taxidermist stuffed him for Cleveland Museum. In April 1925 a letter was sent to the Commissioner of Parks in New York City with a plea that his proposed statue should surmount the names of all the main lead dogs who took part in the run, rather than just Balto's. The plea was ignored; however, the legend below the bronze dog with tongue hanging out and tightly curled tail still serves as a worthy conclusion to the Serum Run.

Dedicated to the indomitable spirit of the sled dogs that relayed antitoxin six hundred miles over rough ice, across treacherous waters, through arctic blizzards from Nenana to the relief of a stricken Nome in the winter of 1925.
Endurance – fidelity – intelligence.

Stuck, Jesson, the Serum Runners. These were the travellers, and theirs was the trail I would be following. I was almost ready to leave. As ready as one can be without a lifetime of experience.

19

IN THE LAST week of January, five weeks before my intended departure, I was still confronted with several serious problems. Silver had been confirmed pregnant and Rosco had suddenly gone lame. Apart from the worry about their conditions, I was left without a lead dog. I had no sled capable of withstanding a long journey. The food the dogs and I would need had still to be calculated, bought, apportioned, parcelled and sent out to convenient pickup points. I had no contacts along the trail. And I hadn't adapted very well to the cold.

Chilblains had been the bane of my childhood winters. Toes, heels and fingers swelled into red lumps, turned dementingly itchy and then split into raw wounds. At the age of thirteen, when I was expecting to turn into one large perennial chilblain, the afflictions mysteriously disappeared. The memory of them nevertheless made me aware that I was not God's most successful design for the Arctic. I carried little fat: I was about the same height and weight as Hudson Stuck, and neither of us would have been a prize morsel for polar bear. What brought me consolation was the fact that the human body freezes at the same temperature whether it is Amundsen's or a Zulu's; the secret is in conditioning, learning the most efficient way of staying warm, and dressing sensibly.

Surprisingly, the coldest spots in the northern hemisphere are found *not* in the Arctic, but in the sub-Arctic. One is located near Verkhoyansk in Siberia and the other ($-84°F$) near Snag, south of the Yukon River on the Alaskan–Canadian border. In the Yukon Territory legislation was introduced after the gold-rush, forbidding both travel at temperatures below $-45°F$ and the locking of road-house doors at night (travellers had been known to freeze to death before being able to rouse sleeping proprietors). Extreme cold *does* bring two bonuses, though one is of questionable merit. Cold air is so heavy that deep lows are seldom accompanied by wind; and, contrary to popular opinion, cold wakes a sleeping person before hypothermia reaches a fatal stage. There is little compensation for mistakes in what is known to the trade as a *total commitment region*, though the Hudson's Bay Company once set prices. In 1674 the loss of a toe to frostbite was valued at £4. I vowed to keep my toes in my bunny boots.

No praise is high enough for bunny boots. They are not cheap at $160 a pair but the alternative is the loss of £40 worth of toes at 1674 prices. The boots were developed for the US Army in the Korean War. Heavy and made of double-skinned white rubber with an air pocket in between, they lace up to the shins. With a single pair of socks they will keep active feet warm when the outside temperature is −60°F. The only problem is that bunny boots don't allow perspiration to escape and there is a danger of trench foot if they are lived in for too long.

For a normal day's mushing I would wear a cotton T-shirt, polypropylene sleeved shirt, fleece shirt, thin wool pullover, thick Icelandic pullover, and parka with wolf ruff; cotton long johns, corduroy trousers, and thick, quilted over-trousers; thin polypropylene gloves, cotton work gloves, goretex mountaineering mittens and, in extreme cold, one-gallon sheepskin mittens; balaclava, noseband, and a muskrat hat belonging to my father, who procured it from a Russian soldier in the 1940s. Needless to say, attending to a call of nature was a major operation.

Thus clad, and with a good sleeping bag, I had camped out at −30°F and got by. What really gnawed inside, however, was the doubt that I could endure night after night of −30°F. What to do with each day's accumulation of frozen dog bootees and my own sweat-soaked clothes, especially if days of snowshoeing were necessary? And then there was the question of food.

In 1880 Frederick Schwatka described sled dogs as having 'the character of thieves, and all their waking moments are devoted to the one object of making a raid.' This is scarcely surprising in the light of a later admission: 'When food is plentiful the dogs are fed every other day while travelling; but if living in camp once every ten or twelve days is considered enough, and often twenty days will intervene between meals.' Schwatka and two companions made a

76

marathon sled journey covering 3,251 miles in fifty weeks. They hitched up forty-two dogs to a load of 5,000 pounds spread over three sleds. The load included: hard bread, 500 lb; pork, 200 lb; compressed corned beef, 200 lb; oleomargarine, 40 lb; cheese, 40 lb; tea, 5 lb, plus 'a huge amount of walrus meat'. On the way they shot 522 caribou, uncounted polar bears and seals, and four musk oxen.

Today hunting is strictly controlled in Alaska so I was not able to include wayward caribou or musk oxen in my food plan. I hoped to buy salmon along the way but I couldn't rely on this and so had to send ahead parcels of food. My dogs were fed daily. In the morning they were given flavoured water, and in the evening a meal of commercial dry dog food. It was watered to a sludge mixed with mulched chicken which was also commercially prepared and came frozen in fifty-pound blocks. In addition there was a daily ration of fat. From five-gallon lumps I made fat cakes the size of matchboxes. They were caught on the toss with an unerring snap by every one of my salivating crew except Sensor, who didn't like his food served in this manner. He would look away as the delicacy sailed over his head and only when I had gone would he retrieve the fat and leisurely nibble at it.

My own food requirements were more complex. Ideally my nutrition should be in forms which were concentrated and convenient, capable of being eaten raw or cooked, would not require lengthy thawing, and would be appetising enough to overcome the apathy towards eating which hits mushers at the end of a long day. I had the opposite problem to the rest of the world, it seemed. Bright red labels on foodstore shelves rubbed the point home: 'Contains No Fat ... Only 100 calories per serving ... Low on carbohydrates...' I was after all the fat, calories and carbohydrates I could get.

My eventual rations included pasta and soups which could be prepared simply by adding boiling water, spices to give strong flavour, oatflakes, salami, beef jerky, salmon strips (called 'squaw candy'), logan bread, dried fruits, trail-mix, chocolate, sweets, coffee and tea. Scott of the Antarctic gave his men a daily ration of a quarter-pound of butter, which prompted me to add this item to my menu. At first I forced the stuff down only by imagining myself at gunpoint. Within a short time the very sight of my butter ration made me yearn for hypothermia. Concurrently, Sensor went off his fat cakes and provided me with an honourable solution. I shared

77

Sensor's fat among the others and gave him my butter, which he eagerly accepted on the snap. I did, however, set aside a reserve of butter for a contingency when it might be all I craved.

At −30°F most food becomes as impregnable as concrete. I would have to wear each day's allocation of fourteen cheese slices, salami, jerky, chocolate and two Mars Bars close to my body so they would be malleable for whenever hunger panged.

An increasingly important concern was to find contacts for food drops between Manley and Nome. Poste restante was out because my parcels would contain frozen dog meat and would need to be stored *outside* post offices rather than inside. A possible solution occurred to me one afternoon when a teacher invited me to talk to her class, and that evening I wrote letters to seven schools along my route. In essence they were the same. 'Dear Children of Elim, I wonder if you would be able to help me ....' I explained my need to find people who would be willing to receive my food parcels and asked about the availability of dog food. As an inducement, but regardless of whether they could assist or not, I offered to talk to them about Scotland and one of my pet subjects, the creatures of Loch Ness.

By this time my bank drafts had been cleared and I was anxious to claim my funds from a bank which had refused me a $200 loan (and subsequently, the papers reported, donated $60,000 to the purse of the Iditarod Race), and pay off my debts. Neighbours offered me a lift to Fairbanks in their Transit van and it was just as well the vehicle was large, for my purchases almost filled it: boxes of groceries, sacks and slabs of dog food, gallons of fat, and a second-hand sled. It was a different style of sled, a toboggan-type designed for rough country and deep snow. Basically it was a bed of durable plastic with an upturned front. It stood only three inches off the ground on runners, made of wood but soled with polyethylene, which extended three feet beyond the rear of the bed. A curved brushbow protruded at the front to act as a fender and handlebars rose at the back. A canvas bag was tied into place and its upper edges ran from brushbow to handlebars. The sled required certain modifications for my purposes: an extra thickness of polyethylene to be added to the runners, the brake to be reinforced, and a sheath knife to be fixed to the handlebars – this in case an emergency arose, such as a bad tangle or a fall through weak ice, when dogs would have to be quickly cut free from their traces.

A roving dog had bred Silver within the first two weeks of my caretaking; I had isolated her at the first signs of her coming into heat but it must have been already too late. The pups were not kept. Destroying them was the most wretched task I had to undertake, and it plagued my conscience for weeks. I was devoted to all my dogs, but Silver was my favourite. We had developed a special bond and I feared now it might be broken. Several hours after the last of her pups had gone I squatted down before her house and called her. She looked at me and didn't move. Then she emerged, much subdued, and after some hesitation she reared up into my lap and pushed her head inside my parka. She rested like this for a full minute.

I have been told that dogs do not think like humans and that it is wrong to infer human emotions from their behaviour. If the first is true then we are fortunate, for they are lessons to us in forgiveness. The second assertion I dispute. I knew I had been forgiven.

While Silver was temporarily out of action and I was questioning whether my trip would ever become reality, Rosco suddenly developed a limp. Working the joints produced no reactions of pain, and no inflammation was apparent. Twice a day I applied DMSO, a deep-penetrating medication with a foul flavour, and twice a day Rosco religiously licked the liquid off as soon as my back was turned. I put him on aspirin and let him rest. Both my leaders were incapacitated.

I can't remember what made me think of trying Alf. By all normal criteria he was *not* leader material. However, one afternoon I put him in single lead and off we went. It wasn't unusual for dogs to hold this position for five or ten minutes before suddenly quitting. I waited for Alf to quit. The minutes passed and on he ran. That afternoon he completed one and a half hours up front. The next day he logged three hours. Alf was a leader. He was not reliable on his commands, but this was only because of his lack of experience. Inspired by this, I found Duran to have equal potential. Neither Sensor nor Kavik would run in single lead, but happily shared the front position with another. It was just the tonic we all needed.

The outlook gradually brightened. 'Dear Alastair Scott,' read a letter with nineteen signatures, 'The third, fourth and fifth grade class of Elim would enjoy receiving your supplies. We would also enjoy hearing about Scotland from you when you arrive here. There is no place here that we know about to buy dry meat or fish. We will try to catch some tomcod, a small fish, for your dogs. We look forward to seeing you and hope you have a safe, successful journey. Sincerely, ...' It was signed by the sons and daughters of the Nagaruk, Moore, Jemenouk, Saccheus, Daniels, Murray, Paul, Takak and Aukor families. Similar replies arrived from other schools and a Manley teacher supplied me with the names and addresses of several colleagues, so that two weeks before my proposed departure I had contacts in Tanana, Ruby, Galena, Koyukuk, Nulato, Kaltag, Unalakleet, Elim and Nome.

The next few days were a turmoil of statistics, logistics and cheese slices. I worked out an approximate schedule of travel, guessed where we might be hemmed in by bad weather, where dog food might be available and where not, how many torch batteries would have been used by Unalakleet, how many fat cakes we'd need in Kaltag, how many Mars Bars, films and antibiotics in Nulato, how much tarpaper for lighting fires – the list ran down to the floor. I planned for twenty-nine travel days, sixteen rest and exploration days, and allowed for twelve emergency days of immobilisation.

Spare sections of gangline still needed to be made up, 380 cheese slices to be unwrapped, and twenty-nine sets of day rations to be prepared. I thawed 230 pounds of mulched chicken, filled and emptied a $2\frac{1}{2}$-pound baking tin ninety-two times and left the chicken bricks outside to turn solid (the advantage of having an open-air freezer). Each brick was a day's ration for three dogs. Finally, I made 376 fat cakes. When all was ready my dogs hauled the resulting parcels to the post office; twenty-six in all, they weighed between twenty and sixty pounds and included fourteen sacks of dried dog food each weighing fifty pounds. I watched with a sense of relief as the mail plane safely took to the air.

For several months I had been running thirteen dogs with a view to selecting the optimum number of eight for my journey. The dogs which came out on top were the original four borrowed from Joee and the four I had bought: Silver, who had fully recovered and was her former perky self though she had to wear a jacket to protect her underside from frost; scruffy Alf, my protégé; Sensor, who always loped and never trotted; and Duran, whom everyone admired. Joee generously waived a hire fee for these four, but I signed an agreement promising to pay two thousand dollars if they became maimed or failed to return. The rest of the eight was made up of Rosco, whose limp had disappeared after ten days' rest; the brothers Sisco and Nanook who always ran together, pulled hard together and used each other as a pillow when resting; and woolly Kavik. I still suspected a latent streak of aggression in him but he was probably the toughest dog in the team and best suited to the journey. Nothing ruffled him. He never let his tugline go slack, he looked comfortable anywhere, ate and drank anything at any time and always loved attention. I was proud of them all. We had travelled 1,170 miles together in training.

My trip was to have one measure of success. It was not the completion of a specific distance, but an arrival somewhere, anywhere, with eight fit and happy dogs. If the place was Nome, all the better. At all costs I wanted to avoid the sort of incident that had once befallen a dog called Nanook and his master, Archbishop Hudson Stuck.

The sad event took place, coincidentally, in Manley Hot Springs at the end of a trip from Nome – the exact reverse of my situation. Stuck had always resented what Frank Manley did to the Balm of Gilead, cutting it down to build his resort ('It is a scurvy trick of Fortune when she gives large wealth to a man with no feeling for trees'), but he was given further cause to regret the place. At the resort Nanook was kicked in the abdomen by a horse and so badly injured he had to be destroyed. A mail-stage driver offered to perform the task.

> Nanook knew perfectly well that it was all over with him. Head and tail down, the picture of resigned dejection, he stood like a petrified dog. And when I put my face down to his and said 'Goodbye', he licked me for the first time in his life. In the six years I had owned him and driven him I had never felt his tongue before, though I had always loved him best of the bunch. He was not the licking kind ... as we crossed the bridge over the steaming slough we saw the man going slowly down the river with the dog, the chain in one hand, a gun in the other. My eyes filled with tears; I could not look at Arthur nor he at me as I passed forward to run ahead of the team, and I was glad when I realised that we had drawn out of earshot.

Preparations can go on forever if allowed, but we had drawn a line and now we were about to cross it. I packed the sled. On 2 March we set off, leaving a small note pinned to a tree in the empty dog lot.

'Gone Nome.'

20

There is always a certain risk in being alive,
and if you are more alive there is more risk.

Henrik Ibsen
(Quoted in Sir Vivian Fuchs, *Of Ice and Men*)

21

I WILL LONG remember the elation I felt as we pulled out of Manley and up into the Tofty hills. The land was still dormant under its weight of white and we were the only signs of life on a trail which snaked through giant candy-flosses of spruce and birch. Now and then clusters of snow tumbled from branches and made the dogs start but their rhythm never faltered. Lingering hints of wood smoke mingled with the redolence of pine; the sun was a shrouded glow and the sky looked like fog. We slipped through the surrounds easily and the log cabins of Manley had disappeared before I thought of looking back. When dog sledding is perfect it is one of life's supreme sensations. It is the spirit and pleasure of travel in highest refinement. Man, animal, earth; a primitive trinity, beautiful in harmony.

That morning it was perfect. The dogs knew something was up, that this wasn't just another training run. As we left familiar ground a sense of mutual interdependence was reinforced within us, we became a single entity from two wet noses at the front to two bunny boots at the rear. My fears dissolved in the relief of being under way.

The temperature was a relatively mild 10°F and we would have preferred it colder. Zero to −10°F are ideal mushing temperatures as dogs and musher don't overheat so readily when working, and snow offers less friction. The sled was carrying about 200 pounds of equipment and supplies, half the 'normal' load expected of a team of eight. Silver and Alf were in lead, Rosco and Sensor in swing, Nanook and Sisco in team, and Duran and Kavik in wheel. We followed the snow machine tracks of trappers on what in summer is a road to the goldfields of Tofty. Tanana was our goal, sixty miles away, but we would camp overnight and take two days for the journey.

'GEE OVER!' Silver nudged Alf over to the right of the trail as a fourteen-dog mirage approached, materialised and passed. Seven pairs of dogs in rainbow harnesses hugged the ground with heads held low, driven by a fat, smiling Athabascan with swarthy skin. We stopped for long enough to exchange names, destinations and motives. Then he miraged and evaporated. Freddy Jordan of Tanana was travelling one hundred miles to race ninety and defend his previous year's win in the 'Minto 90'. A snowshoe hare broke cover ahead of us and my dogs surged after it. Their acceleration was as sharp as if I'd changed gear. They maintained the new pace for a quarter of a mile, even though the hare had immediately disappeared to one side. If there were enough snowshoe hares around Minto, I reflected, we'd give Freddy a good run for his money.

We entered a region of rounded hills which had lost their trees to fire. Scattered across frozen creeks named in the quest for gold, charred trunks stood as desolate totems. Among those hills we rode the ups and downs of lesser hills and looked over to Roughtop Mountain (3,150 ft) on our right. Beyond Roughtop was Eureka, but Susan, Rick and fifty other mushers were in Anchorage at that moment awaiting the start of the Iditarod in three days' time. A raven flew high above us, folded its wings, rolled over and flew on. They are the only birds in the world to fly upside-down for fun.

'Last hill to Kaltag, dogs!' Silver ignored me and continued pointing one ear forwards for trail sounds and one ear backwards − for commands, *not* meaningless chatter. We were beginning the descent to the Yukon River, which we would then follow for 200 miles to Kaltag. Our Alaska would not be the Great Land of 18,000-foot peaks and glaciers; they were far to the south. Our Alaska would be the heartland vastness of forests and rolling hills, and the treeless coasts.

The trail descended into the ghost towns of Tofty and Wood-chopper. Gold was discovered here in 1906 and partners like Long Poke Pete and Crooked Neck Jorgenson flooded in by the thousand. Woodchopper alone once boasted a hospital, fourteen saloons and thirty-five sporting girls, and was probably proudest of the latter. The infamous 'madame' of the Klondike and Nome strikes, the Oregon Mare – so called because her whinnying voice could make dance halls tremulate – was said to have reaped further fortunes here. But this history was now told by nothing more than old upheavals, rotten timbers and rust. There were new excavations too, the scars of D9 Cats. The area had a summer population of around six. We passed three-walled cabins, collapsed wooden flumes, iron sheds and a lubricated dragliner with a fifty-foot boom. Then we were out into flatlands of fire-ravaged spruce and frozen tussocks which jolted the sled.

We passed El Dorado Creek and came to the cleft of American Creek. It was spanned by a bridge of spruce trunks, as perilous for dogs as a cattle grid. I unhitched Silver and walked her over an alternative route which involved breaking trail and a rather alarming drop. Then I added an extra section of gangline and put her in single lead ahead of Alf. 'ALL RIGHT!' The dogs disappeared over the bank and a moment later I was plunging down the drop, braking and struggling to hold the sled upright. Silver and Alf were already over the top of the far bank by the time the sled nosedived the last few feet, to be jerked forwards and upwards without a pause. Within thirty seconds the obstacle was behind us. I had never seen such a demonstration of power by dogs. They were still looking pleased with themselves when we stopped to camp near Fish Lake that evening.

Three hours and forty-two minutes of daylight were accorded this latitude, 65° North, on the winter solstice, but by early March this had increased to twelve hours. Wherever convenient on this trip I intended to stop two hours before dark (7.30 p.m.), because setting up camp and preparing food was considerably easier in daylight than in the narrow beam of a headlamp. An efficient routine was essential but it still required a minimum of three hours' hard work to complete the day's chores. The first necessity was to don snowshoes and set up the dogs' picket line. This was a cable with individual droppers spaced evenly along its length, which I secured between two trees.

Snow had to be compacted so that the line could be stretched out close to ground level. The dogs would then be transferred, the more excitable ones going near the ends where their frolicking would cause less tugging on the others.

The next priority was to cut wood for a fire. Four to six gallons of hot water were required, and it took about one and a half hours to melt and bring to the boil the equivalent in snow. In snatches between tending the fire I would put up my tent.

Again, snowshoes were used to trample a base. The tent was a simple canvas type, spacious, with a conical roof and shallow walls. It provided no warmth, merely protection from snow falls. I suspended it from a cord tied between two trees. Half the floor was left as bare snow because I would be entering and leaving in boots, and half was covered with a groundsheet. When the tent was up I would start my own meal cooking on a Coleman stove, and snowshoe off to collect spruce boughs for the dogs' beds.

Spruce boughs were a special treat. Aside from serving as insulation mats, they imparted a wonderful fragrance to the dogs. Hudson Stuck wrote: 'When the dogs have eaten, ... they retire to their respective nests of spruce bough and curl themselves up with many turnings around and much rearranging of the litter. Feet and nose are neatly tucked in, the tail is adjusted carefully over all, the hair on the body stands straight up, and the dogs have gone to bed and do not like to be disturbed again.' This was true of all except Duran. He disliked spruce boughs. He would stand with three paws on the snow and hold the fourth over the offending material as if I were asking him to sleep on a bed of nails. In time, though, he grew to appreciate them and smelled sweetly too.

By this time the fire would be running short of wood. I'd collect extra and ensure there was plenty of kindling made ready so the morning's fire would light instantly. When the water boiled the dogs' food had to soak for twenty minutes to swell the dried food. After this I would have my supper, prepare hot water for the morning, storing it in a thermos bucket, check the dogs' feet and apply ointment where necessary.

Finally, I would write my diary by candle-light for an hour, or until my hands refused to be rewarmed. This would take me to eleven o'clock or later. I would wear half my clothes in my sleeping bag but take *all* my clothes inside, including the wet ones, to dry them with body heat. My socks, always wet because of the bunny boots, I placed on my stomach, the source of maximum heat. An arctic traveller must have either a defective or a selective sense of smell.

Twenty-eight miles down, six hundred and fifty odd to go.

22

'WOULD YOU CARE to read the first lesson?' Mrs John Starr asked.

She stood before a poster of a Red Indian in the posture of crucifixion, smiled and handed me a note: 'Genesis 44: 1–17'. Saint John's Episcopal Church was an attractive log building with a log belfry, and I had heard its bells tolling on my arrival. Tanana had three churches, the other two being the Arctic Mission (no service) and the Catholic Church. As the congregation of twelve trickled in I watched my dog team through a window. The sled was tied to a post and the dogs curled up resting, still in harness but unhooked from their necklines. At eleven the bells let out a clamorous set of peals. The dogs leapt to their feet in shock. Nanook and Alf barked and Silver began growling. I looked at Genesis 44 and momentarily disowned them.

Mrs John Starr was a lay service leader substituting for an itinerant minister who made only infrequent appearances at Tanana. At Manley it was different. A Methodist minister, Wal Firmin, arrived from Fairbanks each Sunday as long as the temperature was above minus twenty, flying his own bush plane. With guitar under one arm and a combination amplifier–loudspeaker under the other, he walked from the airstrip to the church and his faithful eight. He was middle-aged, wore a Country and Western shirt and string tie, and his smile was benign but bent, suggesting an old operation on a harelip. He played a mean guitar and sang boldly, but his heap of talents was used up by the time he came to his sermon. One week he was a Defence Minister, spelling out the Russian Threat and extolling patriotism. His theme was, 'When the next war comes, dear God, may AMERICA win'. The following week patriotism had been cast aside and he gave

.a lesson on how to break the speed limit without getting caught. He had served as a flying minister in Liberia for seventeen years. As with Hudson Stuck, I suspected Wal Firmin of an allegiance split between God and his means of transport, but it was impossible to work out the respective proportions. So I was interested in Tanana's ecclesiastical slant.

Mrs Starr was a mild, sincere woman who looked as if she would happily step down if anyone else offered to take over. She wore pink trousers, pink blouse, grey sweater, and a pink and green headsquare. She spoke quietly and her words were well-rehearsed. She led the Collect and referred us to hand-me-down songbooks from a church in Detroit. Several additions had been made, and one of these was a bilingual rendering of

> Into my heart, into my heart, Come into my heart, Lord Jesus...
> Uummatimnun, Uummatimnun, Kaiñ Uummatimnun ataviik...

I read my lesson. Mrs Starr led a prayer which began 'Let us pray for the Iditarod mushers, that they will arrive safely in Nome...' and reminded me that the Iditarod had started the previous day in Anchorage. A young girl led the singing, which was unaccompanied, a swinging spiritual which I feared would startle my dogs to their feet and set them howling again.

> Rock-a my soul in the bosom of Abraham...
> So high, ya can't get over it,
> So low, ya can't get under it...

My dogs ignored us. I felt like an intruder and wished I were outside with them. And I forgot to note what it was that ya couldn't get over or under. Finally John Starr gave a five-minute sermon. He wore a suit and shared his wife's sincerity; together they humbly held Tanana's cross aloft. He complained about the way nobody would walk even a block to go to church nowadays whereas everyone used to walk a mile to the Mission in the old days. We were told that the day of judgement was coming: 'Now you can see it,' he warned. 'We have war and famine, it's snowing, floods, ...'

It was a desultory sermon. I wasn't sure how the snow fitted in. He jumped theme every sentence. Brevity was its quality.

Finally we were asked to turn to our neighbours and shake hands. I shook hands with Ken Lilly, who said 'I've got a cabin at Sunset

Creek. Sixty miles from here towards Ruby. Plenty of food in it. Help yourself.'

Tanana was a small place. Everyone knew who you were before you arrived. It had a new and an old half and consisted of two long main streets on the right bank of the Yukon. New Tanana was the downstream end. Its several blocks of state-built houses, with aluminium shiplap sidings painted in light greens and yellows, grew out of the end of the airstrip. A hospital, modern school and the Dinaa Dilnaa Kka Yigh were found here. The latter translates into officialese as Tanana Elders' Residence but means 'Our Parents' House'.

Old Tanana, the heart of the town, comprised tin-roofed log cabins, piles of firewood and a mess of disembowelled snow machines. Alaska is the 'land of spares'. Nothing is thrown away, but is junked close by for the day when bits can be profitably plundered. Comeliness plays no importance in village life and this litter makes practical sense. Here and there fish racks supported shrivelled, dangling shoals. The central hubbub contained two supermarkets, an anonymous guest house, a deflated Stars and Stripes hoisted above the post office and two petrol pumps with fifty-foot hoses for serving river craft in summer. A local information sheet advised 'There are no banking services, but there is a laundromat'. (Obviously my banking experiences were all too common if laundromats were seen as offering comparable services.) And everywhere there were dogs. Tanana was said to have a population of 450 people – seventy-five per cent Athabascans – and 750 dogs.

Opposite Mission Hall, half a mile upstream from the town, was the confluence of the Tanana and Yukon Rivers. The earliest settlement in the area was known as Nuchalawoya, 'where the great waters meet', and it was an important summer meeting place for Athabascans across the Interior. For centuries truces were declared among warring families once a year and a festival of dance and story-telling was held in conjunction with a trade fair. Here Hudson's Bay blankets met Russian knives and changed hands in the northernmost market of east and west.

The three great white traders of pre-gold-rush Alaska, Harper, McQueston and Mayo, all worked out of Tanana. McQueston used a tame moose to pull a snow-plough and clear the way to his trading post, and Harper grew turnips, his prize ones weighing six pounds.

In 1891 the Episcopal Mission of Our Saviour Church was built below the hill and it was still standing, the first building visible to a musher from Manley. The fort, however, had gone.

Fort Gibbon was built separate from but adjacent to the old town in 1901, to garrison soldiers engaged in the construction and maintenance of the telegraph line to Nome; then (purportedly) to keep the peace. Finally, in 1923, the army ran out of reasons and the fort was abandoned. Stuck passed through in about 1910, when a varying force of 200 soldiers was kept in residence at an annual cost of $350,000. They supported as many as eight liquor shops in the town. The sale of liquor to natives was illegal but bootlegging was rife and Stuck noted sadly, 'The evil influence which the town and the army post have exerted on the Indians finds its ultimate expression in the growth of the graveyard and the dwindling of the village.

'The army post will not detain visitors,' he continued, '... there is no stateliness of building ... no military pomp or parade whatever; ... A flag is raised and lowered and a gun is fired every day: the rest is fatigue duty with a moving-picture show twice a week.'

To cap it all, the military reservation burned 3,000 cords of wood annually. When Stuck closed his teeth on a subject, he didn't let go. 'Setting aside the maintenance of the telegraph service, ... it may be said without unfairness that the salient activities of the army in the interior of Alaska are the consumption of whiskey and wood.'

To discover something of Tanana's more recent state of affairs, I went to Silver's old home. She was a Tanana dog by birth, raised by an ex-army man, Will Purvis. He had invited us to stay.

23

SILVER RECOGNISED WILL and gave him an affectionate greeting, then quickly returned to me. 'Your dogs are on the fat side,' Will remarked – which probably accounted for Silver's allegiance – 'but that's okay for the sort of trip you're doing. Best to have some reserves in case they fall sick.'

Will had given up an army career to find adventure in Alaska, and he, Amy and their two children had once lived fifty miles away up the Tozi (Tozitna River). They had recently moved to a handsome cabin they built a mile out of town. Will had a reputation for being able to fix any machinery and he made sleds which he sold to the likes of Joee Redington and George Attla. Amy's mukluks won equal renown and shod Susan Butcher, among others. She was also a trained nurse. Like most rural Alaskans they earned a living from a hotchpotch of toils and skills. In summer they fished. Will operated both a net and a fishwheel.

'A fishwheel? The lazy man's method!' I commented. My host was tall, fair-haired and, fortunately, easygoing. He smiled.

'Then that shows how little you know about fishwheels.'

Contrary to a Scotsman's opinion, fishwheels are not traditional native traps but were introduced by whites at the turn of the century, and they require strenuous management. Anchored in the river, floating on pontoons, they are basically a paddle-wheel with four blades which the current turns. Two of the blades are made of wood and two are net baskets. Will's wheel was the largest size in common use, with baskets twelve feet long. Salmon swimming upstream to their spawning grounds would be scooped up, deflected along a slanting chute near the wheel's axle, and directed into a separate holding box; thus, the baskets were self-emptying on the upward cycle.

'Simple in principle, but the rig needs frequent adjustment. It can slip sideways, driftwood can mess up the works, and a single log can wipe the whole thing away. Then, it needs to be moved according to the rise and fall of the river and the runs of fish. But if things go well, at the peak of a run I can take eight hundred salmon a day with the wheel.'

Tanana's winter unemployment rate of eighty-five per cent was matched by almost every village along the great river. Welfare payments and, to a much lesser extent, the Permanent Fund Dividend provided the financial base of many families. Trapping was a bread-winner for a small proportion of people. Seasonal firefighting contracts brought in considerable money but always necessitated travel outside the region. Tanana crews fought fires in Oregon, California, Southern Alaska – they never knew where they'd be sent next – but they were never paid for fighting fires around Tanana, a state policy aimed at preventing arson in times of scarce work. But it was river fishing which kept the Interior alive.

'The Yukon *is* the economy of the Interior. If the fish stop running, the Interior dies. Every resident has the right to subsistence fishing. The days you can fish are limited, but you can take any amount to feed your family and dogs for the year. If you've got a small dog team, you'll need about a thousand chum salmon a year for them. Some families take seven to eight thousand salmon a year for subsistence.'

Tanana was 700 miles from the mouth of the Yukon and the village populations along this stretch totalled roughly 6,500 people. Assuming that five hundred of them engaged in subsistence fishing and each removed one thousand fish from the river each year, half a million fish would be caught. This figure, a modest estimate, was a small fraction of the overall numbers involved, taking into account the catches made in and around the Yukon estuary, the subsistence catches on the 1,300 miles of the Yukon above Tanana and extending into Canada, the two million fish taken under commercial licences along the entire fresh water course, and the uncaught fish which successfully evaded the nets and wheels and reached the spawning grounds. (In 1986, 90.5 million salmon were caught in Alaskan waters.)

The commercial scene was kept separate from the subsistence. Licences for both commercial nets and wheels were restricted. Will's wheel licence was one of 166 and if he chose to sell it, as he had a right to do, the going rate was $15,000. A net licence sold for $10,000. He had a fish camp which he had used for years. He had no title deeds to it, but most of the Yukon's best fishing spots were similarly 'owned' by families through right of tradition. On certain days Will could use his wheel, on certain days the net and on others he was prohibited from using either. Certain days were for commercial licences only, others for subsistence only. If the fish ran on a fishing day, well and good; if not, that was just bad luck. With a commercial licence he could sell only the fish caught in a commercial period. It sounded an administrative nightmare.

That controls on the taking of fish were necessary was obvious when the demands on a limited supply were so great. However, there was resentment among the majority natives that most of the commercial licences belonged to monied whites. They, the original riverine people of Interior Alaska, were commonly restricted to subsistence livelihoods only. Subsistence was defined as 'the customary and traditional uses by rural Alaska residents of wild, renewable resources for direct personal or family consumption as food, shelter, fuel, clothing, tools or transportation, for the making and selling of handicraft articles out of nonedible by-products of fish and wildlife resources taken for personal or family consumption, and for the customary trade, barter or sharing for personal or family consumption.'

A subsistence fisherman was allowed to *trade* any accidental surplus of his catch. If he caught extra fish beyond his family's requirements expressly for the purpose of selling them, this was a criminal offence. Subsistence rights were essential to the livelihood of Alaska, but they created a wobbly conflict between tradition and profiteering. The issues were often cloudy, as in the case of salmon roe. Will explained.

'This is the big dispute at the moment, and it's real serious.' He sighed and ran a hand through his hair. 'We catch our subsistence salmon. The fish are dead. Some of them are females carrying roe. We've never had a use for the roe and in the past it was always thrown away. Then along come the Japs, who pay a fortune for it. So for years we've been selling our subsistence roe. Why not make money from it rather than waste it? It was illegal but we were allowed to do it. But you always get some idiot who abuses the system, and a few Nenana fishermen were caught selling big quantities of so-called "subsistence roe", only they were throwing away the rest of the fish. That was wrong, but now the state is trying to stamp out *all* sales of roe from subsistence fishermen. They've handed out lots of indictments. I've got one. Most of my friends have got one, even though we've never sold any roe that wasn't from our subsistence catch. It's serious. We stand to lose our permits, our gear, and pay fines. We've taken out a legal case against the state.'

'Will you win?'

'We should get off the charges, but whether we can get the law changed to allow us to carry on selling subsistence roe − I don't know. It's probably too hard to enforce if some people are determined to abuse it.'

Will had put almost everything into his fishing. He had recently sold a top Yukon Quest team, ten dogs, for $6,000 and used the money for a fishing boat. A boat that might now be confiscated. He hoped to raise another quality dog team but it would be a long-term project. He expected only ten per cent of any litter to produce a good racing dog so he would have to breed one hundred dogs to get a team of ten. The first hopefuls were romping below racks of smoked sheefish and salmon. I asked Will if I could buy some fish for the next leg of my journey.

'Sure, only I'm not selling it. I've got plenty, so you can take what you need.' He motioned me towards a rack with enough smoked salmon to make the gourmets of Europe drool. And I'd be feeding them to my dogs. 'By the way,' Will added, suppressing a smile, 'just for the record, these fish I'm giving you are from my commercial stock.'

We spent three days in Tanana. One day I borrowed a snow machine, an 'iron dog' as it was called, and mushed it at fifty miles an hour; but it was nothing compared to the real things. For the most part the real things and I toured the town and explored new trails. We went to the top of a nearby range of hills and visited the last modern remembrance of the military in Tanana. Like a cross between a sci-fi set and a gas works, the towers and radar dishes of a Distant Early Warning Line station stood abandoned. It once alerted the US to invading bombers, but despite its awesome size it was incapable of detecting ballistic missiles and now it was merely awesome junk.

Each day we passed Tanana's failed attempt at agriculture. It was a large flat area on the edge of town where a modern dream of acres of barley was lying fallow. Barley had grown well and all the equipment had been imported, but no one had been interested in working the land. We passed a barely-used combine and other farm machinery lying at an angle in a snowdrift.

On our last afternoon I gazed at a display in a supermarket window. Half my attention was on the reflected faces of the Athabascans who were also looking at the goods. They reminded me of the Greenland Innuit. They had the same long black hair, the same missing teeth and, especially those who drank, the same impetuosity in their eyes. Tanana had a reputation for a more unruly lifestyle than most villages, a hangover perhaps from Fort Gibbon.

I hadn't found people approachable. The colour of my skin seemed to typecast me and erect an immediate barrier. 'It's just as well you know someone here,' one girl had said after we'd exchanged a few words, ''cos no one else would have taken you in.' It was not said unkindly, but simply as a matter of fact. Quiet attempts at conversation produced little response, but I had not expected easy acceptance. The Athabascans were not known for extending warm welcomes to white strangers and, historically, whites had done nothing to deserve them.

The other half of my attention was on the window display. Neatly arranged were jars of Mexican chillis, Californian pickles, Texan corn and a geographical assortment of other goods on a green background. Green was obviously the key, for every product had that colour of label.

'You Irish?' asked a man with Budweiser breath.

'No, Scottish.'

'Happy Patrick's Day to you anyway.'

'You celebrate Saint Patrick's Day here?'

''Course we do.' He looked Athabascan to the core. Not a trace of Celtic. I felt Saint Patrick would have been delighted to know Athabascans celebrated his day with Mexican chillis and dog races. The races took place that afternoon, and there were special events for all classes and ages.

'Get up, Sandy, Sandy go, GET UP, SANDY' screamed one eight-year-old girl who was watching the three-dog trophy slip from her grasp as Sandy stopped to lift a leg on a marker. The day's highlight, however, was the baby category. On the starter's orders a dog sprinted 150 yards pulling a wide-eyed toddler bound horizontally to a small toboggan. At the finishing line half a dozen catchers stood ready to dive *en masse* at the outfit and seize any part. If they missed, it was 1,300 miles to the far end of the race track.

One hundred and twenty-five miles of questionable trail lay between these festivities and Ruby, the next settlement along my route towards Nome. This stretch and the one across Norton Bay were the sections which held the most fear for me. Silver and Sensor led us through the town and away on the fourth morning. Figures with bundles on their backs were on their way to bank their laundry. A notice-board announced a church raffle in which first prize was a gun. Several of Tanana's video outlets were doing brisk business, and through an open window I glimpsed Jane Fonda contorting on a TV screen and being mimicked by a sturdy silhouette. When we came to a snow berm I imagined McQueston's moose ploughing a way through for us until we were back on a fine trail, and then, inexplicably, I caught myself humming 'Rock-a my soul in the bosom of Abraham'.

24

ALASKAN MAPS ARE, by their own confession, only moderately reliable. The USGS 1:1,000,000 map of the Fairbanks area currently on sale is not an unreasonably remote example, as it centres on the state's second city. The map's reliability guide in the legend shades four per cent of the area as 'good' and ninety-six per cent as only 'fair'. It omits three major roads (two of which have been in existence for thirty years) in a region which has only five, and is strong on sled routes which have long grown over. A lover of wilderness could hardly ask for anything more, though I would have appreciated a few more landmarks on this particular morning.

'Rock-a my soul' didn't last very long. As a result of a mis-understanding I took a wrong turn on leaving Tanana and several miles later found myself separated from the Yukon by a bank so steep ya couldn't get over it. We tried to find a way round but eventually had to return to Tanana, two hours later, where a gentle gradient led down to the Yukon. My maps were 1:250,000 and perfectly adequate as long as I stayed on the river. It was a mile wide here, though frequent islands forced splits into narrower channels. Below two feet of compacted snow, below four feet of ice, the mighty river worked away at transporting an annual eighty-eight million tons of Canada and Alaska to the Bering Sea. The trees it toppled from its banks in summer were still a major source of wood for Eskimo communities on the coasts – once it had been their only supplier of wood for harpoons, kayaks, paddles and firewood. In winter the Yukon van-ished and became one long sinuous snowfield.

Tanana shrank behind us until only Mission Hill stood out against a wash of greens and browns below distant blues and the odd white summit. Cottonwood and spruce crowded the edges of banks which dropped steeply as faces of sand, sandstone, shingle or puddingstone.

The foreground was an expanse of snow, pure or sullied but always snow. This would be our view for the next two hundred miles, a world of white with a fringe of colour.

The trail, so far, was a perfect surface prepared by the paws of iron dogs. The rubber track that powered them along rolled the snow flat. We ran alongside one bank and avoided the mid-river jumble of ice. Every so often triangular slabs had been squeezed up like shark fins and sometimes the trail crossed fissures where ice crusts had parted. These were the only hazards. Our trail must have been a motorway compared to what Ed Jesson and his 'wheel' had encountered on this section ninety years earlier.

> I got my papers [newspapers] and hit the trail to try and pass a preacher and a man with 2 horses pulling double-enders and cuting the trail all to pieces. This was worse than the rough ice. The horses broke thru every step and it was the hardest riding I have ever seen. I had to get ahead of these horses. The horses feet were bleeding and every little ways the sleds would slide off the heigh trail that was packed by dog teams... In trying to get back up ... they would twist 8 foot sections right out of the trail. Most of the dogs had broken many of their toenails off having caught them on the edges of these horse tracks and holes. The trail was bloody for miles from the bleeding and limping dogs.... Many men had sprained their ankles and were limping.... What those dog men said and thought about the 2 men and horses would burn up a ton of asbestos fireproof paper.

In Jesson and Stuck's time there had been cabins every few miles along the river and road-houses strung out at twenty- or thirty-mile intervals. The stampedes at the turn of the century had brought massive migrations of fortune-seekers into the land. They had left as the strikes declined, but so great had been their invasion that sixty years were to pass before Alaska's population once more equalled the peak level of those gold-rush days. The population is considerably greater now than it was then, but it is also considerably more concentrated. Forty-three per cent of Alaskans live in the borough of Anchorage. Five per cent live on or north of the Yukon River and occupy the few cartographic dots on roughly half the state's territory. In Tanana I had heard of six people who *might* be living somewhere along the next 125 miles. The Interior of Alaska is actually 'wilder' now than it was ninety years ago.

My map marked some cabins which had gone, washed away by the river or reduced by rot to the forest floor, but some were still standing. At Mile Twenty we passed close enough to Folger's Camp, a cluster of cabins, to read scrawled on a gable 'Enter at your own risk. Andy's Pad along the Yukon. $100 a night rent.' We looked for Andy but he was absent, his Pad locked, his price a tired protest against abused hospitality. It was an unwritten law of the far north that cabins were left open, with kindling and dry wood prepared and a stock of food set aside, for the hapless traveller seeking to escape the cold. No payment was expected, but by the same token the traveller was required to leave the cabin as it was found and, at the earliest opportunity, replace the food used.

We stopped here to rest and drink. I had a thermos of coffee, and the dogs half a bowl of 'soup'. (Each morning we set off with two gallons of hot water and food scraps in a thermos bucket. The bucket also held the day's ration of chicken bricks, sealed in plastic bags, so that they would be thawed in time for the evening meal.) Only a few of the dogs drank. The others each gave his reflection a cursory glance, dimpled it with his tongue and then stretched out to doze in the snow. Every day I had to note which dogs were off their water on a regular basis and test them more often for dehydration. The problem was the heat. Twenty degrees of frost constituted summer to them but instead of drinking more, they drank less. It was just another sled dog quirk to safeguard mushers against nights of restful sleep.

We moved on after half an hour. High above us cirrus clouds were being teaseled into wisps, twisted into whorls and allowed to drift off as imitation mother-of-pearl. I was looking around for cumulus which might threaten snow when the sled suddenly stopped. My stomach hit the handlebars and I was pivoted into a complete somersault, landing on my back on a patch of glare ice. Fortunately my parka and hat helped cushion the blow, but I lay there for a moment struggling for breath. The dogs turned to look at me, wondering what had happened. Their expressions accused me of negligence, and it was undeniable. My momentary preoccupation with the clouds had coincided with an end of driftwood sticking up through the ice.

At Mile 35 a cabin hove into view on our left, and Darvin Island on our right. At times it seemed like that — as if we were on a treadmill, standing still and revolving the scenery towards us. The cabin was blackened with age and stood a hundred yards off the trail atop a steep bank. A glance at the snow and chimney told me it was unoccupied. I parked the sled on the river below and made nine snowshoe trips up and down ferrying supplies and equipment, and relaying the dogs to a picketing spot close to the cabin. It was a simple weatherproof structure stocked with saws, axes, three pairs of snowshoes, two beds, sleeping bags, blankets, clothes, books, food and a fitted stove. Any solid shelter was preferable to a tent, but this one was almost four-star by my rating. Poor access, no immediate firewood and a barrel stove so dented that a pot sitting on top was barely in contact – these resulted in lost points. This criticism came later, on a full stomach and in a warm bed, and under such circumstances was a grand indulgence.

Before blowing out the candle I read a few pages of *The Unabridged Jack London*, which stood out on a shelf of desert westerns, but didn't persist. 'To Build a Fire' is not a story to comfort a lone traveller watching minus twenty grow frost gardens on his windows.

Instead I took out my notebook and jotted questions on mammoths, in anticipation of an encounter the next day.

25

Mammuthus primigenius HAD no need to reach tall for its food so evolved smaller than a modern African elephant, standing no higher than eleven feet at the shoulder. Its body was proportionately elongated and covered in a dense fleece, an undercoat six inches deep and outer guard hairs forty inches long. Short legs held it close to the cottongrass, mosses, sedges and dwarf trees on which it fed, and it had bog-browser's feet. These were spongy pads of fat tissue and elastic fibre, marvellously broad and fitted with horizontally extending toes. Forty-five thousand years ago this creature, the woolly mammoth, had duplicated the migration of the more ancient (and by then extinct) mastodon and was a prolific species. Plodding softly on its cushioned feet it had walked from Europe to Siberia, crossed the Bering Sea Land Bridge and taken up residence in Alaska.

Two immense tusks up to ten feet in length provided adequate defence against its main enemies, the sabre-tooth tiger and, later, man, but were useless against deep bogs and the last Ice Age. By eleven thousand years ago *mammuthus primigenius* had died out, but a remarkable number had tumbled into baths of natural preservative and been quick-frozen.

Permafrost is a continuance of the last Ice Age and it affects the boreal lands within, and in some cases even far south of, the Arctic Circle. Under existing snow, ice or the insulating mat of vegetation that constitutes tundra, the ground remains permanently frozen to depths of 2,000 feet. In 1901 a 'devil creature' was discovered being eroded from a mud bank at Beresovka in northern Siberia. It turned out to be a perfectly preserved woolly mammoth. The contents of its last meal remained undigested in its stomach, its luxurious fleece was caked and matted but still intact, and its flesh had deteriorated so little that when thawed a portion was fed to the scientists' dogs without ill effect. In Alaska the remains of mammoths and mastodons turned up frequently enough for Eskimos to incorporate them into their myths as a large form of mole. In 1882 Edward Nelson recorded: 'The bones of the mammoth which are found on the coast country of the Bering Sea and in the adjacent interior are said to belong to an animal known as the *kĭ-lûg̃-û-wûk* (*ko-gukh-pûk* of the Yukon). The creature is claimed to live under ground where it burrows from place to place, and when by accident one of them comes to the surface, so that even the tip of its nose appears above ground and breathes the air, it dies at once. This explains the fact that the bones of these animals are nearly always found partly buried in the earth. The Eskimo say that these animals belong to the under world and for that reason the air of the outer world is fatal to them.'

Mammoths are believed to have been difficult to enmire, and why quite so many ended up in the same bog remains a mystery, but mammoth graveyards do exist. One site at Berelekh in Siberia contained 140 bodies. (Mammoth and mastodon ivory is currently one of the Soviet Union's more unusual export items.) Another site, as yet unexcavated, was on the Yukon River. It was marked on the map as the Palisades but was known locally as the 'Boneyard'. We passed it on our second morning out from Tanana.

26

THE PALISADES WERE a colonnade of lurid sandstone triangles, eroded from the river bank and standing in relief. Their finely chiselled shapes and regularity conveyed an impression of design, a touch of Classical Greek in the Yukon's architecture. They ran for three miles, and the Boneyard was at their upstream end. It was nothing to look at: indistinguishable from any other crumbling wall of mud and stones, almost sheer and between two and three hundred feet high. I scrutinised the lumps and protrusions for signs of ten-foot tusks and fatty feet, but the *ko-gukh-pûks* remained hidden. Many people had been lucky enough to come along after a rockfall and find themselves face to face with a piece of mammoth. It was illegal to excavate here, because the cliff was poised to collapse and apparently waiting for a slight pull on a tooth. A further reason for keeping our distance was a dark slash between us and the Boneyard, a sucking rush of open water.

'ALL RIGHT, Rosco!' He was in single lead and enjoying it. His tail wagged even when we crossed a snowbridge over a stream. This was at Birches, where we came to a cardboard sign 'Ken, please post these, thanx.' It was easy for a stranger to know everyone in this thousand-square-mile block and be on first-name terms with them all. Often that was the only name one had. I knew that somewhere up ahead were Rod and Jan. This sign had been written by Lenny, who had a cabin at Birches. Everyone knew that Lenny was not at home because he had taken his dogs to Nome to watch the end of the Iditarod race. 'Ken' was the Ken Lilly who had shaken my hand in church and offered me his cabin at Sunset Creek, about halfway to Ruby at Mile 60. One of the beauties of a wilderness is that by virtue of being a part of it you are accorded a certain status and privilege. Here, I was admitted to an extended family.

Several miles later the dogs' ears suddenly stiffened. I had heard nothing. Their noses tested the air and then, as decisively as a weathervane, swung round 60° to the right. All morning I had noticed the frequency of large cloven-hoof prints in the snow and miles of savaged willow beds. These signs had made me wary, for I had no gun. I distrusted firearms, considering them a greater potential threat to myself than whatever I might select as a target. But then I had not yet come face to face with an irate moose.

These were the first moose we had encountered. Three hundred yards away a cow and half-grown calf had heard or winded us and were struggling up a snowed-in bank. The mother ploughed a way to the top and the calf followed until it lost its footing and floundered for a moment. Its mother paused to stare at us. She held her long pantomime face five feet off the ground and stared, a behemoth caught blowing a raspberry when the wind changed.

Historical sources are confused as to when moose first appeared in Alaska. Some maintain it is only in the last fifty years that moose have migrated from Canada in substantial numbers – certainly, elderly Interior natives affirm none were ever seen during their childhoods. Yet moose have been in Alaska for considerably longer than this, and their disappearances can be explained by dramatic declines in their population, some approaching virtual eradication.

Schwatka noted that severe winters in the early 1880s had killed many moose and that they had been scarce since then. He also remarked that prior to 1867 moose noses were dried by the Russians and eaten as great delicacies. Schwatka shared my fascination with this part of the animal's anatomy. 'I never comprehended what immense noses these animals have until I got a good profile view of this big fellow, ... his nose looked as if he had been rooting the island and was trying to carry away the greater part of it on the end of his snout. The great palmated horns above, the broad "throat-latch" before, this animal might tilt forward on his head from sheer gravity, so little is there apparently at the other end to counterbalance these masses.'

Other creatures had also left their traces alongside the trail. Double dots inside double obliques signified a snowshoe hare had bounced lightly here, barely breaking the surface even on the longest hops. Spruce hen and ptarmigan had strutted around in a dither. Foxes had stalked them. Once the rough indentations of a scuffle led to bloodied snow. Searching here and there, resting, backtracking, circling, constantly changing direction ... each sequence told a story on a single theme. The quest for food was intense and dangerous.

I stopped to examine some unusual prints. They were identical to dog tracks only much bigger. 'What d'you think? Wolf?' The dogs offered no definitive opinion.

They *were* wolf tracks, but final proof had to await the arrival of Bud Strong an hour later. He appeared as a distant light in the afternoon. I thrilled at the sight. An approaching snow machine or dog team was what every cross-country musher wanted to see, not so much for the meeting, but for what it signified. With luck this driver would have left a trail for us all the way to Ruby. Bud pulled over well ahead to avoid frightening the dogs and I halted the sled alongside. He removed his helmet to reveal an otter-skin hat underneath, and seemed keen to have a rest and a chat.

'What's that dog's name?' he asked, pointing.

'Duran.' It was normal for mushers to introduce their dogs before themselves.

'Nice lookin' fella. Ah had me a dog jist like 'im once. But that was a lawng time ago. Chrissakes, what in creation's that ...?'

'Alf. And he's a great dog.'

Alaska is too young to have developed a state accent. Its accents are imports from the Lower 48, and as varied. Minnesota is probably the most represented state. Bud's accent might have been Minnesotan, clear and animated, but *lawng* was southern. The accent, like the owner, was more likely a unique blend, personalised by years of solitude. Its identification was not helped by a wad of chewing tobacco which made a goitre-like bulge in one cheek and was responsible for an amber icicle encrusted in his beard.

Bud Strong was seventy-eight years old and looked the anachronistic prospector. He lacked felt hat, gold pan and burro but he had the right face, what little was visible. Wrinkled brow, bushy eyebrows and sharp eyes all set within a devil-may-care halo of beard as long as a mammoth's undercoat. His padded jacket and matching trousers were modern, but his mukluks looked to be out of the Middle Ages. Made of grease-stained moose hide, they swelled each foot into a bloated lump, extended up to the knee and were bound on by an extravagance of criss-crossing thongs. Judged by his footwear, Bud might have been on his way to slay a dragon or burn a witch.

'Did you have many dogs?' I asked.

'Twenty-eight was the most. Started off with two bitches. Nineteen twenty-four, it was. Chained 'em outside. Wolves bred 'em. Built me a team that way. Those dog-wolf pups sure made good sled dogs.'

In 1924, aged fourteen, Bud went to join an uncle who was trapping up the Porcupine River, north of Fort Yukon. He took to the lifestyle easily. When his uncle died the following winter, Bud decided to continue working the traplines on his own. He was then fifteen years old and the only company he had that grim winter was his uncle's body, kept in an outside shed to await burial in the spring thaw.

For the next four years he worked a cloverleaf configuration of traplines centred on his main cabin. Each trapline was about one hundred miles long and furnished with ten cabins for overnighting. They were substantial cabins, eight feet by ten feet, double-walled and insulated with moss. He operated a rotation system, working one line each year and letting the other two lie fallow.

The best quality furs he stretched, scraped and stored in permafrost where they kept well for years. Each spring he took the poorer furs down to the Yukon in Canada and gave them to a passing RCMP patrol, along with a shopping list of dried foods. The RCMP took the furs to Dawson City, sold them, bought his provisions with the proceeds, and returned. They left the food supply *and the change from the fur sale* at a prearranged cache for Bud to collect when he was next in the area. Once he missed out this spring trip and went almost two years without seeing another soul.

'When ah quit in nineteen thirty ah had me a sixteen-foot sled loaded high with prime furs. Took twenty-eight dogs to pull it to Fairbanks. Guess what ah got for them furs, go on, guess....'

'Three thousand dollars...'

'Ha!' A huge grin split his beard and tugged at the icicle. Whatever else, he had obviously got fifty years of fun out of this story. 'Ha! Twenty-eight thousand five hundred dollars, they fetched. A lawt of money in them days.'

It wasn't until he put his helmet back on that I noticed what he was carrying on the sled in tow.

'Hey! ... a wolf!'

'Yep. Ah shot 'im ten miles back. That's four hundred dollars' worth lying there.'

It was much larger than I had expected, and wilder-looking than I had wanted to believe. I was a defender of these maligned animals and prepared to argue that no authenticated case of a wolf attack on man exists. The head before me explained how the evil reputation originated. It was black and shaggy. A lip was rucked back to expose a fearsome array of teeth. Its tongue lolled out, a ghastly and very human pink. Thick hair sprouted between the paw pads.

'Don't like these things much,' Bud said, kicking the Yamaha with a medieval foot, 'but when they go, they go.' He straddled the machine. 'By the way, ah've made you a trail to Koyukuk.'

'I've made you one to Tanana.'

The Yamaha roared to life. When they went, they went.

I spent the night at Sunset Creek. Ken Lilly's cabin was five star. Good stove, plenty of firewood, trail-to-door access. I felt slightly depressed. It was a rare mood for me, but I couldn't help thinking of a fifteen-year-old boy running a trapline beside his dead uncle, a young man and his frozen wealth being pulled to Fairbanks behind twenty-eight dogs, a seventy-eight-year-old man on a lone hunting trip in winter. The Great Land, and Great Landers, could make one feel very small.

And what would Rod and Jan be like? I rather dreaded meeting anyone else in the heroic mould. With luck Rod and Jan would be degenerate. They would watch videos, use microwaves, have rust on their guns and be intimidated by winter. They would be newcomers and stay-at-homes.

27

It is as though the land slowly works its way into the man . . . The land becomes large, alive like an animal; it humbles him in a way he cannot pronounce. It is not that the land is simply beautiful but that it is powerful. Its power derives from the tension between its obvious beauty and its capacity to take life. Its power flows into the mind from a realisation of how darkness and light are bound together within it, and the feeling that this is the floor of creation.

Barry Lopez, *Arctic Dreams*

28

Snow fell in soggy lumps; not single flakes but clusters. They found ways through my ruff and hit me in the eyes. They plastered a layer over my parka, my sled, my dogs. Every now and then a dog would shake on the trot and burst into colour – except Sisco and Sensor who merely appeared to be moulting – but at once would be reclaimed by this all-consuming whiteness. I had never seen snow fall with such malevolence. It was an attempt at burial.

We lost the trail. Visibility was down to less than a hundred yards. There was no horizon, no sense of gentle gradient and no awareness of bias to left or right. For six or seven miles we had been able to follow Bud's day-old trail. Where it ran through deep snow it had not yet been filled and was discernible. Where his snow machine had crossed patches of hard-packed snow its marks had vanished. On hard-packed snow a sled can go anywhere. We must have veered off in a new direction for a mile or so. The firm surface came to an end. Soon the dogs were up to their shoulders in soft snow and forced to porpoise. It was pointless trying to retrace our tracks because they were already covered.

I called a halt and fitted belly jackets to the front four dogs. A dog's underparts were provided with little natural insulation and so were susceptible to frostbite in deep snow or cold wind. The rear four dogs didn't need jackets in this case because the trail would already be trampled for them. Then I had to strap on my long Victorian tennis rackets.

The choice of snowshoes for breaking a trail is a compromise between comfort and kindness. A large pair makes easier walking because they prevent you from sinking too deeply, but they do nothing to flatten the snow for your dogs. A smaller pair is kinder on the dogs because you sink to the depths of your knees and compact the snow, your leaf-shaped prints overlapping to form a narrow but relatively smooth lane. In particularly deep snow you might have to tie cord to the toes of the snowshoes and work your feet like a puppeteer. My snowshoes tended towards kindness rather than comfort.

A further problem was that my dogs were instinctive trotters when placed in harness. They were not like trappers' dogs, who are trained to plod along in line matching a snowshoer's pace step by step. Rosco was a severe test to my stamina. I would find myself about to step ahead, weight pitched forward and off-balance, but the foot I needed wouldn't move because Rosco was standing on the tail of the snowshoe. He could never understand why I fell over every time he wanted to show some affection. The problem was compounded by the rest of the team wanting to join in the fun.

The only option was to anchor the sled and leave the dogs while I snowshoed a trail for half a mile or so and then came back to collect them. The snow was too soft to anchor the sled with any degree of certainty and although a loose dog team was unlikely to run far under such conditions, above all else I dreaded losing my team. I had devised my own method of securing the sled when the snowhook proved useless. I unclipped one of the leaders and Kavik, my strongest dog; then I turned them about and clipped them back to their lines in reverse. With these two facing the wrong way there could be no co-ordinated attempt at flight.

The snow continued. Snowshoes on and off, walking, driving — for two hours we made slow progress in an unknown direction. It was exhausting work. Sometimes we hit crusts that held our weight for a few yards. We never knew when we would break though but we always did, and ended up floundering once more.

Then the snowfall thinned and stopped. An hour later we had worked out where we were, found the trail half a mile away and were gliding along under blue sky. Under these conditions it would have taken us fifteen minutes to travel what had just taken three hours. Spruce forests and undulating hills once more offered safe passage. It looked a harmless scene, incapable of the sort of disappearing trick we had just witnessed. Yet this land allowed no room for complacency. It was beautiful, but in Lopez's terms; and it demanded respect.

We travelled on to Moose Point where we stopped to look for what sounded like the opening lines of a fairy tale. It was said two brothers lived somewhere near here in cabins they had built a mile apart, opposite each other and on different banks of the Yukon. I looked around but could see no signs of habitation. Then the sound of barking emerged from woods on the left bank. The river snow was a firm crust here and Silver led us straight towards the sounds, up a trail in the bank and to a cabin set back in the woods.

My route from Manley to Nome was the same taken by the telegraph wire laid by the US Army Signal Corps in 1903, although no remnants of it had so far been visible. Here at Moose Point the old wire was still in use. Rod Kocsis used it for snaring beavers.

29

OF THE FUR-BEARERS trapped in Alaska, the weasel-like marten and the beaver are the species most commonly taken. The set for a marten consists of a fishhead wired to a branch and a gin trap placed before it on the only line of access. To catch a beaver under several feet of ice is a much more challenging proposition. These dumpy aquatic rodents, master engineers of the animal kingdom, lead extraordinary lives. They are intelligent and highly adaptable and it is believed they were formerly diurnal until the trapping onslaught of the early nineteenth-century induced them to become predominantly nocturnal.

In those days beaver pelts were in demand for their underhair which, being barbed, was particularly suitable for processing into felt. Beavers were also much sought-after for their castors, pear-shaped scent glands found near the base of the tail. Castors secrete castoreum, an acrid, dark orange alkaloid. This substance acquired near cult status as a panacea, and not without some justification, as modern research shows it to contain the active ingredient of aspirin.

The prehistoric ancestors of beavers were nine feet in length and as brawny as the largest bear. Today they grow up to four feet long, one foot of which is a solid leathery tail six inches wide, and they weigh between thirty and seventy pounds. The tail serves as a third point of support while felling trees, and as a rudder, being used to compensate for torque when swimming with branches. Beavers have no means of defence and must flee from danger. They can stay under water for fifteen minutes, though in winter they extend this by rebreathing bubbles of expelled air trapped under the ice.

'Busy as a beaver' refers not only to the hectic lifestyle of these animals, which never hibernate, but also to their need for intensive gnawing to offset the rapid growth of their teeth. Their four curved incisors are clay-pot orange and self-sharpening. Left unchecked they would soon extend to a fatal length. Beavers have transparent eyelids which adjust their optical system for underwater vision, and a flap of skin behind their teeth which acts as a watertight valve. Special valves also seal off nostrils and ears.

They are the only mammals besides man to undertake large-scale development projects to create a special environment. Their dams are built to extend their water access to trees and to make a suitable pond for their lodge and food store. Dams are precisely engineered to fit the topography of the land, and the water surface is used like a builder's spirit level. Tree trunks and sturdy branches form the basis of the wall, then twigs are added and the holes plugged with grass and mud. In three minutes a beaver can nibble through a five-inch-thick willow log. One creature is known to have felled a tree 110 feet tall and forty-two inches in diameter. A substantial dam can be constructed in four or five nights. The largest ones, six hundred feet long, forty feet wide and twelve feet high, are the work of decades. Once built, dams require constant attention. Breaches are repaired at once and spillways are created in times of flood.

Beavers eat only bark, up to two pounds a day, and this explains their prodigious consumption of trees. (At an estimated 216 trees per beaver per year, it exceeds that of the army at Fort Gibbon.) Aspen tops the menu, followed by willow, cottonwood and alder. Branches are anchored in an underwater heap some distance from the lodge and fetched piece by piece to be eaten at home. Home is underground, a three- or four-roomed agglomeration of wood and mud with built-in air vents and two submerged tunnels for access. Its design is intricate and interior water levels are regulated to the nearest inch by peripheral dams and special sluices. Furthermore, the living quarters are positioned at specific levels relative to each winter's thickness of ice, and beavers apparently have faultless powers of prediction.

Beavers pair for life but take a new partner if the old one dies. An average of four kits are born each year but litters may contain as many as eight. They enter the world tail first, ready furred and with eyes partially open. Within three hours they float happily. Two weeks later they can swim awkwardly but lack sufficient weight to overcome their buoyancy, and the breath control necessary for staying underwater. The first weeks of their lives are spent feeding on milk and bark shavings, sleeping and romping. They learn to read water vibrations and the squeaks, whines and bassooning of communication, and waterproof themselves by rubbing secreted oil through their fur. After three or four weeks kits are taken on excursions from the lodge. They will stay in the area for two years before being driven off to build their own lodges. Thus an average lodge contains ten beavers: two adults, four yearlings, four kits.

Beavers leave their lodge by one tunnel, swim the twenty or so feet to their food pile, remove a branch and return to the lodge via the other tunnel. Trappers endeavour to place snares under the ice close to these routes on the outskirts of the food pile. They use chainsaws or power-augers to cut a two-foot-square hole in the ice. A food branch fitted with snares is lowered into the water, the ends of the snares being secured to a strong pole laid across the hole as an anchor. The hole is then covered with spruce boughs and a pile of snow to prevent it from freezing over. An ensnared beaver will be drowned.

A skillful trapper can skin a beaver in sixty minutes, scrape the pelt in five and have it stretched out and nailed in a perfect circle in twenty. In good years a beaver pelt of standard quality is worth twice its diameter in dollars. An average-sized pelt thirty-five inches across fetches seventy dollars at current prices. A trapper may take beavers only in a limited season and to a variable quota of around forty.

Beaver castors are still saved and sold for commercial use. Castoreum is a base constituent of expensive perfume. Doubtless few of the glamorous elite realise that what they are dabbing behind their ears is a beaver's anal secretion.

30

THEY CAME GLIDING through the woods about an hour after my arrival. It seemed that Rod and Jan were standing four yards apart on a conveyer belt; their single team of dogs and two sleds hitched in tandem were hidden by shrubs as they approached. Rod Kocsis was tall and strongly-built. He had a dense black beard, and when seen in the red fox hat he customarily wore he cut the sort of figure thrown into the air by Cossack dancers. He was one generation out of Hungary, though more recently Connecticut had been his home. At thirty-four he held several years over Jan. An Alaskan by birth, she was almost the same height; slim, finely-boned and with straight black hair which tumbled out of her hat and reached to her waist, she mirrored his festive personality. They made a handsome pair.

'Hi there, stranger!' Rod shouted, showing neither curiosity nor suspicion, and adding, 'You should have helped yourself to the cabin — it's open,' when he noticed my fire and pot of dog food.

'What a neat surprise,' Jan exclaimed. 'I think we'll bring out the broccoli tonight. You *are* staying, I hope?' The spontaneity of their welcome reinforced my image of Bush Alaska's open family.

Their cabin was largely taken up with a sled Rod had made out of ash. It lay across the central table and spanned eleven feet, almost from wall to wall. The final coat of varnish was drying and it looked immaculate, far too precious actually to use. The cabin's interior was also immaculate. Even the many books lining the walls drew attention to the way they held their ranks. A plump beaver hung by a paw from a rafter and thawed over a bucket. Rod and Jan added four more, the day's profit, and the cabin became a veritable obstacle course.

The opening lines of the fairy tale were true. Rod's brother, Rolf, did have a cabin on the other side of the river. Rolf had come to the region first, eleven years earlier, with two friends. The 'open-to-entry' system of land allocation had been in operation then, enabling anyone to enter certain remote regions and stake five acres. The three cheechakos had done this, built a cabin and spent a winter trapping. Rolf and one of the others had left shortly before breakup. The friend who stayed wanted to see the Yukon slough its skin, a renowned pageant in ice. He was never seen again. Several weeks after breakup suspicions mounted and a search party was sent to check on the cabin. They found an unfinished meal on the table and a paraffin lamp which had burned dry. The body was never found but it was assumed the missing man had been compromised by a bear and either eaten or chased on to weak ice.

Rolf returned to trap the following winter and Rod, fresh out of Connecticut, joined him. He liked the lifestyle and returned in late summer 1978 to build his own cabin opposite. In this way the brothers were able to suit themselves between being independent and companionable. Rod's cabin went up in three weeks, just before the advent of winter and the redesignation of the region as the Nowitna National Wildlife Refuge. Existing cabins were permitted to remain in the refuge but no new ones could be built. Rod was the last legal squatter and had since cleared fifty miles of trails to work as a trapline.

'Can one make a living off trapping here?' I asked.

Rod was sandpapering an imperfection off the sled. 'Here, no. Elsewhere you could maybe scrape by for a few years if that's all you wanted, but you wouldn't get rich. It's up and down. I couldn't depend on trapping for my existence. I love winters out here but I also love some of the comforts I grew up with. We grow our own vegetables in the summer – we're pretty proud of that – but there are too many other things we have to buy that trapping wouldn't pay for.' Most of their supplies, including fruit, were bought wholesale by mail order from Seattle and stored in a frostproof cellar below the cabin.

'Is that why you use dogs rather than a snow machine, as an economy?'

'No. I like them. They always start in the morning, they don't get bogged down. They're more fun to use, and they also extend my trapping season by two to three weeks at each end. Dogs can pull a sled over thin, patchy snow and through water where a snow machine would get wrecked real soon. But I've got a snow machine too. That's what I mean, I like the best of both worlds.' Rod was a carpenter by trade. Each summer he travelled to find work, sometimes as far afield as the North Slope, and Jan worked in fish factories. They had a house in Ruby fitted with all the comforts of an average American home. In winter they left the conventional life behind and became trappers. 'I don't reckon it's possible for someone born outside a wilderness to wholly revert to a primitive lifestyle and be happy with it. The question is how much of a compromise you want to make. We've found a solution that suits us, alternating between different worlds and mixing them to a certain degree.'

They took their two worlds seriously. This was no half-hearted cop out. After supper they began skinning beavers as if the next day's meal depended on them. Their hard work in no way detracted from the contentment they found in their 'solution', yet they had fears for the future. They had only squeezed into their dream at the last moment. A few weeks later and the wildlife refuge would have denied them this cabin and their relatively exclusive backyard of hundreds of square miles. And there was no guarantee they would be allowed to keep it indefinitely. The cabin was theirs but it was on federal land. Any change of heart in Washington could result in eviction.

'We've no right to get possessive about this place but it's inevitable since we've found what we were looking for. We felt glad when they made this a refuge because it stopped others from coming in and we figured fewer people would bother us. Now we're afraid that it was only the first step in closing the region to all forms of residence and that next we'll be told to leave.' Not even here, in the heart of Alaska, were they safe from the relentless march of bureaucracy. The land had now become small and delicate enough to fit the concept of management. I felt their dilemma. They saw themselves as protectors of this wildnerness. They knew it intimately and cared for it. They never took more than two beavers from the same lodge in a season, and over the years the beaver population in the area had shown an increase. They recognised the need for controls but hoped, against all odds, for ones that would discriminate between the land's con-scientious and selfish tenants.

Earlier in the conversation, when dwelling solely on the present, Rod tried to persuade me that I too should make my home out here. Scotland, he maintained, was too populated and too organised, and it had too few challenges left. 'Just paint the fence and it's finished,' he said. Alaska's fence wasn't ready for painting, but construction was well under way.

'We just have to make the most of what we've got while we've still got it.'

At a quarter to seven the radio was turned on, as were other radios all over the Bush, and tuned to Trapline Chatter on KJNP (King Jesus North Pole). 'For Sam and Willow at Eightmile Creek. I'll see you Sunday. Love you lots, Sal.' 'From Wendy and Jim Peters, to all at Rampart. It was a boy!' 'Doug. Am grounded. Will drop your supplies on Tuesday. Steve.' Trapline Chatter and KIAK's Pipeline of the North were notice-boards for the many hundreds of families beyond the reach of telephones. It was rare for a listener not to know vaguely of at least one name mentioned, and even then it was a comfort to share in the births, arrivals, delays, cancellations and lost shopping of others.

We stayed tuned for an Iditarod update. When it came it left us little the wiser. The reporter muddled the information from two checkpoints, lost his place, shuffled his papers and apologised for the mess. Joe Runyan, one of the favourites, had apparently lost his lead, and his dogs had fallen sick. We weren't told who was now setting the pace, but learned that Susan Butcher and Rick Swenson were in the front pack and, to everyone's surprise, so was Old Joe Redington. In two days' time I would learn the results at first hand.

The day had started at 6.30 a.m. for this trapping couple, and it ended around 10 p.m. Jan spent the last hour sitting on the cabin bed reading aloud from a novel while Rod skinned one more beaver.

'Come visit us again,' Jan said, as I set off the next morning.

'You bet. When I'm next passing.' The reality of when that might be crushed all humour out of the remark. I had never come across so many acres of contentment. Rod and Jan may have reduced my self-esteem further, but they showed that the Spirit of '24 lives on.

31

RUBY ROAD-HOUSE was offering free meals and accommodation to Iditarod racers; to others, a bed cost one hundred dollars a night and a cheeseburger with fries cost ten – roughly a dollar a mouthful. Only members of the media leap-frogging from checkpoint to check-point could afford these prices, and the town was full of them. Their planes had taxied spaghetti marks on the Yukon and now stood in ranks beside fish wheels.

One table in the road-house was occupied by three men and a woman: a young black man enjoying explosive spasms of laughter, a cameraman, his sidekick holding a mop wired to a recorder, and a thirty-one-year-old woman, formerly from Wisconsin, with long blonde hair and a ready smile. Hers was not the sort of face one would expect to see emerging from a blizzard, rather from the soft-focus of a cosmetics advertisement (for a bottle of refined beaver, perhaps). A slender build gave Libby Riddles a delicate look. This year 'the first woman to win the Iditarod' was not a competitor, but following the race as a commentator for ABC television.

The 1985 race had been Libby's third attempt at the Iditarod. In previous years she had finished nineteenth and twentieth. The race got off to an unusual start with bad weather halting the mushers for a day at Rainy Pass, Mile 223, and preventing the airdrop of dog supplies. The race was officially 'frozen' for a further two days. Libby had a strong team that year, but so had many of her rivals. Susan Butcher had already scratched after her encounter with the moose, but Rick Swenson and ten other top names were with Libby in the leading pack when the race restarted. By the time she reached Shaktoolik on the coast she had a narrow lead of a couple of hours, and 229 miles still to go.

The Iditarod changes its character when it reaches the coast. Mushers swap the rugged toboggan-style sled for the lighter and faster basket-style, and a 'final dash' mentality governs strategy. This is the most exposed section of the course and the polar wind strikes unhindered from the north. Each year mushers suffer frostbite and get pinned to the spot somewhere along the final 250 miles. In 1985 the weather proved decisive.

Libby rested her dogs for two hours at Shaktoolik and set off for Koyuk as the next musher arrived. Koyuk was fifty-eight miles away across flat sea ice. A blizzard was raging and the temperature was slightly below 0°F but winds gusting to between sixty and seventy miles an hour produced a chill factor the equivalent of − 56°F. It was late afternoon and only three hours of daylight remained. Other mushers arrived in Shaktoolik, but no one else ventured into the storm that night.

The trail was flagged but visibility came and went with each burst of wind, and Libby was often forced to stop the team and hunt for the next marker on foot. She zigzagged from one marker to the next until dark and then stopped for the night. Each of her fourteen dogs was thrown a whitefish and left to curl up against the drifting snow. She unloaded her equipment on to the ice and spent a cramped twelve hours inside a sleeping bag in a 5 ft by 2 ft by 2 ft sled bag.

The next morning showed no improvement in the weather but Libby made it to Koyuk, twenty-four hours after entering the storm. Other racers were already on their way (one was later marooned for thirty-six hours on the sea ice) but Libby had a five-hour lead, which was enough to win her the race. She also won that year's Leonhard Seppala Humanitarian Award for the care she had shown her dogs all along the way.

As a result of her victory the Iditarod received much wider publicity in the Lower 48 and ceased to be seen as a he-man event. And the significance of her win was hardly lost on Libby herself. She ends her book *Race Across Alaska* describing a microphone being thrust towards her as she crossed the finishing line in Nome.

'How does it feel, Libby?'

'What I feel is, if I died right now, it'd be okay.'

When Ruby's fire siren sounded shortly after midday, the ABC crew scrambled. The first musher of the 1988 Iditarod had come into sight.

32

Silver was always in single lead when we entered a village. Only she was able to cope with a sudden geometry of trails going everywhere and the distractions of people, snow machines and dogs. She led us into Ruby on our fourth day out from Tanana. Having had too much snow on one of those days, on the last we ran short. For several miles the Yukon was a mess of grey smudges where sandbanks had been stripped by the wind. The sled alternated between dragging sluggishly and grating as ice-fast grit rasped the runners. Ruby's situation was the opposite. Its streets were so steep and polished that in order to descend any gradient in the town I had to 'roughlock' the runners. Wrapping a couple of turns of chain around each runner was a simple and efficient trick to turn a frictionless sled into dead-weight.

Inexplicably, Ruby is the only settlement of any kind on the *left* bank of the Yukon for the last 800 miles of its flow. Its box-like timber houses, some painted, occupy a gap in wooded bluffs. The gap is not flat but a steep flank of hillside, and the houses are notched into it in such a way as to give everyone equal opportunity of tumbling down to the Yukon or to a small tributary which has its confluence here. Only in Sukkertoppen, Greenland, have I seen a village crush slopes into its streets with more alarming success.

The adjacent bluff is too steep to build on but it provides Ruby's cemetery with a cliff-top panorama of town and country. Hills compact to the south and a summer road wends through them for eighty miles to Poorman, serving minor goldfields along the way. 'Ruby sprang up early in the summer of 1911, as a mushroom springs up in the night,' Stuck wrote, '. . . and will dwindle and die . . . when the placers in the hills behind it are exhausted.' The placers still produce, a slow and steady yield, and Ruby survives with 233 inhabitants. The Iditarod reaches it from Poorman.

A talk on the Loch Ness Monster was scrubbed from the school agenda that morning because a spontaneous holiday was declared so pupils could welcome the racers. The community hall acted as the checkpoint and was swamped in piles of sacks containing the supplies each musher had sent ahead, marked with bold colours for quick identification. Inside, steam rose from tureens of soup and an endless supply of coffee, a chef was changing into white garb, and a radio operator was frequently raising his earphones to visitors interrupting his work. To the one question they all asked he replied, monotonously, 'Joe Redington'.

The excitement about town was almost palpable. Children were hurling snowballs, in what was a rare game; normally snow is too dry to hold together, but an unusually mild spell of 45°F had turned it wet and sticky. Not all Ruby was favourably infected by Iditaroditis. My host did not rush out when the siren sounded.

'To me it's no big deal,' he said; and then he might have been Caesar pronouncing *veni, vidi, vici* for he used the same solemnity: 'A bunch of dogs come, they shit, they leave'.

Joe Redington, sen., was first into town and he and his ten dogs were immediately engulfed by the cheering crowd. The 'Father of the Iditarod' was heading the field through his own prowess. Fifty-two mushers had left the start at Anchorage, two had scratched (including the oldest entrant, eighty-two-year-old Norman Vaughan) and Old Joe had held the lead since McGrath, a distance of 241 miles.

He was one of Alaska's great characters. He spoke bluntly, always made time to chat and had a reputation for generosity. A kindly, smiling man who for years had been contracted to recover equipment and US servicemen – alive or dead – from plane crashes in the bush, Joe had himself walked away from at least eleven plane crashes. With Susan Butcher he had mushed dogs to the top of Denali, and with his sons he had hitched one hundred pairs of dogs to a single gangline and mushed a bus during the 1976 Alaska Centennial celebrations.

Most Iditarod mushers had raised their dogs from the Redington bloodline; Joe kept a kennel of 400 huskies and each year leased five quality teams to other Iditarod racers. He didn't always keep the best team for himself but this year he had, determined to improve his previous highest placing of fifth. His age was against him, however; for this race was physically and mentally demanding, particularly the lack of sleep. 'Hard Luck Joe' had become his nickname, as a result of things going wrong and his habit of falling asleep at the handlebars.

Whatever happened, he always emerged with a grin and said he'd enjoyed himself.

Iditarod rules allowed racers to receive hospitality in people's homes, if invited, and to fetch water, if available. Otherwise no assistance was permitted. They had to collect their own supplies and feed their dogs as if they were in the wilds. By custom, the first musher into Ruby was exempted. Old Joe's dogs were led off to be bedded in straw and fed by someone else, and he was escorted to the community hall.

Unwashed and suffering from lack of sleep after five days on the trail, Old Joe adjusted his braces and stepped out of the race to take a seat at a white table-cloth decked with silverware and lit candelabra. Behind him the equally white executive chef of the Clarion Hotel, Anchorage, sautéed and *flambéed* the first item on the menu; the manager of the hotel fiddled with a Laurel Ridge Sauvignon Blanc-Semillion 1986; and camera crews and press photographers advanced. During the prolonged meal which followed Old Joe was offered three more bottles of wine and one of sherry, all of which he refused, and seven courses.

Shrimp & Wild Mushroom Sauté
Jumbo shrimp and wild mushrooms sautéed and *flambéed* with brandy served with a rich crayfish cream sauce.

Double Beef Consommé
Rich clarified beef broth served with fresh julienne of vegetables.

Rainbow Trout Macadamia
Fresh trout fillet rolled in macadamia nuts pan fried and served with brown butter and lemon sauce with fresh parsley.

Fresh Fruit Sorbet
Fresh melon and strawberries accompanied with Lemon Sorbet.

Veal Oscar
Tender veal medallions sautéed in butter *flambéed* with cognac topped with Alaskan king crab legs and fresh asparagus in a pool of rich demi-glaze topped with béarnaise sauce.

Garden Salad
Fresh butter lettuce and spinach topped with tomatoes *concassées* dressed with a fresh cream and herb vinaigrette.

$$$ *White Chocolate Cheesecake* $$$
Wanda's own New York style cheesecake with a chocolate pecan crust served on a pool of raspberry sauce and one thousand crisp one-dollar bills.

After the meal the manager placed a hollow fox on his head, for some reason, and made a speech. He talked eloquently about blizzards, pioneers, hardship, endurance and the Clarion's bedrooms. Because it was Joe who was first here, the fox announced, he was doubling the value of the sweet. It was an impromptu gesture and he hadn't a cent on him, but he wrote an IOU for $1,000 on the back of his business card and stuck it in the remains of Joe's cheesecake. Old Joe smiled, as well he might. Two days earlier he had received no cheesecake but $3,000 in silver for being first to the half-way point of Cripple Landing.

Other mushers wended into Ruby several hours later. Second place was a surprise, a man of Swiss origin called Martin Buser. He fed his dogs, who lapped half-heartedly while stretched out on beds of straw, and then he curled up in the snow and slept beside them. Herbie Nayokpuk of Shishmaref (north of Nome), one of the few native mushers taking part, came in third. He said he was short of socks, and within minutes half a dozen pairs were being offered to him. The Iditarod didn't always elicit such a response in the villages, for in the past hospitality had sometimes been abused. But the people of Ruby enjoyed the race and if they couldn't run it themselves, having their socks run it was the next best thing.

The arch-rivals, Susan Butcher and Rick Swenson, came in one after the other that evening. They parked their dogs outside the houses of friends. Each had scouts keeping an eye on the opposition to give warning of an unexpected departure. It was a race of great strategy. Mushers worked different routines to try to strike an optimum combination of resting, feeding and driving which would cover distance and yet conserve strength. They concealed these routines, changed them and played on them, in the hope of panicking their rivals into making mistakes or exceeding their abilities. The order of arrival at a checkpoint was an unreliable indication of a team's condition, for first in might be exhausted and second in might be fresh after resting out of sight on the way.

Rick, stout with a ginger beard, joked with onlookers as he lit his alcohol stove to heat dog water. He was the master tactician. He had been known to arrive at a checkpoint, pretend to set up camp and then suddenly take off. This had panicked others who were at advanced stages of preparing meals. They had hastily ditched hot water, packed, roused their dogs and set off in pursuit, only to find Rick camped round the first corner.

He replaced his set of Quick Change Runners in ten minutes and discarded the old ones even though they looked barely scratched. Every second counted, as he knew only too well. His mind was fixed on beating Susan and gaining a fifth Iditarod victory. It would already have been his if he had won in 1978. That year, towards the end of the fifteenth day of the race, Rick lost *by one second* in a sprint finish down Nome's Front Street.

Susan tended to her dogs and patiently answered incessant media questions. Did she think she would win? Did she get cold? Did she always feed the best bacon to her dogs? Had she had a rough time? She pointed to her broken sled. This was the third checkpoint she had reached, hoping a replacement would be waiting, only to be disappointed. When a film crew switched on a floodlight above Granite and made him sit up in surprise, it was too much. Susan asked them to leave. The wonder leader, with two consecutive Iditarod victories under his collar, groaned and slumped back into his straw.

Many years earlier, Susan had offered him for sale. Lacking in confidence, slow at learning and stubborn, this black-and-tan dog showed little promise. No buyers were forthcoming so Susan kept him and worked on his faults. He still had a 'self-image' problem, she believed, but now $50,000 wouldn't buy him. He simply wasn't on the market. Granite was needed for the hat trick which, at that particular moment, appeared to be slipping out of reach.

By the time Susan and Rick entered Ruby, Old Joe had rested for six hours and was already two hours further down the trail. Luna, his main leader, had been reluctant to leave town and it had taken Joe half an hour of cajoling to persuade his team that they were still winning the Iditarod and with only 402 miles to go. Eventually they had trotted off into a sunset the colours of tomatoes *concassées* and *julienne* of vegetables, served over a frozen pool not dissimilar to the world's most expensive cheesecake.

On the sea ice of Norton Bay, between Koyuk and Elim

Manley road-house under moonlight, shortly before Hallowe'en.

An efficient routine was essential when camping at − 20°F. My tent and picketed dogs near Eureka.

Above: Susan Butcher and Granite.

Right: Joe Redington, sen., 'Father of the Iditarod', on arrival at Ruby during the race.

On the sea ice of Norton Bay, between Koyuk and Elim.

Resting on Manley Slough. In lead are Silver, wearing a belly jacket, and Alf, wearing a bootee.

Rosco (*left*) and Alf (*right*) in a ground blizzard on Topkok Hill.

Good weather, smooth trail, eager dogs – mushing at its best.

Cosy on a bed of spruce boughs. Nanook asleep.

'Endurance – fidelity – intelligence.' In the barren Kigluaik Mountains, Seward Peninsula.

The Yukon, Alaska's great river and my road, at Nulato.

Little Diomede boy ice-fishing. Behind him, two miles away, is the forbidden territory of Soviet Big Diomede.

Little Diomede village (with polar bear skins drying on racks), where West meets East in the Bering Sea.

Following the silvery trail, between Kaltag and Old Woman.

33

DURING MY TWO days in Ruby, Iditarod racers continued to pass through but the mood of people and event changed. The bustle and curiosity surrounding the front-runners had evaporated and by the time the midfield arrived, children were back in school, Ruby had reverted to its normal routine and the media had flown on to blunt their pencils at another checkpoint. Despondency hung over the dog teams resting on a quiet main street. These were the teams whose drivers had held higher expectations and one was Bill Cotter, lying in nineteenth place, with no more tricks up his mittens. 'I've put ten thousand bucks into this race and I'll be lucky to win five thousand in Nome,' he lamented. 'And it'll cost me another thousand to fly this outfit back from Nome.' He talked of quitting.

I prepared my own team for the resumption of our journey. We were all packed and ready. My dogs looked fresh and healthy compared with their racing colleagues, but in this respect my opinion was always biased. No one ever came up to me and made loud covetous noises about my companions, but they still made me brim with pride.

A thaw followed by a sudden freeze produces a hazardous running surface, and over twenty-four hours the Yukon basin experienced a 70° shift in temperature, from 45°F to −26°F. Ice crystals became sharp and abrasive, and quickly caused severe laceration to paw pads unless bootees were fitted. Bootees were small pouches of durable bunting, usually Polarfleece, worn like socks and held on with a wraparound of velcro. They had to be fitted tightly enough to stay on without restricting blood circulation.

Putting bootees on a whole team was no musher's idea of fun. Fingers got cold and had to be warmed after every one or two dogs. In cold weather it took me twenty minutes to bootee eight dogs. If the dogs rested for more than fifteen minutes, I had to loosen all thirty-two bootees. If the dogs ran through water, all bootees had to be changed. Polarfleece could be expected to last thirty or forty miles but footwear had to be checked regularly because a hole let in ice and rendered a bootee potentially *more* damaging to a dog's foot. They were a lot of work, and unpopular.

Silver hated wearing bootees. She always held up her first booteed foot as if I had just injured it. When I booteed the second, she disregarded the first and held up this newly damaged limb. With four bootees on she lay down, totally disabled. She had no fear of other dogs, glare ice, deep snow or wind, but she drew the line at footwear. And yet at the command to go she always leapt up and never gave them a second thought.

We made a handsome team – thirty-two feet in socks of red, blue or mock-tartan (and two more in bunny boots) – as we pulled out of Ruby at midday, gatecrashing Iditarod rankings in about thirtieth position. The trail was clearly marked by flags at one hundred yard intervals and these would continue all the way to Nome. It was marked by lost or discarded bootees even more regularly. I leaned over and snatched them up on the move, keeping only the best, for it appeared mushers had been reducing their loads and discarding unused bootees by the dozen. The novelty soon wore off even though – at seventy cents apiece – here were some of the richer pickings of the rush.

For fifteen miles we followed Ruby Slough and were sunk in a trough in spruce forest. Alf shied when we came to a parked snow machine and a man raising a beaver through a hole in the ice, and shied again when a whiskey jack (a species of jay also called, for its sins, 'camp robber') swooped low over us out of spite or boredom. When the trail turned off the slough we climbed a bank and ran through forest. It felt exhilarating to be on a trail wending through trees again but after a mile we emerged on to the expansive Yukon. A huddle of cabins soon appeared far off on our right. Whiskey Creek.

Alaskan 'water of life' was once produced here, uniquely and impatiently. The Bush distillers of Whiskey Creek wanted to speed up the maturation process and to this end they constructed a large water wheel. Full casks of spirit were strapped to the wheel and made to revolve constantly in the hope that it would do the trick. It didn't. This must have taken place before 1925, because by that year the creek's name was established; 'Whiskey Creek to Galena' was the

Serum Run leg driven by Ed Nollner. In two days I hoped to meet him, because he still lived in Galena.

'HAW. Good girl.' When we were well clear of the trail we stopped for a rest. A fourteen-dog team approached from behind, an Austrian musher, it transpired, running the Great Race for the first time. The minimum credential required for a rookie musher to take part in the Iditarod was proof of having completed the course of any two-hundred-mile race. This rookie team plodded and looked exhausted. The lead dog tried to turn off the trail and follow my tracks. Horst Maas stamped on his brake and shouted 'GEE'. He repeated it again and again. The dog stood still and stared at me with a statue's pretence of vision. Then it slowly turned and moved off.

Horst looked along my line of dogs and stopped fifty yards later.

'All of them?' he called. 'I also must do?' He raised a boot, tapped it and pointed at my team.

'I'm not sure. I think this snow is bad for their feet.'

Only a few of his dogs wore bootees. He wrestled his shoulders inside his parka. 'It's very cold.' His voice came low and listless. I called 'Are you all right?' but he didn't hear me for he had already turned, and with much shouting the gloomy procession drew away. I stood lost in thought for a while. That lead dog's eyes.... The Iditarod shed some of its glory in this brief encounter.

I spent the night camped in Jimmy Malamute's cabin. It earned one star through having a roof. Jimmy Malamute, whoever he was, had not maintained it for a long time. A quarter of one wall was missing and drifts had recreated the Alaskan landscape inside. If my sled had been able to negotiate the Yukon's steep bank I could have driven the team through the wall, across the floor and out the door. One advantage of this was that my snowshoes could stay on the whole time, and the surrounding snow was so deep and soft that it was impossible to do anything without them. I wore the Big Feet to relay my supplies up from the river, to picket the dogs, to gather wood and to cross the cabin to add salt to my porridge.

I found another advantage to wall-less cabins; if the views are good, they are unimpeded. The setting sun sent fingers of spruce shadow reaching across the Yukon and faintly pinked its surface. Willows on the far bank turned to rust and glowed. Across this scene, moving from right to left, a dog team travelled close to the middle of the river. It was no more than a silhouette of seven small dots in line and a large one misshapen at the rear. It moved steadily and silently, undulating over the bumps in the trail with mesmerising fluency. It looked so delicate when set in this vast billowing land, and yet in no time it had glided past and slipped out of sight.

When a second team passed I went for my camera. I could feel that the temperature was unusually cold but my camera showed me just how cold it was. Bush lore offered a cornucopia of crude devices for gauging temperature. Some worked on principles as extreme as a miner's dead canary. Others were more humane and discerning and one of the most famous was McQueston's thermometer. It was common knowledge among bushmen of the time that mercury solidified at $-40°$ (Fahrenheit *and* Centigrade, for at this point the two scales intersect) and that pure alcohol, such as Davis Painkiller, froze at $-70°F$. Certain other commodities had freezing points in between. McQueston's thermometer consisted of four small bottles and a note of recommendations placed on a shelf outside his trading post. The bottles contained mercury, whisky, kerosene and Davis Painkiller. Travellers shook the bottles in sequence. If the mercury was frozen, the note recommended not being caught out on the trail at night; if the whisky, it was unwise to leave camp; if the kerosene, a person should not leave his cabin; and if Davis Painkiller turned to ice, it was dangerous to step away from the fire.

My thermometer was my camera. For it to function at all I had to use an external battery pack which I wore close to my body along with the daily ration of snacks. A cord from the battery pack had to be retrieved from my many layers and screwed into the camera each time it was used. If a film splintered and broke when I tried to wind it on to the next exposure, the temperature was $-30°F$ or lower. This was the bottom end of my scale. That evening my film splintered and broke. I had to warm the camera by the fire and then remove the damaged film in the darkness of a sleeping bag.

It was even colder the next morning when I awoke. My sleeping bag enveloped me except where a small hole was allowed for breathing, and overnight this became a crust of ice. The moments contemplating getting up were always agonising, preparing to release the draw string and allowing in that shriek of cold. My bunny boots would have an ice lining from the previous day's perspiration, but there was a trick to eradicate this problem. I emptied a thermos of hot water into one boot, swilled it around, emptied it into the other, drained them both, leapt into them, donned parka, gloves and over-trousers, and then launched into a frenzy of physical jerks. Leaping up and down on the spot, swinging my arms in arcs and slapping myself on the back – this had to be done vigorously for several minutes. It was effective but painful. There is no way around this. Mushers come either battered or frozen.

In extreme cold everything became complex, stubborn or stuck. Simple tasks became protracted events and the least of them suddenly demanded the most testing degrees of dexterity. Every aspect of a routine now contrived to make you remove your gloves and when you finally succumbed, your fingers immediately chilled and your gloves froze to grotesque shapes. My solid-fuel hand-warmer reliably produced heat an hour after I needed it, my Coleman stove refused to work at all. It made me envy the dogs.

Snow would have settled on them during the night and by morning they would be hard to spot. One by one they would look up and shake their heads on hearing the commotion of my violent slapping. They would continue dozing and yet keep a periodic check on my progress, watching me blow into cupped hands as the fifth match expired before lighting the tinder and watching me generally fetch, saw, melt, stir, stoke, serve, tidy and pack. When they smelt their morning soup and snack coming, they would spring to life, rock back into the posture of an up-ended sphinx and luxuriate in a stretch. In twenty seconds they would devour what had taken me an hour and a half to prepare, and two minutes later they would be dozing again.

On cold mornings such as this one, when we were about to set off for Galena, my dogs depreciated. Anyone could have had them for a song, with harnesses thrown in.

34

FIVE MILES BELOW Jimmy Malamute's cabin the Yukon turns sharply north and bends itself round the abandoned settlement of Louden. In Stuck's time this was 'a native village with a trading post and government school', but only the cemetery remained. Its four hillocks, one for each of the area's principal families – Nollner, Evans, Demoski and Huntingdon – would have passed for any other bumps and dips in the river bank had they not been marked by a solitary pole and a spanking Stars and Stripes. I parked the dogs and snowshoed over. The snow crust sometimes sank several inches, causing a cobweb of fractures to shoot out several yards under my feet, but fortunately it was just bluffing.

The grave markers were wooden and bore names and dates. Few had lines of sentiment or explanation. Crosses, headboards and what resembled large doll's houses were scattered about, according to the lie of the land rather than symmetry, and many were decorated with plastic flowers. Among Athabascans it was customary for a favourite possession or an object which had been meaningful in the deceased's life to be placed on top of a grave, and through 'house' windows it was often possible to see a tool, pipe, pair of spectacles or the like. I had once come across two modern graves whose mementoes had been an unopened can of Olympia beer and a new belt-drive for a snow machine.

This cemetery was still used, as evidenced by the flag, but as in most of the world's northern villages, frozen ground made winter burials impracticable in Alaska. The dead were stored, for burial on the last Monday of May, Memorial Day, which was also a traditional occasion for village cemeteries to be tidied and maintained.

The northbound Yukon led us below Cave-off Cliffs, which were doing just that, and swung round west again into a new topography, the Koyukuk flats. The river was a mile wide at the approach to Galena. The town was hidden, but that something important lay among the trees was betrayed by military antennae on a sandstone ridge. Galena had fuel tanks, cabins, dogs, snow machines and F15 fighter jets.

The town had a population of 950, of which about 300 were the personnel of Campion Air Force Base. The original settlement was founded in 1919 on the strength of nearby lead ore (galena) mines and it expanded after the building of a military airstrip in 1940, to the detriment of such villages as Louden. New Galena was set back out of sight at the upstream end of the community. Old Galena bordered the river as a narrow strip of cabins, several on log stilts in anticipation of floods. The fenced-off military base was immediately behind and as regards floods, *it* was all right, Jack, having built a protective embankment which excluded Old Galena by a matter of yards. Old Galena might wash away, but not over Campion A.F.B.

As we crested the river-bank and entered town the first word to greet us was 'SUZUKI'. Japan is Alaska's greatest trading partner. Others were quick to follow.

'THAT WAY, THAT WAY!...' yelled a young woman. She was running towards me and gesticulating frantically. 'THAT WAY TO THE CHECK-POINT!...' — and then, after I had thanked her and confessed that we were not part of the Iditarod — '...in that case, you'll have time for coffee, won't you?' So I was welcomed to Galena and being delayed under the SUZUKI sign when Ed Nollner happened by.

Of average height and dressed in modern anorak and trousers, he was easy to identify because he wore his name written on the front of a grey peaked cap with its earflaps pulled down. He had a youthful face for his eighty-four years, not gaunt but full and rounded except around the mouth, which was drawn in, deepening his cheek furrows and making his chin protrude. He wore a large pair of spectacles with translucent amber frames. In quiet moments his expression tended to a thin smile, as if he were the sole proprietor of a joke whose time was almost right, but not quite.

'The Serum Run. You want to know about the Serum Run.' They were not questions. Mentally he seemed to heave a sigh. 'I guess everyone still wants to know. It was a long time ago now. I was twenty-one then. We had good dogs in those days, good feet. These dogs nowadays, they're fast, but they're not tough like our dogs were. We never used no moccasins. My older brother George and me, we had fast teams. I raced at Ruby once, six miles it was. Won by six minutes. *Six minutes.* You understand that? That's a long way over six miles. That was with Dixie in lead. Dixie led with the serum, too.' He spoke softly and in the native manner, short phrases delivered in a rush, but without the usual aggressive, demanding intonation.

He couldn't remember who had told him, but word had come along the telegraph that two fast mushers were needed and he and his brother George had been selected. He had seven dogs in harness, big grey malamutes, and mushed twenty-four miles to Whiskey Creek to wait for the serum. The date was 29 January 1925. His was the tenth of the twenty legs between Nenana and Nome. The ninth was run by Bill McCarty. Bill McCarty and Ed Nollner were the last of the serum runners still alive.

'It was real cold that day. Minus forty. I waited – I can't remember how long, but a long time. Bill came about six that evening. Of course it was dark at six. We warmed the serum by the stove. It was just a box and furs. I left soon after. It was just a normal run. We never knew what the fuss was when the papers called us heroes. We just done what we had to, helping others when we could. That's the way we were. Then they called us heroes.' He chuckled. Sixty-three years later he was still incredulous about this.

His brother George had married a few days before, but he turned out that night to take over from Ed in Galena. George drove the same team eighteen miles to Bishop Mountain. He rested the dogs there and then returned with them. The Nollners' dogs covered eighty-four miles for their part in the run. By the time the serum reached Bishop Mountain, dog teams had carried it 325 miles in fifty-four hours, an average of six miles an hour, including the delays necessary for warming the package.

George Nollner handed over to the eleventh musher, Charlie Evans, who left at 5 a.m. to run the thirty miles to Nulato. The temperature was a perilous − 64°F. Lung scorching was one inevitable consequence of forcing dogs to inhale such cold air rapidly and over a long period of time, but a greater hazard was frostbite. Charlie Evans had borrowed two dogs to increase his team to nine, even though he had no extra rabbit-skin covers to protect their undersides. The groins of these two dogs were severely frostbitten and they later died of their injuries.

'There was another serum run, about a month later, it was. In March. No one ever mentions it. I ran it, too. It was colder then, minus fifty-four at Whiskey Creek. Most of us ran it again, but some didn't. And a woman took part this time, the only one to run the serum. Maggie Smoke, it was, from Tanana.'

This second run delivered the 1,100,000 units of serum sent from Seattle by sea, aboard the SS *Alameida*. Ten years later, Ed went on to explain, another relay was arranged along the route but this time for sport, to see if the Serum Runners' time could be beaten.

'Did they do it?' I asked.

'No,' he beamed. 'No, they never beat us. We had good dogs in those days. Nowadays these dogs are okay, but . . .' he was interrupted by someone and reminded that his plane was leaving in less than an hour '... I've got to go. You were lucky to catch me. I'm taking the plane to Fairbanks. To go dancing. I like dancing.'

35

ALASKA'S SCHOOLS ARE the most modern and best-equipped and have the largest budgets of any in the USA, if not in the world. However, this has only come about recently and previously the opposite was true. The federal government did nothing for the education of Alaskans before the granting of territorial status in 1912 except hand the issue over to Sheldon Jackson. At his own insistence – and he was an extremely insistent man – this Presbyterian minister was appointed General Agent for Education for Alaska in 1885. It was a hastily invented post, without portfolio, salary or funding. Sheldon Jackson remained undaunted. He was five feet and two inches of uncrushable zeal. His eloquent speeches won over the hearts of good American women, his cause won over their purses, and he went to Alaska, against the orders of his Church, to indulge in his own brand of misguided philanthropy. He believed the highest ambition of Alaska natives was 'to build American homes, possess American furniture, dress in American clothes, adopt the American style of living, and be American citizens ...' Having ascribed their ambition, Jackson aimed his crusade at making them achieve it.

The first schools were operated under the tutelage of missionaries and resident priests and ministers of the various denominations. Pupil attendance was minimal and generally ended after elementary levels because the subsistence lifestyles of the people required children to help at home. The educational slant was towards removing children from native influences, and accordingly native dress, religions, languages and customs were banned. When government schools were instituted the same policies were enforced, until as recently as the late sixties. Only the most gifted children received higher education and for this they had to leave their villages and attend one of a few

129

key boarding schools, such as those of Anchorage, Fairbanks, St Mary's and Sitka.

The status quo cartwheeled in 1976 as a result of litigation brought against the state by the parents of Molly Hootch. She was a student of high school age in the Eskimo village of Emmonak. Her parents contested that it was a violation of human rights to force children away from their homes and cultural environments in order to receive a secondary education. Furthermore, they asserted, it was unconstitutional.

They won the case and as a result of the subsequently-named Molly Hootch Decree, the state became obliged to provide secondary school programmes in any community which had an elementary school and at least *one* child of the right age requesting further education. The decree was expediently timed as regards financing, for it coincided with the state's booming oil revenues. High schools were built wherever there was a school district with six or more eligible students. Today few of Alaska's 127 villages entitled to high school programmes are without their own specialist staff and buildings. Manley's High School, for example, with five students (the roll has fallen since the school was built) cost one million dollars to construct, and it was one of the cheapest. The schools in villages without road connections were many times more expensive.

In all the villages I passed through, high schools were immediately apparent. They were always the largest and newest buildings in the community. Their lines bore the stamp of industrial starkness, functional rather than aesthetic, and they resembled windowed warehouses. Made of wood and sheet metal, they were raised above ground and permafrost on concrete pilings. A full-sized gymnasium was incorporated into each complex; basketball games held there were the social highlights of winter. They gathered villagers together in a way seldom seen in post-television days.

In these schools I rediscovered the all-but-forgotten convenience of flush lavatories and central heating. Schools were equipped with carpets, squadrons of computers, desks with fold-away electric typewriters, and all modern teaching aids. They provided pupils with free toothbrushes, toothpaste, pencils, biros, paper, books, and health checks, hot lunches, snacks and (on exam days) breakfasts. Isolated schools with gifted or handicapped children were visited on a regular basis by fly-in specialist teachers.

130

Education in Alaska is an expensive affair. High transportation costs make this inevitable. The price of an item bought in Anchorage may increase ten times by the time it has been delivered to a remote community. In order for a school basketball team from Galena, for example, to compete against their rivals in Nome, a plane from Fairbanks has to be specially chartered for the excursion – if it is a three-day tournament, this would involve two charters. School budgets are nevertheless sufficient, because education is now a priority expenditure. Barrow School District's athletic budget alone was said to be in excess of $250,000 per annum. Teachers can expect minimum salaries of $40,000 per annum. Qualified teachers on casual contracts are paid $200–$240 a day. The high school superintendent of Galena earns $80,000 a year.

One morning the creatures of Loch Ness and the British Royal Family were introduced to Galena High School in an eclectic discussion. I presented a factual account of the evidence and research connected with the investigations of Loch Ness, moved on to discuss Britain as a whole, passed around a Scottish one-pound note and some postcards, and wound up with the Royal Family and children's customs, such as rolling eggs at Easter, building Guy Fawkes bonfires and leaving teeth under pillows for fairies. Only in retrospect did I realise they must have found my homeland very strange.

'Would anyone like to ask any questions?' I concluded.

A rush of hands went up. What did the animals in Loch Ness eat? ... What did the Royal Family eat? ... Did I like the Queen? ... Did *everyone* like the Queen? ... Why didn't Britain have dollars like everyone else? ... Did people keep sled dogs in Scotland? ... What did the fairies *do* with all the teeth? ...

And then one which surprised me. It was asked by an eleven-year-old girl. 'Is AIDS a problem in your country?'

Yes, I said, it was a serious problem. I returned the question to her even though I knew the answer. 'And how about in Alaska. Is AIDS a problem?'

'No, not here ...' she replied.

'Yes,' interrupted another. 'It's the same here.'

A few days before Christmas a newspaper had reported the first HIV positive case in Kotzebue. Situated just inside the Arctic Circle and with a population of 2,630, it was second to Barrow as the world's largest Eskimo community.

I changed classes after this and spoke to older children, aged fifteen and sixteen. They showed little enthusiasm for any subject, and no questions were asked at the end.

'Now you've had the full Alaskan teacher experience,' remarked Grace, a youngish teacher. 'When the pupils are young they are bright and lively, always eager to learn. Then they hit a certain age or a certain stage of awareness – and they just give up. They won't work and won't show any interest. "What's the use," they all say, "I don't need to learn more than writing my name to be a trapper." Of course, none do any trapping. Trapping is only done by a few old people now. It makes teaching terribly depressing, but there seems no way around it. We have to learn to live with this sense of failure.'

In the evenings the teenagers hung around the community halls, bars or recreation rooms. They killed time talking, drinking if they had been able to procure supplies, smoking and hitting the knobs of space invaders. Children of any age were allowed to drive snow machines up to a maximum of 20 m.p.h. Yet they drove snow machines at high speed, out of boredom. They saw a meaningless future for themselves in their villages, and dreamed of Anchorage. In Anchorage they would have a chance of making it big, or at least of being offered a life. They were the new wave of redundancies in villages which received welfare payments and relied less on subsistence activities. Life had become more comfortable; there were fewer chores to do but no alternative occupations, paid or otherwise. Native children had low self-esteem and they felt white Alaska was prejudiced against them. They measured themselves and their futures against the extremes of *Dynasty*, fast cars and a world of hype satellited from beyond a golden horizon. Television never portrayed success as a full quota of beavers; and if it occasionally suggested happiness as a log cabin and a hunting and gathering lifestyle, their own experiences were often contrary.

'At my last posting on the Lower Yukon I saw children waiting to enter school the moment the doors opened in the morning, and having to be asked to leave at the end of the day. Not because they liked school, but because they had miserable home lives. They live with alcoholism, arguing, fighting, swearing, assault – all these things go on in these villages. They are microcosms of city problems, only

132

their effect is magnified through isolation and having no means of escape.'

Grace saw this as a severe disadvantage of the Molly Hootch Decree. The stress children had once suffered being sent away to schools in alien environments was much less than some children now experienced through being forced to stay at home. The children previously sent away to schools in the cities had been given a broader insight into life, a gradual introduction to cities and the ways and attitudes of whites, all of which, Grace believed, was knowledge they could later use to advantage, to help them find their place in a radically changing society. Since the Molly Hootch Decree fewer native children experienced city life. Those who experienced it first as young adults were less able to cope with the pressures and the prejudices, both real and imagined.

'So they come back to their villages. They take to drink and drugs because there isn't much else and that's all they know. Having had lousy parents as role models, they become lousy parents. And so it goes on. The problem is, how to break the circle? Teaching a new way is the answer and providing great schools is the first step. But somehow we've got to give these kids a *reason* for learning.'

She knew of two fourteen-year-old girls who had become alcoholics and were now undergoing treatment, and she cited the case of a fifteen-year-old girl called Mary. She was an extremely talented pupil and a keen learner, then she gave up. She began playing truant and drinking and smoking dope, and had a child. 'Unmarried native girls get a child allowance of six hundred dollars a month from the state. Mary threw everything away, and now she says that having kids is her job. If her lifestyle doesn't kill her first. It breaks my heart to see the waste. As things stand, we're watching genocide, we're looking at the death of a people.'

'What about the languages, Athabascan and Koyukon? Are they still spoken and being taught?'

'That's another sad story. But if you really want to find out, then go and talk to Madeline Solomon. She's the expert. And the other thing I think you ought to do is visit an F15. I've got a contact at the base and can set it up for you.'

36

THE 'SOMETHING THAT is talking in there' was talking when Madeline Solomon showed me into her living room. She immediately went over and switched it off, a gesture almost unique in my Alaska experience.

'Is Koyukon a progressive language?' I asked. 'I mean, will it originate a new word for a new concept, such as television? Or will it import a foreign word?'

'It is progressive. Television is *bi 'yeekìhadinaayee* in our language.' She breathed the word rather than spoke it. 'It means "something that is talking in there". We see things different from you, so we give them our own name. Same with people. I got two names. Madeline is what everyone calls me but my Indian name is *Halohoohunh*, after my grandmother. It means "good seamstress". They never give Indian names, now. In twenty years I think no one can speak Indian any more.'

She lived in a typical Galena house with a snow machine (*tsobeleek* – 'iron dog') parked outside. Permafrost prevented the town from having an underground system of pipes or septic tanks, so once a week water was delivered and waste tanks were pumped out. It was a compact wooden house on one level with four or five small rooms. The interior was well-equipped with modern accessories, even a microwave oven (*beyee hoolohuteldeyhdlee* – 'that in which there is lightning now and then') and made homely by a varied assortment of the colourful and sentimental: a painting of the Last Supper in undiluted pigments, a mirror with an impressionistic image of a bare-legged girl holding a dope pipe, a Garfield poster, a 'God Bless This House' sampler, and framed photographs of some of her nine children, thirty-five grandchildren and thirteen great-grandchildren.

She was born on the Kateel River (a tributary of the Koyukuk) in 1905. Her father was an Irishman named Harry Lawrence and her mother an Athabascan, but she never knew them for she was given away to a Nulato family for adoption. Of her seven years' schooling, three were spent at Nulato and four at the Jesuit mission in Holy Cross.

'We were punished for speaking Indian then. I just forgot the language completely in four years. Things were tougher in those days. There was no work on Sundays. There was no moose either, no easy meat. I never saw my first moose till 1928. Kids have it easy now. We had to work hard. In the First World War we knitted a lot of stockings for the Red Cross. Once we saw a ship with yellow funnels pass. It was full of conscripts. We were in the war for one year, three months and eleven days. I always remember that. I don't suppose they cared what language those conscripts spoke.'

In 1921 Madeline was married to a widower fifteen years older than herself. It was an arranged wedding, as was the custom, and she met her husband for the first time on their wedding day. It was a happy marriage until his death in a sledding accident in 1943. She married again and continued trapping, fishing and working in a shop until 1964, when she was offered a teaching post. In 1965 she became the first native language teacher to be appointed in Alaska.

There were twenty native languages in Alaska, she explained. Besides those of the southern natives (Haida, Tlingit, Tsimshian), languages were divided into two main families: Eskimo-Aleut and Athabascan. The former included Aleutian Aleut and four branches of Eskimo: Inupiaq, Sugpiaq Aleut (Yupik), Central Yupik and Siberian Yupik. Athabascan, in broad terms, was related to the languages of the Navajos and Apaches of Arizona and New Mexico – suggesting a shared past and tribal migrations. Athabascan subdivided into eleven distinctive forms whose extreme degree of difference could be compared to that of German from Dutch. No native language had a written form before the arrival of white men. Aleutian Aleut was the first to be converted to print, using a Slavonic alphabet, and its first book was published in 1834. All native languages were subsequently translated into script.

'Koyukon is a form of Athabascan. It's very beautiful and very expressive. But it's not easy and its vocabulary is big. Of all the languages, they say it's dying the fastest.' Madeline's shoulders rose and slumped as she sighed. 'For sixty years they tell us not to speak our language. They punish us. They tell us not to let our children speak it because it slows their learning. So we speak English and forget Koyukon. Then they change their minds and tell us our language is good and we must not lose it.'

'They' were the territorial and state authorities. 'When did they change their minds?'

'When they made me a teacher in the sixties. Then they brought in this Bilingual. That was in 1972. They made a law for a bilingual teacher to be appointed at any school with more than fifteen native children. But often they can't get teachers. Only the old people speak. Sometimes they're too old to teach, or don't want to.'

'Do the children want to learn?'

'Some, they like to learn. But they can't practise because their parents don't speak it. But most kids now, they don't care. They just don't see any point in learning the language again.'

I kept hoping she was going to say 'But my great-grandchildren ... they can speak it, they like to learn ...' but as we talked, no hint of optimism suppressed the spectre of a lifeless Koyukon.

'What about your great-grandchildren? Can they speak it?'

'Some of them understand a lot, but they don't speak. They don't get any practice. I don't know what happens in twenty years.'

She wore a silvery blouse marbled with purple, brown and blue. Sandy streaks tinted her otherwise white hair, worn short and naturally waved. She was small in stature and portly, with an enduring prettiness that was most apparent when she removed her glasses, as she did occasionally while conversing. She raised her eyebrows and smiled as an old Stones' record suddenly began pounding in an adjacent room. She smiled weakly, an heiress without successor, as if the sounds added weight to her heritage.

37

MEANWHILE, THE IDITAROD was hotting up. Two predictable names had jostled their way closer to the front. Old Joe had dropped a dog, lost the lead and then regained it. He and his team of nine pulled out of Kaltag two hours ahead of the Swiss Alaskan, Martin Buser. With fifteen dogs still in harness, Buser was now recognised as the man to beat. Seventy-five minutes behind him came Susan Butcher, who was one hundred minutes ahead of Rick Swenson, who was five and a half hours ahead of Joe Garnie of Teller. These three teams each had twelve dogs. In sixth place, with eleven dogs (and three pairs of borrowed socks) was Herbie Nayokpuk.

The last competitor to reach Nome would be awarded a red lantern inscribed 'I swept the Iditarod Trail clean'. Currently sweeping it clean, travelling together and already six days and fourteen hours behind the leaders, were two unusual teams. One was partly composed of poodles and the other was driven by a former hairdresser and the only British contestant, Leslie Ann Monk. In Galena I met her husband, Roy, a tall bearded manufacturer of dyes for the chemical industry, and he related their Iditastory.

Their interest in running sled dogs had been sparked by the acquisition of a pet husky ten years earlier. At that time there were about two hundred Siberian huskies in Britain. Over the years this number had increased to two thousand and their kennel had expanded even more rapidly. Mushing was fraught with problems in Britain, Roy grumbled. Fences and few rights of way restricted training runs, quarantine laws effectively prevented running dogs abroad, and lack of snow made the use of wheeled buggies necessary. The British, in keeping with their history, mushed chariots, not sleds.

The Monks dreamed of conquering Alaska. The previous winter Roy and Leslie Ann had come out to gain experience, and for $15,000 they had bought an eighteen-dog team from a retiring Iditarod musher. They returned to Britain for the summer and left the dogs in the care of another musher. In their absence the caretaker picked the best dogs for his own Iditarod team and substituted inferior ones. Legally there was nothing the Monks could do about the matter.

Once back in Alaska at the start of this winter they sorted through the remains of their purchase, borrowed and rented other dogs, and patched a team together. On the day the race started, the six female dogs in the team were all in season and during the many undisciplined stoppages, all six were bred on the trail. Near McGrath Leslie Ann came to a collapsed ice bridge and lost heart. She backtracked twenty-five miles to the village but was then persuaded to return and find a way round. While Roy and I were talking, Leslie Ann was leaving the half-way point of Cripple Landing.

'She hasn't got a strong enough mental approach,' Roy remarked. It wasn't hard to tell he wished *he* were out there running the race, and that, inwardly, he was proud of his wife. They had already survived an Iditarod of sorts to run an Iditarod.

The poodles were in the team of John Sutter of Chugiak. There were six of them, standard-size black creatures with wiry curls, and instead of yapping they were said to bark like the huskies which made up the rest of the pack. He had never cared for the breed until asked to look after a miniature – the middle of the range – belonging to his father-in-law. That dog could run! John had started training standard poodles to pull a sled as a novelty and after eleven years of suffering derogatory jokes, he had amassed fifty minor trophies. Poodles made fast intelligent sled dogs, he maintained, but at times they were too intelligent. They knew when to give up. They lacked stamina and robustness. 'John Sutter started his poodle program with obedience training,' the *Anchorage Daily News* reported, 'which to a hard-core, liver-eating musher is about as logical as charm school for pit vipers.' Good sled dogs simply pulled, the paper argued, and that left no room for other refinements. John Sutter was out to prove poodles could complete the 1,150-mile race. It wasn't certain who would have the last laugh: the liver-eaters or the poodle-programmer.

Thus the Iditarod was shaping up as a keen contest at both ends, for $30,000 and for the Red Lantern.

38

HER CABIN'S EXTERIOR was a fascination of bric-à-brac. Freak bits of bent and twisted wood, birch burls, four 'kicker' (outboard engine) propellers, glass insulators off telephone posts, antler oddments, a rusty whip saw, and I can't remember what else. She had laid fresh spruce boughs as a doormat. Inside darkness prevailed except in the corner where Hazel Strassburg, wearing a light blue smock, was at work. She was short and stocky, her face pointed and serious. Blood was smeared up to her biceps.

Sunlight slanted in the room's only window, covered by a sheet of plastic to effect double-glazing, and illuminated the beaver Hazel was skinning. Within a semicircle of scattered knives she slit and ripped, and occasionally nudged her spectacles back into place with the hook of her elbow. Four more beavers lay on the floor by her feet.

'The young people don't trap any more — just us older people,' she said.

She was sixty-three and a widow. Credited as the best trapper in Galena and a tireless worker, she ran twenty-one sets and was now skinning the last of her beaver quota a full month before the season closed.

Plastic flowers glowed on the window-sill. Behind her a poster listed nine instructions on what to do in the event of a nuclear attack, each advising on the necessary action to cope with an increasingly severe situation. The ninth was double-size: 'Kiss Your Ass Good-bye...'

'The young don't trap any more,' Hazel repeated.

39

CAMPION AIR FORCE Base looked like any other hardship posting, a hive of inactivity inside a guarded fence. Part of it served as Galena airport and the rest as an outpost of Operation 'Top Cover for North America', housing F15 Eagles of the 43rd and 54th Tactical Fighter Squadrons. With my sled packed and ready for the journey to Nulato, I drove my dogs to Campion's main gate and anchored them to its fence. Grace had given me the name of a pilot, Mike Donahue, who led me to a combined hangar and living quarters. We climbed a set of stairs to the pilots' mess-room. It was an elongated room with desks, bookcases, sofas, a television set and, at the far end, a 'fireman's pole' to the lower level. There were only two Tactical Fighters at this outpost of Top Cover. Don, the other pilot, was lounging before a videoed soap.

'The Air Force mixes *old* and *young* pilots,' Mike said, the implication being that he was the old one. He was about forty, a hand short of six feet, with dark hair, bushy eyebrows and a wiry strength. Don was perhaps twenty-eight, tall and blond-haired. The old one was calm and quietly self-assured, whereas the young one was excitable and loud. Don took over and conducted the tour in a jocular vein.

'When I think people won't understand if I tell 'em I'm a fighter pilot by profession,' Don said, 'I tell 'em I'm in sole charge of a thirty-two million dollar chemical processing plant.'

'Is that what an F15 costs?'

'Yes, sir. And it goes up as we speak. The Youess Air Force has a thousand of these little plants.' *Youess.* A slovenly drawl. His casual manner made him seem an unlikely trustee of a precious plant.

Pilots spent most of their time watching television. It was a stressful period, waiting for a scramble, so they worked rotas of five and one: five weeks at their headquarters in Anchorage and one week on standby at the bases of either Galena, King Salmon or Shemya Island. Their main task was to intercept Russian 'Bears', F95 bombers, which frequently entered US airspace. Mike pointed to a wall map of Alaska and Siberia which was studded with pins.

'Each pin is a Bear contact. Galena has more alerts than any other base. Last year we intercepted fifty-seven Bears, though actual scrambles were half that figure as Bears generally fly in pairs. This year we've had four scrambles.'

'They like to keep testing the system,' Don added. 'C'mon, let's go see our little babies.'

One by one we slid down the pole which deposited us in a corridor a few paces from an entrance to the hangar.

'Our scramble time, from alert to take-off, is between five and ten minutes. Most of that is taken up with getting into our arctic survival suits. They're not much good though ... are they, Don?'

Arctic survival suits seemed a standing joke. 'They sure aren't. Only good to minus twenty. After that your butt freezes. We reckon it's official policy. Sort of encouraging us to stick with our machines.'

'Do you wear bunny boots?'

'No, they'd be best, but wait till you see the cockpit. No room for bunnies. If we had to eject, there'd be no guarantee our feet would come with us. Even with less bulky boots, we've got no guarantee.'

140

The two F15s stood side by side and were much taller and longer that I had expected. Sleek and of a dull metallic grey, their wing tips almost touching, they posed like a couple of mutually admiring mosquitoes.

'A test F15 stripped of even the weight of its paint can go from a dead start to 110,000 feet in a little over two minutes. For the first minute it's quicker than an Apollo rocket. The planes you see here each weigh 60,000 pounds, and half of that is fuel.' Flying at low altitude and at their top speed of Mach 2 – twice the speed of sound, or 1,500 miles per hour – they guzzled fuel at a maximum rate of 50,000 gallons per hour. The situation was evidently hypothetical, for under these conditions an F15 would run out of fuel in eleven minutes. 'Normally we cruise at subsonic speeds and can stay airborne for five and a half hours on one fuelling. We carry extra fuel tanks on the wings and can jettison them if we need more speed. We usually have to fly between five and fifteen hundred miles to meet enemy planes.'

'You've given this tour before, haven't you?' I prompted. He laughed, and we moved under the wing to view the armoury. I pointed to two slim projectiles, eight feet long, with plaster of Paris noses and fins at middle and rear; they looked more like bits of plumber's piping than missiles. 'What are those?'

'Heat-seeking Sidewinders, for air-to-air strikes. We can throw out foil and flares to combat enemy heat-seekers. So can they, of course. F15s carry four Sidewinders and four radio-controlled air-to-ground missiles. And see that hole in the wing next the fuselage? Behind it is a machine gun with six revolving barrels. It carries one thousand rounds which it'll exhaust in nine seconds. That's about one hundred bullets a second. We don't have any radio contact with an enemy plane so that's our first and cheapest means of persuasion. So far it's always worked.'

I climbed a ladder and looked into the cockpit. If the clutter of gadgetry was not quite as dazzling as might be expected, it still looked laughably simple to jettison your fuel tanks, let fly a Sidewinder or eject yourself completely while trying to turn on your radio. There were panels of buttons and gauges for flying control, weapon activation and navigation. It was all terribly cramped. I imagined myself strapped to the seat. If I put my hands on my hips, my elbows would protrude through the fuselage. There was no way my bunny boots would come with me if I tried to bail out. Under my seat, I was informed, in an area seemingly too small for a football, were vacuum-packed rations, a life raft and a sleeping bag. They said my seat would eject with me – fortunately, for I would still be strapped to it – and that it would be released automatically by the jerk of the parachute opening. I was so overawed by all this that I forgot to ask *how*, having just watched my jettisoned seat plummet towards Siberia, I was meant to retrieve my life raft and sleeping bag. Perhaps that was all part of 'the policy' too.

'If the engines fail, will it glide?'

'Yes,' Don replied. 'Like a stone.'

I had underestimated him. Below that boisterous façade there had to be a man of exceptional nerve and ability. I think I would have a nervous laugh and a tic of understatement if every day I faced the prospect of donning a ropy survival suit, asking Russians to go away in the language of a hundred rounds per second, and being snagged by a pair of boots doing twice the speed of sound. I didn't envy him.

I shook hands, thanked them both and hurried back to my dog team. No, I didn't envy them. I had no ambition to be in sole charge of a thirty-two-million-dollar chemical processing plant. It was enough being manager of a two-thousand-dollar food recycling works.

40

From Mach 2 to eight miles an hour. An F15 could fly the Iditarod in forty-five minutes. Yet it would devour 37,500 gallons of fuel and require its tanks to be refilled three times on the way. I was happier with my dogs. They devoured chicken brick stew and required refuelling only once a day, and they could glide beautifully. With eight dogs, a brake and an anchor I had all the responsibility I wanted.

Blue sky, sun, 2°F. The northern hemisphere was ours, or so it seemed, as we glided along an endless ice rink. The villages here – Galena, Koyukuk, Nulato, Kaltag – were close enough to encourage regular traffic and this was probably the most travelled section of the Yukon. Not that it was busy – we encountered a total of eight snow machines over thirty-five miles. Three of them were fully laden with Kaltag teachers and pupils on a three-hour drive to take part in a cross-country skiing competition.

The Koyukuk Flats made any landmark prestigious and the only one was a vague and squashed sugar-loaf hill called Pilot Mountain. Sunk as we were below the flats and in the wide cut of the Yukon, our view was of wooded islands and wooded banks. Then we rounded a corner and confronted Bishop Rock, a dramatic crag-faced bluff with spruce along its crest. In summer its base would take the full force of the current, causing the flow to bunch up and surge aside. A heavy iron cross had been erected near the top; and lower down, surmounting a lesser crag, was another, made of wood and painted white. The Bishop of Vancouver Island, the Reverend Charles Seghers, was murdered near this spot.

He first came to Alaska in 1877 and preached to the Indians of this region on 5 August, the feast of Our Lady of the Snows. He was so gratified by the response to his sermon that he vowed to return some day, build a mission in Nulato and name it for that propitious occasion. In 1886 he set out to do this and was within thirty miles of Nulato when he camped near this rock for the last night of the journey. He had with him an assistant called Frank Fuller, who had been subject to fits of strange behaviour ever since the party set out. He seemed convinced the priests were plotting his undoing. Once he accused them of trying to drown him, and on another occasion of attempting to burn him alive. Fuller went berserk. He entered the bishop's tent screaming and waving a gun and, when Seghers awoke and rose to his feet, shot him in the chest. Seghers was found dead, slumped across his bearskin rug. (Fuller was put on trial in Sitka, found guilty and sentenced to life imprisonment, but was apparently released after doubts about his motive and sanity were raised.)

It was hard to believe this land had a human history because, in visual terms, history is a heritage of scars. If I had searched around the many creeks we passed I would have doubtless come across old tailings and mining conduits, but the desecrations of man's involvement appeared to have healed here. How many other past events, unmarked by crosses, were around us? These thoughts entertained me as we approached Last Chance.

We passed the summer fish camp of Yistletaw, a dozen cabins with a name so lyrical it echoed for a mile in my mind, and we passed the turn off to the village of Koyukuk which shared its name with the mountain at its rear, 900 feet of crags and cornices. By then a strong breeze had arisen and was whipping the snow into a moving blanket around the dogs' legs. Their feet iced up quickly in these conditions and I had to stop frequently to clear them. With my mind still lodged in the past, I imagined Last Chance to have been named for a prospector, down on his luck, who had tried here for a final pan. That, I was later told, was fanciful. Last Chance was essentially a well-stocked shop, nine miles from its nearest customer, with its goods flown in from Anchorage and ordered by mail from Seattle. For the last twenty-two years this log-cabin supermarket had made its profits from the sale of beer and spirits. It was said to offer the Yukon traveller the 'last chance' of legally buying booze between Galena and the Bering Sea.

Trading in Alaska's current epidemic was big business.

41

Something is stalking the village people. Across the state, the Eskimos, Indians and Aleuts of Bush Alaska are dying in astonishing numbers. By suicide, accident and other untimely, violent means, death is stealing the heart of a generation and painting the survivors with despair. A toxic brew of booze and boredom combines with isolation and changing cultures to claim the lives and spirits of the people at an alarming rate.

Culture is not an item – an artefact to be lost or pawned, or a memory that might be forgotten like the words to an old, no longer popular song. It is the anchor that holds each individual to his or her place in a vast and uncaring universe. When the culture is gone, the individual stands face-to-face with apocalypse.

'A People in Peril', *Anchorage Daily News*

In Nulato I came across a recent eighty-page report by the *Anchorage Daily News* highlighting alcoholism and its consequences in rural Alaska. It had as its cover a photograph of a sunset silhouetting the grave of one of Alakanuk's suicide victims. In a period of sixteen months this Eskimo village of 550 people was the scene of eight suicides, over forty suicide attempts, two murders and four drownings – all alcohol-related. The figures were lower in other villages, but sometimes not by much.

For years the extent of the problem had been concealed as a result of poor record-keeping and the practice of registering suicide deaths as 'accidental' out of deference to the shame felt by victims' relatives. When investigated, native suicide figures increased by as much as seventy-three per cent over those previously recorded. When the statistics were correlated, a tragedy of horrifying proportions was exposed. For American men between the ages of twenty and twenty-four, the national suicide rate was 25.6 per 100,000; for white Alaskan men it was 44; for native Alaskan men, 257. Native Alaskan women also took their lives at rates markedly higher than average, and among them the incidence of Fetal Alcohol Syndrome – physical and mental defects produced in an unborn child as a result of drinking during pregnancy – was two and a half times higher than the USA average and twice that of other Indian populations. Alaska, as a separate entity, ranked fourth in the world for per capita consumption of hard spirits: behind Hungary, East Germany and Poland; and ahead of Czechoslovakia and the USSR.

In the days when Alaska was Russian America, St Petersburg prohibited the trade or gift of alcohol to the natives. The ban was unenforceable and regularly flouted. By the early eighteenth century the Indians in the south-east of the country had learned to concoct their own brew, and they exchanged furs for the ingredients. Their distillate from a mash of flour, sugar, molasses and dried apples was drunk hot from the still. They called it *hootchinoo*, a Tlingit word meaning 'happiness', which white tipplers shortened to 'hootch' and adopted into English. From the middle of the nineteenth century onwards the flow of alcohol into coastal communities steadily increased as more and more American whalers chased their quarry in northern waters. A skipper in the employ of the government went to Port Hope in 1889 and reported that 'Each visit of a whaling ship was followed by riot and drunkenness; the women were carried off to serve the lusts of the sailors and officers', and as a result the Eskimos were 'in a most degraded state, physically, mentally and spiritually'.

Following America's purchase of Alaska in 1867, a law was passed forbidding natives, intoxicated persons or habitual drunkards to buy or sell liquor. In these early days selling whisky to natives was regarded as a more heinous offence than murder, and almost as serious as violating a cache. In Forty Mile such trade was punishable by banishment, or execution by hanging. There were nevertheless ways around the law, as W. H. Pierce noted in his book *Thirteen Years of Travel and Exploration in Alaska*, referring to the year 1886:

> ... it had a dance floor for what were locally known as 'squaw dances' ... Indian women were the only female partners available to most of the miners. Selling or giving liquor to Indians was illegal at that time but the law did not do much of a job of stopping either sale or gifts. One old-timer explained: 'You see,' he said, 'when you took an Indian girl to a dance, she wanted a drink, just like anyone else. But there was usually a deputy marshal hanging around and we had to be careful. There wasn't any law against kissing a squaw, *so* what you did was go to a bar and buy two shots of whiskey. One of them you drank – and swallowed. The other one you drank but didn't swallow. Instead you went over to your partner and transferred it from your mouth to hers.'

National prohibition affected white Alaskans between 1920 and 1933 but natives were subject to an unbroken period of selective prohibition from 1867 to 1953. For legislative purposes they had always been regarded as living on an Indian reservation, and in 1953 Federal laws banning alcohol for Indians were repealed. Suddenly beer and spirits became readily available. Chronic drunkenness became rampant.

In 1980 village councils were given powers to impose restrictions on alcohol sales in their own communities. 'Wet' communities elected to confine the sale of alcohol to licensed retail outlets which were owned either privately or by village corporations; 'damp' communities prohibited the sale of drink but allowed it to be imported (for example, through mail order or by a run to the nearest wet village) for private consumption; 'dry' communities banned the sale, importation and, in some cases, even the possession of alcohol. Of the systems, 'dry' was the only serious attempt at eradicating the problem of alcohol abuse, but in practice 'dry' meant 'secretly wet'. Bootleggers saw to that.

Bootleggers had markets only in dry and damp areas. They based themselves in damp villages and ordered drink to be flown in from the wet. This was undertaken by private, chartered or commercial freight planes, and was legal. A case of Windsor Canadian Whiskey (a popular brand whose producers cater to the Bush by using unbreakable plastic bottles and advertising in the *Tundra Times*) could be purchased in the city and delivered to the Bush at a total cost of $130. Then it was secretly distributed and sold for a minimum of $360. Bootlegging brought huge profits – as much as $3,000 a day on special drinking occasions such as the Fourth of July – and was allowed to persist through community apathy and complicity. In villages where everyone knew everyone else and lived close together it should have been relatively easy for a concerted effort to curb the flow of drink, but no one ever wanted to stir trouble or get involved. The evidence required to prosecute a bootlegger was so weighty and hard to gather that cases often failed to make the courts or collapsed into acquittals, leaving witnesses exposed to retaliation.

Last Chance was a privately-owned, licensed retailer but it no longer held a monopoly over the Lower Yukon. Another out-in-the-sticks booze shop had opened nine miles downstream from Nulato. (The inhabitants of Nulato had signed a petition asking for it to be closed – their own village corporation, Gana-a' Yoo, owned the land on which the store was sited. To their astonishment, Gana-a' Yoo ignored the petition and approved the lease.) Excluding beer, total *liquor* sales of these two stores was estimated to be 2,630 gallons annually. Their nearest customers lived in Koyukuk, Nulato and Kaltag, and numbered 790 men, women and children. These three villages were 'soggy'. Vacillating between wet and damp, they had not banned the sale or importation of alcohol, but simply refused permission for retailers to operate within their municipal boundaries. Other villages had adopted an 'if you can't beat the bootleggers, join 'em' approach. Tanana had elected to be wet. The community ran the only alcohol outlet in the village and used some of the handsome profits to treat the victims of alcohol abuse.

The demon is ethylalcohol, and there are both cultural and bio-genetical reasons why its rampage among native peoples is so severe. The chemical make-up of native Americans (and of Indians, Chinese and Australian Aboriginals) is different from that of Caucasians. Natives lack an enzyme, acetaldehydrogenase, which is crucial in regulating the effects of ethylalcohol. They absorb alcohol more slowly into their systems and this, coupled with the common practice of intermittent binge-drinking, results in higher blood-alcohol levels and the potential for more volatile behaviour. They are more prone to blackouts than to delirium tremens, more prone to the sudden than the gradual impulses alcohol causes. Drinking is a recent phenomenon in native history, and it takes many generations for a degree of tolerance towards alcohol to be developed.

These inherent traits are given full play in societies which have lost their direction and self-respect. Young native men often find they have no place in the community. Women and elders can bring in more welfare money; the subsistence tasks which once occupied all their working hours have become either obsolete or simplified through technological advances; and of the few jobs available, most are clerical positions for which they must compete against women and elders. For these natives, the Young Blood of the community, the future looks particularly bleak. Ethylalcohol – the gilded poison – offers respite.

Anthropologists recognise three critical stages in the process of acculturation, commonly a native culture being assimilated or annihilated by 'Western' culture. Firstly, a native culture receives new goods and technology and incorporates them into its traditional way of life. Attitudes stay the same and the only changes are material. Respected values and definitions of success stay the same. The second stage occurs when attitudes change. By then a new native generation has acquired the material aspects of a western lifestyle and it begins to regard traditional values and customs as backward and inferior. It adopts western definitions of success – money, career, possessions – but finds itself in a gulf between a culture it has discarded and one in which it is ill-equipped to compete and not always accepted. During this stage hope and self-respect diminish, and spirituality degenerates. The third state, when and if it is reached, is to find a place in society once more.

In any community there are good and bad, drunkards and tee-totallers. The statistics tend to brand every native as a drunkard, a waster on the brink of suicide. This is emphatically not the case. Many native Alaskans never drink alcohol, but they are in the minority and few, if any, can distance themselves from its effects on relatives and friends. The tragic distinction of the problem here is that an entire people is involved. Hudson Stuck witnessed the same plight in his day and it depressed him, but he remained optimistic: 'In the midst of such a crowd of healthy, vivacious youngsters, clear-eyed, clean-limbed, and eager, one positively refuses to be hopeless about the race.'

I searched for hope in the writings of others. In *Arctic Dreams* Barry Lopez wrote: 'We sometimes mistake a rude life for a rude mind; raw meat for barbarism; lack of conversation for lack of imagination. The overriding impression, I think, for the visitor in the Arctic who walks away from the plane, and waits out the bouts of binge drinking, the defensive surliness and self-conscious acting in the village, is that a wisdom is to be found in the people. ... This is a timeless wisdom that survives failed human economies. It survives war. It survives definition. It is a nameless wisdom esteemed by all people. It is understanding how to live a decent life, how to behave properly toward other people and toward the land.'.

I believe this wisdom does exist, but am unconvinced that *young natives* believe it exists.

In one place, a native community called Alkali Lake in British Columbia, alcohol has gone. Fifteen years ago the total adult population was addicted to drink. Then one couple reformed and made a stand; the husband turned in his bootlegging mother, and gradually they won support. The remaining bootleggers were driven out, as was the alcoholic priest, and a fifteen-year struggle ensued at the end of which the community had swung to ninety-eight per cent abstinence. The people of Alkali Lake turned their experiences into a programme called 'New Directions' which taught communities to rebuild themselves by developing trust, communications and mutual support. They found that stopping drinking was the easy part, healing the wounds was what made it last. New Directions was not a magic formula, but a strategy against a hard mental conflict — and they proved it could work.

As with any alcoholic, the desire to be cured has to develop within the native communities before any cure can be effected. The only sure way of stopping the supply of drink is to dry up the demand; support programmes on the lines of New Directions then have to be instigated to assist the delicate metamorphosis, ease the initial loneliness and depression of sobriety; and a whole new attitude has to prevail. This epidemic is not like the previous ones of measles, influenza, tuberculosis and diphtheria. This one can be, indeed *has* to be, fought from within. More than ever this is an occasion for communities to rally and help each other in time-honoured tradition.

The people are up to it, but the time is not right for a united sense of responsibility to emerge.

I wonder if perhaps an enquiring mind is not enough and whether, because I happen to be white, I am incapable of picking up the songlines of native Alaska. Bruce Chatwin believed the Australian Aboriginals, for all their physical degeneration, were in communion with their past through song. A network of songlines covered the land, stretching back through time to link the Aboriginals with the forces of creation. The songlines brought them strength and gave them direction, and their world could be sung into a new existence.

I looked for the hope which Struck and Lopez found, and saw it; but the sounds of an old and no longer popular song eluded me. The alcoholocaust was apparently not yet done.

42

MRS OSWALD COLLECTED barbed wire.

'Southern Oklahoma, 1922,' she would say, pointing to a strand. Then to another, 'This one's ma oldest, Texas 1876. It was only invented in 1873, you know? Now, this fella, found him in a garbage tip in Detroit.' She had over 200 different examples, though she had only brought about fifty with her. They might have been friends from the way she referred to them, and she gave the impression of having spent all her seventy years rooting around Detroit's garbage tips and dismantling Oklahoma's fences. The strands were sewn to lengths of canvas which she unfurled whenever she lectured to clubs, schools or wayward mushers. She was besotted with the stuff and when she had described each piece, she leaned towards me and confided, without a hint of humour, 'You know, when people hear I'm going to talk about barbed wire they aren't at all interested, but in no time at all they get all wrapped up in it.'

Mrs Oswald was on vacation from the Lower 48 and visiting her son, Tom, a teacher at Nulato High School. He and his wife had willingly extended their hospitality to me. My dogs were tethered outside, royally stretched out on leftover Iditarod straw and defying me ever to mention spruce boughs again. One end of their picket line was attached to my sled and the other to the Oswalds' twelve-foot satellite dish.

Teachers always occupied the best houses in the villages – central heating, running water and flush lavatories. The rest of the villagers had wood stoves, hauled water from a hole in the river (they had a wellhouse, but in Nulato no one liked the taste of its water) and used outhouses or honey buckets – the charming term for plastic-bag lavatories whose contents were dumped in the sort of places 'fellas' from Detroit were sometimes found. Village houses were comfortable and better suited for a winter traveller's needs. I would have been happier in one, or even in a crude cabin. It seemed wrong to be hopping from one island of suburban comfort to another, and I found it hard, stepping out of a primitive landscape which enthralled and inspired me, to be confronted by the dulling amenities of a twenty-first-century house. It seemed a betrayal. Yet my convictions were never so vehement as to forsake a bed for Iditarod straw, and I was always grateful for the extraordinary kindness of my various hosts.

'Susan Butcher stayed with us,' Mrs Oswald the Fence said, proudly. 'During the race. That's her straw you're using.' She took me into her confidence again. 'And do you know what . . .?

I imagined Susan hadn't liked her barbed wire.

'. . . She didn't have a shower. She was here for two hours, talked for most of them, *and she didn't have a shower.*'

'But she was racing. A shower would have made it harder to face the cold, dirty prospect of racing again.' I said this gently. 'Incidentally, do you know how the race is going?'

'Last we heard it was between three of them: Susan, that man Swenson, is it? and that Swiss man, Boozer, or something.'

The satellite dish was Tom's own investment, and the only private dish in town. The Oswalds and their neighbours, also teachers, said they had a 'need' for television here. The big dish received a potential twenty-four channels from each of ten satellites. Their television was used mainly for kaleidoscopic effects and background noise, though one morning we watched it; a practice of doctors was advertising for ricked necks. They asked us to call them. We were in Nulato and they were in Phoenix. Then we had to leave. The day was scheduled. First I would talk to the school about monsters, then I would take

151

my dogs to hunt for what Schwatka described as '... a small wooden cross, ... bearing the following inscription:

Lieut. J. J. Barnard, H.B.M. Ship "Enterprise"
killed by the Koyukuk Indians Feb. 16/51',

and in the evening we would visit the Adult Recreation Centre.

The children seemed to enjoy my talk though only, I suspected, because I was taking the place of a more tedious subject. I slipped out of school and left them being wrapped up in barbed wire by the second guest speaker of the day. Once behind my dogs I felt a new surge of life and as though my destiny was my own again, except when the sheet ice of Nulato's streets sometimes took over. We headed for the graveyard, not only because Barnard's cross was possibly there but also because it afforded the best views of the village.

Nulato was at the end of a long wooded hill flanking the Yukon, long enough to hold an airstrip on its crest with several miles to spare. The graveyard occupied the extremity of the range, where it dropped to the village at an angle which must have alarmed many a pallbearer. Most villages consisted of an old and a new section, and Nulato was no exception. The new was a mile away where the land rose sharply into hills. Beyond the hills was the direction of Nome, but there was no easy way through going overland; and I would have to continue on down the Yukon for another thirty-five miles to Kaltag, where a portage struck out over the mountains for the coast. The Yukon was first obstructed by this range of mountains at Last Chance, and there, having flowed westwards across almost the full width of Alaska, it was forced to turn south and make a long detour to the Bering Sea.

Old Nulato hugged the river on which its importance as a trading community had been founded. Its cabins of dark seasoned wood were separated from New Nulato's brightly varnished ones by a tract of snowfields dotted with pine trees and scrawled with snow machine tracks. The area held a population of 350 natives and about a dozen whites, the majority of whom were teachers. The school was in the old section, looking garishly modern in its surroundings of long-dead wood and fishwheels frozen to the shore. In the eighteen miles between Koyukuk and Nulato, Stuck had once counted fifty fish-

152

wheels. My route had been marked less by fishwheels than by 'Oly' beer cans.

'The winters are very mild nowadays,' remarked an elderly man who had walked up and introduced himself while I was scanning the view. 'Very mild. They've been mild ever since they landed on the moon.' Stan said that several years ago a science teacher had arranged for a sample of moonrock to be sent to the school. It had come in a solid cube of perspex and pupils had gazed into it as one might into a crystal ball. The old people had thought it a bad omen.

When asked what I was doing, I explained about Barnard's grave.

'It's not here. It's at Gazaalma, about two miles downriver. But you won't find nothing. It's gone.'

I thanked him, and headed there nevertheless because my dogs were eager to run. 'Gazaalma' is a Russian word for 'barracks', and a reminder that Nulato was the first site of Russian occupation in the Interior and the deepest point of their penetration into America. The Nulato Indians had for centuries used the Kaltag Portage to trade with Eskimos, from whom they received seal and whale oil and, via Siberia, tobacco and copper spearheads. Nulato had twenty-nine Indians when a Russian Creole, Malakhov, arrived in 1838 with instructions to set up a trading post on the Yukon. *Youcon* is an Indian word meaning 'big river'. To the Russians it was known as the Kwikpak.

Malakhov was received by Chief Unilla and allowed to set up shop. He left it undefended and found it burned to the ground when he returned the following year. He also found he had unwittingly killed off his market. An epidemic resulting from his first visit had left insufficient villagers to place the dead on traditional burial platforms. Starving dogs had eaten the corpses and scattered their bones. Unilla's family had died and, grief-stricken, he had taken his own life by shutting himself in his house and setting it on fire. Malakhov rebuilt the post and again left it undefended. It was burned and rebuilt two more times before things settled down in 1842, when a detachment of soldiers became permanently garrisoned nearby. A new representative of the Russian American Company, Derabin, began turning in a profit.

This was the situation when Lieutenant John Barnard came up the river in February 1851. He was with an expedition – one of forty in a ten-year period – searching for traces of Sir John Franklin and his party, who had disappeared three years earlier on Britain's last serious attempt to find a North West Passage. Barnard had heard rumours of white men up the Koyukuk River (probably Russians connected with the post) and thought it possible Franklin had found a way over the Brooks Range from the Beaufort Sea. Barnard stayed with Derabin and a Russian messenger was sent to the Koyukuk Indians to request the chief to come and discuss the rumours. According to an unsubstantiated account, one which contradicts normal practices, the messenger was eaten. At any rate, he did not return.

The Russians were detested because of their penchant for brutality, and Barnard had unwittingly walked into a long-standing feud between the Koyukuk and Nulato Indians. The latter had left the score uneven after an attack in 1846, and the Koyukuk Indians chose that night for revenge. They attacked three large houses where some hundred Indians were sleeping, and then moved on to the trading post. Fifty-three people died in the Nulato Massacre, including Barnard and Derabin and his family. Gazaalma was abandoned after this and three years later a new fort with a stockade and a new Indian village were built upstream where Nulato is now sited. The trading post continued to prosper under Russian control until the Purchase.

When Stuck visited the site of the massacre in about 1915, he wrote: 'many skulls and bones and copper household utensils and beads and buttons have been uncovered from amongst the rotting, charred timbers, and carried off by "souvenir" hunters. I, myself, though not of that great company, dug out of the bank with a stick a brass button bearing the imperial Russian double eagle – evidently from a uniform coat – and was interested to see, with a magnifying glass, on the back of it the word "Birmingham", and I wondered if official brass buttons are still imported into Russia.'

Stan was right; Gazalma was lost under snow when I surveyed the part not yet washed away by the river. No Birmingham buttons for me, but I was not of 'that great company' either. Just when I was about to mush off for the sake of mushing, a snow machine came by with two Franciscan riders. This was not apparent until they stopped, removed their helmets and introduced themselves. The driver, Father Sam, was a slight man approaching fifty with a heavily pitted complexion. He spoke so softly it was a struggle to catch his words before they floated off. Brother Clem was in his mid thirties. Tall and overweight, he had a benevolent, fleshy face and was fond of exclaiming 'Oh! Shoot!' and 'Holy Cow!'

'Barnard wasn't buried with the others. He wasn't Orthodox. Even in summer there's not much to see,' Father Clem whispered. 'Do come and call on us before you leave Nulato. We'd enjoy your visit.'

43

THE ADULT RECREATION Centre was relatively quiet that evening, and possibly every evening. It was a modern frame building off the same blueprint as the schools, with an abundance of tables and a shroud of cigarette smoke in its main room. It was in the new sector of the split town and I drove there by dog team as the Oswalds had decided not to come after all. Eight people between the ages of twenty and eighty, though predominantly at the older end of the range, were seated round a table playing pan. A woman was watching. Her sweat shirt read 'Stickdance for Lorraine McGinty'.

Pan, short for panguingue, appeared to require fixed concentration, long schooling and at least five packs of cards. The game originated in the Philippines and somehow made it to Alaska and become extremely popular. This was not just another card game, however, for it had assumed a special social function. It was played during all-night vigils at funeral wakes, accompanied by story-telling. In fact, pan was said to be the last preserve of the story-telling tradition. The game was often played for small stakes; a player might lose five dollars or win as much as forty. Lotteries, raffles, bingo, boxing, racing – any form of gambling won enthusiastic participation in native communities. But money stakes were not allowed in the Adult Recreation Centre, and the play that evening was for counters.

I asked the other spectator if she understood the game.

'Sure.' She didn't take her eyes off the play for a while. Then she turned and gave me a down-up scan. 'You some kinda reporter?'

'I think any newspaper would get fed up waiting for my story – I'm travelling slowly with dogs.'

'Yea? We get a lotta folk like you here – weirdos, some of 'em.

155

Once had a guy *walkin'* to Siberia. Crazy, man! He was real spaced out. Galena paid his way here to get rid of him. We paid it to Kaltag. They got him a ride to Fairbanks. Last summer a nut came floatin' down handin' out Jesus sheets. Yea, we get some weirdos here.'

She said few people in Nulato were *pure* Athabascans now. Irishmen on steamers had apparently been a major cause of the change. McGinty was a common name in the area. She said she had five children and didn't get out much now. But then, she never had. She had been twenty-six when she crossed the Yukon for the first time, and the far side was only two miles away. She was unmarried and lived off her child allowance. I asked what her boyfriend did.

She scoffed. 'We're all the same, man. Just doin' our best survivin'.'

We continued watching pan. Between games the players might talk of good or bad hands, but otherwise they remained silent. For forty minutes the rhythmic patter of cards hitting the table told the only story.

I drove the dogs back home and almost lost Silver and Rosco to a snow machine. It came round a corner fast, lost control on the ice and careered towards my leaders. I watched in horror as a collision seemed inevitable, but the skis caught rough ice at the last moment and the machine roared by only a few feet away. The driver turned, let out a rodeo cry and punched the air. I was still shaking when we reached the Oswalds' house.

That night I lay in bed and imagined a Nulato inundated with reporters, foreigners and weirdos. This Nulato had decided to get its own back. Each evening eight stooges, by rota, would play pan at the Adult Recreation Centre. They wouldn't talk, wouldn't laugh, wouldn't share arcane wisdom with any passing rubberneck. A ninth would be there waiting and willing to spout the sort of nonsense rubbernecks love to hear. And so intruders wouldn't detect the village behind closed doors, the real Nulato: the real pan, the story-telling, the makers of snowshoes, the designers of kicker engines, the hatchers of marketing strategies, the teachers of the hunt, the planners of tribal sovereignty . . . . They wouldn't hear the last laugh.

Then I was able to fall asleep.

44

'HOLY COW!' BROTHER Clem exclaimed, when he heard I was mushing to Nome. 'Through all those blizzards? Haven't you heard the news?' I shook my head. 'We only caught a snippet about the Iditarod ... a musher's lost in a storm. Buser. He was lying second but he's not shown up.'

This only added to my apprehensions about the next stretch. I was having second thoughts. 'If I don't go to Nome, where would you suggest I head for?'

'Like, Hawaii, maybe ...?'

Brother Clem was the incumbent of Nulato, while Father Sam assisted for two weeks each month and then ministered to another community an hour away by snow machine. We sat talking in Brother Clem's sitting room, a small simple room decorated with posters bearing Biblical quotes. We had just been to church, and Father Sam had preached to seventeen elderly and two young Nulatons, and offered a prayer to those with drink problems. Now he was reflecting on the Church's work in Alaska.

'When the first Russian priests came to Alaska with the fur traders and translated a simplified version of the Bible into Aleut, they omitted all references to Hell. They reckoned the natives suffered enough here on earth.' This was understandable, he added, because the only natives the priests met were enslaved to the Russian fur trade. By eradicating native religions and not succeeding in replacing them with a substitute the priests had contributed to the suffering. 'One priest is recorded as having converted ten natives to Christianity in nineteen years. The people were left without spiritual support.'

The Orthodox Church left its triple bar crosses wherever the Russians went, but great tracts of Alaska remained untouched. Into one of these came the Reverend Robert MacDonald. In 1862, five years before Alaska became American, this Church of England itinerant entered the region around Fort Yukon. A remarkable man, later to become an archdeacon, MacDonald was the first to discover gold on the great river; but he had no interest in such a trifle. He learned the local language and translated the complete Bible, prayer book, hymn book and several other works into Takudh (Athabascan), and his translations are still in use on the Upper Yukon and Porcupine River.

Elsewhere things didn't change for twenty years until the diminutive Sheldon Jackson came onto the scene and events took an unusual and dramatic turn. He took it upon himself to divide up Alaska into approximately one dozen sections and these he packaged as ecclesiastical monopolies, in much the same way as drilling rights are currently offered to oil companies. Each section was contrived as a fair apportioning of easily-accessible and remote regions. Jackson allocated sections to as many different denominations as he could muster, and into whom he could instil interest. Each had to agree not to trespass on the grounds of another.

The result was that the Episcopalians received the Upper Yukon and the southern reaches of the Arctic Coast; the Roman Catholics got the Lower Yukon; the Presbyterians won the northern Arctic Coast and most of south-east Alaska; the Congregationalists moved to the most westerly tip of the mainland, Cape Prince of Wales; the Swedish Evangelists took the villages around Norton Sound; the Quakers of Philadelphia were awarded Kotzebue and precincts, and a patch near Juneau; the Moravians of Pennsylvania went up the Kuskokwim River; the Methodists were to work the Aleutian Islands; and the Baptists were given Kodiak Island and Cook Inlet.

The Churches were slow to move into their new domains at first, but after 1886 they increased their efforts. If Jackson could have found dozens of sympathetic evangelists like MacDonald, then this ingenious idea might have produced a blend of native culture and ecumenism strong enough to support the people through the woes of the twentieth century. But the new invasion of missionaries, such men as the unfortunate Seghers of Bishop Rock, carried Jackson's 'Americanisation of the Natives' as its ethic. There were exceptions like Stuck, and the Jesuit Fathers Jetti and Rossi who travelled the Nulato area and preached in Koyukon, but most missionaries upheld all things western and packed a lot of soap.

'The role of the Church has changed,' Father Sam said. 'We now recognise that if the Catholic Church is to survive here, it has to beat alcoholism – and soon. The only thing stopping the people from drinking themselves to death now is a lack of money. In 1992, when natives have the right to sell land allocated to them under the Settlement Act, many will then have the money to do it. Our role is now more as counsellors and self-help organisers than as preachers.'

'Are things *really* that bad ...?'

Brother Clem nodded. 'I don't think I could cope here without Father's help. We have to deal with everything from child molesting to suicide. We've had four suicides here in the last year, and other drink-related deaths. One time it seemed we were going from one funeral to another.' He said drunks came to talk to him, but in such a state it was impossible to reason with them, and they never came to him when sober. No one would talk about it. No one liked to hear the subject mentioned. It was regarded as their problem and they would sort it out in their own way and in their own time. 'All we can do is try our best to help, and just be here for when we're needed. We never lose sight of hope ...' he hesitated and looked down for a moment, '... though sometimes it seems very far away.'

45

'STICKDANCE IN MEMORY of ...'

The stickdance and potlatch are two enduring traditions which outline a fundamental difference in philosophy between native and western cultures. Potlatches are festive gatherings organised by an individual family and characterised by extravagant displays of generosity. They are essentially a way of thanking those who have helped the family at some occasion in the past – a wedding or a funeral – but they can stem from less decisive events, such as a successful hunting season. 'Potlatch' is a Chinook Indian word meaning 'giving'. It was previously the custom for families to spend years making fur clothes for presents and then to give *everything* away, including the last of their money. The more they could give, the higher they rose in status. Only the more successful families could

159

host these occasions on the scale demanded. The fact that they would be destitute at the end was of no significance – they would gain immense and lasting prestige through such a show of generosity. They would be lent tools and utensils for living, and they would benefit from the potlatches of others. Thus individual success was defined as popular esteem and acquired by bringing material advantage to the community as a whole.

The break in tradition is that potlatches no longer leave the host family destitute. They are still extravagant affairs and fulfil the same functions: expressions of gratitude and shows of wealth which reinforce bonds of kinship and renew cycles of distribution. They are also damn good parties. 'The white man likes to pay for everything with money,' it was commonly argued, 'but we like to pay for it with potlatch, and have fun.'

Stickdances are occasions specifically for thanking those who have helped at funerals. The Roman Catholic Church put a stop to them for many years, but in the 1960s it agreed they were not idolatrous and allowed them to start up again. Stickdances generally cost around $10,000 to host and are held two to four years after a person dies, to allow the bereaved family to save the necessary money. They take place in the village hall where a spruce pole – the stick – stripped of branches and decorated with streamers and fur pelts is set up in the middle of the floor. An abundance and variety of furs is also hung around the walls, and the room contains heaps of presents and clothes which the family will have made or bought. The scene is said to resemble a department store.

Everyone is welcome at a stickdance. The dancing begins on a Friday around midnight and takes the form of a circular flow around the stick. The dancers' movements are not energetic but suggestive of being in a trance, and the floor is occupied for between twelve and sixteen hours. During this period the closest friends of the deceased and those who gave the most support during the family's bereavement are given a complete set of new clothes, including handmade mukluks, an expensive parka and a hat of prime fur. Sometimes the face of one of these people is covered, and this person becomes the representative of the deceased.

On Saturday afternoon the stick is taken to the river, broken into pieces and thrown into the water along with the old clothes of those who have received new. This represents the spirit, now finished with our world, leaving earth and passing on. The furs that decorated the stick and the dance hall are cut into strips suitable for ruffs and given away. The remaining presents are also distributed, and sometimes these include sweat shirts specially printed 'Stickdance in memory of . . .'

Stickdances are only performed in two villages, Nulato and Kaltag. Kaltag was to be my last stop on the Yukon.

46

ALF STILL GREETED me each morning with a yawn which he extended into a little song, but he was sick. Although he remained eager to run he had lost his appetite, and a dog which is not eating soon loses condition. Rosco had gone off his fat cakes, Sensor scarcely drank, Duran had soft stools, and Nanook and Sisco (among others) had web splits. Only Kavik stood as a paragon of huskiness. It was, I reflected, a fairly normal morning for a dog musher.

Just to be sure about Alf I tracked down an Iditarod vet who was waiting for the Red Lantern contestants, and we struck a deal: a sled ride for a consultation. Alf's temperature was found to be normal (101.5°F) but I was told to keep a close eye on him. I had become proficient at reading tails, checking to see if they were being held true to character at work and being wagged at rest. Once under way that morning the team ran strongly with no hint of disorder, except for Rosco who held back slightly. He always required half a mile to warm up and I allowed him this because he was older than the others. When his warm-up was done, all tail gauges registered normal.

These dogs at least *had* tails, unlike many earlier in the century. The Athabascans hitched their dogs so close together that, according to Stuck, the breath of one frosted the tail of the next in front and tails rapidly became weighed down with ice. Indians avoided the problem by docking their huskies' tails. Stuck considered the practice cruel, depriving the dog of protection when sleeping and forcing it to breathe cold air. He disliked the way Indians treated dogs in general: another popular custom was cutting off a husky's canine teeth to reduce injuries when fights arose. Once he had a Great Dane pup which proved useless for mushing and he decided to shoot it. 'Indian after Indian begged for the dog, but I had more regard for him than to turn him over to the tender mercies of an Indian. There are exceptional Indians, but for my part I would rather be a dead dog than an ordinary Indian's dog.'

Aside from the monitoring of tails, my attention was drawn to a landscape which reminded a Scotsman of home. In the early stages of the run the hills supported a weight of forest and drew themselves up reluctantly. Later they became bolder lumps whose riverine sides had been undermined and toppled, leaving steep inclines where only a few hardy trees found a hold. Later still, where the immediate blockade of land parted, a loftier mountain range formed the horizon. What reminded me of Scotland was the texture of the view, the combination of leafless branches and muzzy pine, and the dull tweed of its colours; the treeline was set at the right level, the mass of exposed mountain was correctly proportioned and the snow-crusted ridges were suitably modest in profile. The vista was wholly undramatic in shape, but quite the opposite in appeal. It lacked the forbidding element of the Rockies or Pyrenees and came across, to me, as familiar and homely.

As Lopez wrote: 'The differing landscapes of the earth are hard to know individually. They are as difficult to engage in conversation as wild animals. The complex feelings of affinity and self-assurance one feels with one's native place rarely develop again in another landscape.' And accordingly, with a similar landscape conversation, affinity and self-assurance return.

This was my biased relationship with the right bank, but the left bank remained secretive. It had been this way since Galena, a low timberland which I could only know from the map. Beyond my wall of trees, apparently, was a region which was either a lake with many islands or a swamp with a lot of water; it was hard to tell from the chart's mosaic of greens and blues. Waterways such as Wounded Cub Creek and the Khotol River seeped across the land looking for a way out, and their meanderings formed such a serpent's nest of squiggles that on any other piece of paper they would have been considered a waste of crayons.

Mountains to the right of us, serpents to the left, and underneath a snow machine highway. The hard-packed trail had been ribbed and diced by rubber tracks. Periodically it climbed and fell over sandbars, cut through a crust dented like pumice stone and ran beside stubborn snow fingers which the wind had burnished, back-filled, tapered and left as elevated wedges. At −15°F the air quickly chafed exposed skin, so I kept my gloves on while studying the map and noting the mileposts: Ninemile Island, Halfway Island, Sevenmile Island. For a thirty-five-mile stretch the arrangement of islands could scarcely have been handier.

Kaltag commanded a fine panoramic view, a wide sweep of Scottish mountains and a good long look up the Yukon. The first row of cabins was lined atop and hazardously close to the edge of the river's sixty-foot banks, and the rest of the village was dispersed across a moderate slope behind. The school and a ball park occupied the highest spot at the rear. Houses looked more neatly and proudly maintained here than in other villages, except Ruby, and for prettiness the two were evenly matched, though I felt Kaltag had a practical advantage in that its streets were less likely to break a neck. Kaltag claimed 278 people, two shops, four video outlets, a massive community satellite dish, many stray dogs and a post office almost buried under snow. The prevailing wind had swept clean the streets in its path, but it had left deep piles of snow in the lee of each house. Snow machines had roller-coasted along these hummocks and now the streets in this direction were continuous corrugations with troughs six feet deep.

By the time we rode Kaltag's corrugations we had been travelling for three weeks and had covered 378 miles − including many rest days and the distances of several side-trips. I had begun to feel impatient to reach the Eskimo communities of the Bering Sea and to confront the enemy, the coastal weather, to measure it against my fears. I decided to spend only one night in Kaltag and set off for Unalakleet the next morning, if Alf was up to it.

Several men waved as we undulated towards the post office and I took these to be spontaneous gestures. It was not until I entered the subterranean entrance to buy some stamps that I realised my arrival was expected.

'You must be the Scotsman, are you?'

'... how did you know?'

The postmaster smiled. 'Bush telegraph. Another musher's just come into town. He came down the Koyukuk and heard you were coming down the Yukon. He's heading the same way as you and thought you might like to travel together. A white guy. His name's Dick and he's staying near the school. You'll see the dogs.'

'Thanks. I'll go and look for him.' I bought my stamps, and imagined he didn't sell too many of them. Bush telegraph seemed the more efficient service.

It took some time to find Dick and in the process I was directed from house to house. The first house belonged to Franklin Madros who had been chief of the village since 1953. A chief was elected to his post and then held it for as long as he wished. His responsibilities were similar to those of a mayor. A fit seventy-year-old with distinguished white hair, Franklin Madros was said to be popular among the Madroses and unpopular among the Esmailkas — inter-family power plays were common in village politics. He kindly invited me in for coffee and we sat below an army of sporting trophies and statuettes. The shelf supporting them looked insecure and I feared we would be assailed at any moment. The chief was suffering from jet lag after a trip Outside on village business, and our conversation was brief. He talked of village councils, native councils, regional corporations and 'ANCSA', the Alaska Native Claims Settlement Act — none of which I could understand.

In another house ANCSA cropped up again, only in a more antagonistic atmosphere, and I was railed for my part in it. These were not my first encounters with the subject but I hadn't managed to untangle the intricacies of the situation. If drink was the major issue on the minds of native Alaskans, then ANCSA was not far behind. I excused myself, and eventually found Dick buying dog fish from a house near the river.

He was in his late twenties and looked capable of a fair discus throw. Dark-haired, clean-shaven and with a serious manner, he said he worked for a native corporation in Kotzebue. He enjoyed running dogs and persuaded the corporation to let him travel by dog sled when conducting business in outlying villages. Now he was on vacation. From Kotzebue, up the Kobuk River to Nulato, Dick had covered a distance equivalent to my route, but in less than ten days and over much wilder terrain. His dogs were tired after many sixty-mile-days and he was thinking of flying them home from Unalakleet.

I could only count eight dogs but he said he had left Kotzebue with ten.

'I lost two on the way. One wasn't pulling so I shot it, but the other was an accident. I'm still pretty sick about it. The picket line broke during the night at Shungnak and two dogs I always keep apart got into a fight. By the time I heard the noise, one was so chewed up I had to shoot him – one of the best, at that.'

Ninety miles of trail formed the 'portage' connecting Kaltag with Unalakleet, the Yukon with the coast. Dick was aiming to reach Old Woman cabin the following day, a run of fifty-four miles. This suited my plans, except Dick wanted to leave early to allow a leisurely pace while I had arranged to talk to the school the next morning. We agreed to travel separately and meet at Old Woman in the evening.

'If you work for a native corporation, can you explain to me what ANCSA is all about?' I asked.

He frowned and blew air between his teeth. 'I'll try. How many days can you spare . . .? But let's leave it till tomorrow.'

47

THE PUPILS OF Kaltag's Grade Five showed me their zoo. They had a tarantula and a chameleon – in separate enclosures. The tarantula's poison glands had been removed and it ate flies. Life was hard for a tarantula in Alaska, they explained, because of the seasonal scarcity of flies. Each winter the tarantula struggled through a famine. But things were obviously worse for a chameleon in Alaska. It was dead. I didn't like to ask why they kept the shrivelled remains but assumed that, being a rarity in Kaltag, bits and pieces of a chameleon were better than no chameleon.

'Some you win, some you lose,' said a cheery wee soul, and in the grim contest for Grade Five's flies, the chameleon had lost.

48

A −25° NIGHT warmed to a 0°F day. Alf ate half a meal, but he had sung a whole song beforehand and this indicated that he was game to run. We left at eleven in bright sunshine.

'First hill since Tofty, dogs. Go for it!'

You could shout anything at them and believe they understood it − this was a private belief, a lone musher's consolation − but this time they really acted as if they did. They trotted along a track incised into the slope of a snowfield and climbed a thousand feet as easily as if they were still on the Yukon. It was hard to believe these were the same dogs I experienced so many problems with five months earlier. They were pulling a heavy load for fifty-four miles into mountains and treating it as a jaunt.

'You're all right, you bunch.' I toned down the praise because I didn't want them to become conceited.

The track jinked through copses of pines and round tight curves and over long series of bumps which rattled pots, pans and stove. We stopped to look back for a last view of Alaska's great artery, now only one finger wide and disappearing into forest long before the horizon; then we dropped into the ups and downs of a shallow, open valley on the fringe of the treeline.

Two parallel lines had been forged in the trail ahead. On and on they ran, always faithfully together and always luring us deeper into an unknown of corners, humps and dips, and then out again into the loveliest scenery of the journey. As the day progressed the lowering sun enhanced these lines. The trail dulled, the twin bars glinted silver and we felt like locomotive Sixty-Six without wheels, smoke or cowcatcher.

On several occasions our railroad made a sharp descent followed by a sudden turn. Twice the sled flipped and I was thrown off, and twice a wide sweep resulted in the demolition of saplings, but the only other casualties of the day were lost cheese slices and a crushed

Mars Bar. Nothing could detract from the thrill of that run. We rested for an hour and a half over lunch, and when running averaged nine miles an hour. Again I realised how perfect it was. Enough distance, enough speed, enough time to look and think. There can be no question about it; give or take a unit or two, this is Man the Nomad's designated speed.

Old Woman was formerly a maintenance depot on the old telegraph line. Its working life proved short, however, because the section of line between Nulato and Nome was replaced with new-fangled wireless stations in the 1910s. Old Woman Mountain, tent-shaped, loomed over Old Woman cabin with the menace of a slagheap. The cabin was a modern shelter. When we arrived Dick was stoking Old Woman stove and the place was roasting.

I will not paraphrase my conversation with Dick as we dissected ANCSA beside the fire. It would be tedious repetition on his side and tedious questioning on my part, and besides, much of it had to be sorted out later through research. The Alaska Native Claims Settlement Act has the bulk and complexity for a thousand Arabian Nights, let alone one of Old Woman's.

'Well, have you got it?' Dick asked at around one in the morning.

'I think I've got the basics, but I'm not clear on ...'

He laughed. He said he didn't think anyone fully understood ANCSA, except perhaps some of its chief beneficiaries: white lawyers.

The right to claim ownership of land falls to whoever is there first, living on it and using it before a second interested party arrives. This is the quintessential precept of occupancy and the root of nationality. This is the argument the Britons would have put to the Romans; the Australian Aboriginals to the Europeans; and the Alaska natives to the Russians – had the former in each case been consulted. When there is no longer enough land of suitable quality for all, the forces of 'might is right' come into play. The pattern is always the same. The weaker party – referred to in law as the 'uncivilised' party – is pushed aside until such time as protests call for a compromise. The key questions then become 'how much land, which land and exactly what uses of land' are the first occupiers justified in claiming? It is inevitably a bitter debate, for the issues at stake are the homes and futures of two people – Native and Incomer – whose fundamental definitions and concepts of land are often at variance.

Many persons are inclined to dismiss Native claims of every kind as so many attempts to secure present advantages by the revival of ancient wrongs. Why should anyone today feel guilty because of events that occurred long ago? The question is not one of guilt, past or present. The question is one of continuing injustice. The Europeans came to America, and on grounds that would be unacceptable today, they occupied lands that belonged to the native peoples. The Russians did the same thing in Siberia and Alaska. International law now requires a fair accommodation of indigenous people in their own nations.

Thomas Berger, *Village Journey*

Native land claims in Alaska date back to 1867, to the Treaty of Cession which conveyed Alaska from Russian to American 'ownership'. At the time the Tlingit Indians protested, asserting that America had no right to buy what Russia had no right to sell. Their land belonged to no one but themselves, they stated, but Article III of the Treaty termed them and their kind 'uncivilised Native tribes', without citizens' rights, and they were ignored. In 1935 Congress had a change of heart and allowed natives to sue the federal government for land it had taken. The Tlingits and Haidas filed for $80 million in compensation for 16.8 million acres lost to Tongass National Forest. The case was shunted about for *twenty-four years* before the court found in their favour. They were awarded forty-four cents an acre, after a further nine years' delay. More importantly, though, the US Court of Claims had passed verdict that aboriginal title existed and was not nullified by the Treaty of Cession.

When Alaska was declared a state in 1958 aboriginal title was obliquely acknowledged, but not addressed. Over the next decade conflicting interests in the land brought the issue of native claims to the fore, and in 1966 all major land developments and transactions were frozen until the matter was resolved. The Alaska Federation of Natives was formed to press for a settlement; the state was prepared to come to an agreement because without one it was unable to select the 103 million acres it had been granted under the terms of the Statehood Act; and oil companies, trade unions and employment lobbyists wanted the way cleared for the exploitation of the North Slope and the construction of the trans-Alaska pipeline. The 1971 Alaska Native Claims Settlement Act was the result.

ANCSA, and its subsequent amendments, awarded natives 44 million acres and 962.5 million dollars, the latter being paid in various instalments over eleven years. Congress did not regard tribal governments as efficient or desirable means of implementing the multifaceted Act and made its award conditional on the natives setting up profit-making corporations. The move was designed to create employment in isolated areas, and to steer rural Alaska into mainstream American commerce. Twelve regional corporations were to be the principal overseers and they were to be assisted in local administration by more than 200 village corporations. Once created, both types of corporation were subject to the normal forces that determine profit or loss. ANCSA's land and monies did *not* go to the natives individually but to these corporations, and they had divided responsibilities in arranging conveyances, investments and expenditures.

The natives became shareholders. They had to have twenty-five per cent or more native blood to be eligible. Typically, a villager received 100 shares in both village and regional corporation. Someone living outside a village – called an 'at-large' shareholder – received 100 shares in the regional corporation only. Natives living outside Alaska could become shareholders of their former region, or join the 13th Regional Corporation which was created later and based in Seattle. It received no land allotment but a pro rata share of the money. A few villages, those in reservations, were given the choice of opting out of ANCSA's provisions, receiving full title to their land but no cash, and five chose to do so.

A major problem remained. How were the native corporations to cope with new natives, the rise in population? If they were to continue issuing shares on fixed stock, in no time the shares would be worthless. The number of shareholders had to be limited, and so a cut-off date for eligibility was imposed. Those born before midnight on 18 December 1971, the day Congress passed ANCSA, were eligible; those born thereafter were excluded. A freeze on the disposal and transfer of native stock was imposed for twenty years, to allow the youngest shareholders to reach adulthood before shares became marketable. Approximately 80,000 natives were eligible when the deadline fell. The afterborns, as they became known, now have no legal interest in ANCSA or its allocations; their parents have, their older brothers and sisters may have, but they have not.

The 44 million acres were not massed together in the form of a reservation but spread across the entirety of Alaska as a sprinkling

169

of units around each village. In accepting their 44 million acres the natives extinguished all claims to aboriginal rights of ownership, hunting and fishing over the remainder of Alaska – the 321 million acres, or ninety per cent of the land, ultimately retained by the state and federal governments. The payment of $962.5 million, or $3 an acre, was made to compensate for this loss. ANCSA was not a total severance – it did not give the natives land and money and then divorce them from the state; it was a settlement which reduced their status from *citizens with aboriginal title* to one of citizens only with continuing citizens' rights.

Even the allocation of the land was fraught with problems. Dividing the land on a regional basis was not always fair. For example, an acre of tundra given to NANA, Dick's corporation at Kotzebue, was scarcely comparable in economic terms with an acre of prime forest given to Doyon, the corporation of most Interior Athabascans; the tundra might have oil underneath, or have no commercial value. In order to equate such disparities ANCSA directed that a corporation could keep any revenues accruing from the *surface* exploitation of its land but must share seventy per cent of any *subsurface* revenues among the other twelve corporations. (To confuse matters, timber was classed as subsurface material.) This was sensible in theory but it had unforeseen consequences.

ANCSA was acclaimed as a breakthrough in land-claim settlements. What distinguished it from others was that it let the natives administer the settlement themselves. At the time native negotiators saw the terms of the settlement as far from ideal but the best it seemed likely they could achieve, and much better than the first offer of four million acres and $500 million. It took a decade for ANCSA's flaws to be revealed more fully.

To begin with things looked promising and there was no shortage of enthusiasm or money. Native corporations built offices, set up companies, paid high salaries, flew directors, advisors and lawyers between Barrow and Florida, and invested both inside and outside Alaska. One Eskimo corporation revealed plans to build a resort in Hawaii. All of which was fine if, at the end of the day, the corporations produced a profit. Only two did. For the others, the money has been running out. Doyon, once seen as a model of ANCSA's success, lost $21 million in one year and its assets are now at risk.

ANCSA threw natives into a financial world they were not prepared for. Corporations lacked experienced management and made costly mistakes. Seventy per cent of their shareholders lived subsistence lifestyles. White professionals flocked north to give advice, sometimes bad advice, at a high price. But a key flaw was that ANCSA forced businesses to be set up in areas where they were simply not viable, no matter how skilled the management. So many administrative details were left undefined and open to dispute that constant litigation further squandered time and money. Is gravel, for example, a surface or a subsurface resource? Corporations which own a gravel deposit assert it is 'surface' material and therefore any revenue from it is theirs. The other corporations maintain it is 'subsurface' and seventy per cent of revenues must be shared among them all. The legal contest has cost an estimated $35 million over five years and still has not been resolved.

Village corporations were faced with the monumental task of sorting out the conveyance of the new land. First they had to assess the area and ownership of existing plots in their villages. For the most part cabins had simply been built and occupied, and everyone knew who owned them. No one knew or cared exactly where his patch ended and his neighbour's began. There had never been any need for precise demarcation. Village corporations now had to define each family's plot. Surveyors had to be sent in, disputes arose, litigation ensued – all at the corporation's expense. The real cost of implementing ANCSA was never anticipated, and it has bankrupted many village corporations. Native Alaska has been described as a 'legal landscape littered with the debris of innumerable lawsuits'. The Act has set in motion all possible rivalries between shareholder, afterborn, village and region.

The native people as a whole understood little of ANCSA at the time of its introduction and later felt angered that they had not been consulted directly. Instead, the agreement had been made with the Alaska Federation of Natives and it, many argued, had not represented their views. Of the $962.5 million awarded, the average at-large shareholder received a cash payment of $6,525, and the average village shareholder a mere $375. No further cash payments were made to shareholders after 1976.

Under ANCSA's terms, on 1 January 1992 (or twenty years after the date of receiving title to its stock, if later than the date of ANCSA's inception) each corporation will issue replacement certificates and native shares may then be sold or transferred, in full or in part, to anyone. This is the 1992 fear. That native land, which everyone thought ANCSA had safeguarded for future native generations, will pass out of native control, either through voluntary sales by individual stockholders, or through forced collective sales – for in 1992 the natives will be legally responsible for the debts of their bankrupt corporations. In 1988 ANCSA was amended and the restrictions on the sale of stock extended beyond 1991. Yet natives see this as a postponement and their fears remain.

'Didn't anything good come out of it?' I asked.

'It brought money into the state, but mainly white professionals benefited. Native standards of living have certainly improved since 1971, but more as a result of increased state spending than because of Ancsa.'

'So what do you think should be done?'

'There's no easy answer. I think Congress has to regard Ancsa as an experiment which didn't work, and wipe the slate clean. The one mistake Washington and Juneau always make is in thinking natives must be saved from their subsistence economies. Subsistence in Alaska is not an impoverished state of existence the way it's thought of elsewhere. Ancsa should have been geared to subsistence ways of life rather than to commercial corporations. I'm not for full-blown tribal sovereignty but I think a move has to be made towards some autonomy. Native morale is low. They always see themselves as underdogs. Ancsa gave them a first real go at looking after their affairs, but it dictated the terms and the terms proved loaded.'

'But if natives are given control of hunting, fishing and such subsistence rights, what about whites?'

'That's the crux of it. They'd be pushed out, and they have rights too. You'd also get abuses such as walrus being killed just for their tusks – or more of it, it goes on even now. So Fish and Game would still need to retain control. I said it wasn't easy, but I think towards subsistence is the way to go.' Dick paused and read my expression. 'Well, have you got it?'

The next day we drove our dogs in convoy, downhill to Unalakleet. In Nome, 269 miles further on, the Iditarod had ended and we were anxious to hear the results. I watched Alf closely because he had stopped singing and was refusing all food.

49

SUSAN BUTCHER TOOK the lead on the sea ice between Shaktoolik and Koyuk. At Elim, with 123 miles to go, she reduced her team by one dog to eleven, and left two hours ahead of Martin Buser and six hours ahead of Rick Swenson. When Swenson saw his hopes fading and that Buser had a chance of beating Butcher, he allegedly sent a message ahead offering Buser a fast sled he had arranged to be waiting at a future checkpoint. The offer was not taken up. When Buser was crossing the Kwiktalik Mountains beyond Elim, 'wild, whipping winds churned up a virtual whiteout' and he holed up for twelve hours. Swenson gained on him during this delay and later passed him.

Susan Butcher's lead was never threatened after Elim. She and Granite and the others won their third consecutive Iditarod in a third consecutive record time: 11 days, 11 hours, 41 minutes, 40 seconds. Rick Swenson came in second, fourteen and a half hours behind. He still held title to the 'most ever' wins in the race, but his record was largely forgotten while the media focused on some unpleasant remarks he had made about Butcher several days earlier.

The total purse of $151,500 (down from $250,000 the previous year) was shared between the first twenty mushers in the usual way.

Place	Racer	Hrs/mins behind winner	Winnings
1	Susan Butcher	—	$30,000
2	Rick Swenson	14:29	$21,000
3	Martin Buser	16:40	$16,000
4	Joe Garnie	21:40	$13,200
5	Joe Redington, sen.	39:44	$9,000
6	Herbie Nayokpuk	39:45	$7,200

Bill Cotter, who in Ruby had bemoaned the ten thousand dollars he had put into the race, took fifteenth place and $3,300 in prize money. Horst Mass, the Austrian, finished twenty-third. John Sutter was thirty-eighth across the line, arriving 158 hours behind the winner. Three of his poodles completed the race and made Iditahistory. The Red Lantern was won by Leslie Ann Monk (forty-fifth place, 193 hours b/w) in a time of 19 days, 13 hours, 22 minutes, 55 seconds. Seven entrants did not finish. Two dogs died during the race, near Ruby. An autopsy failed to reveal the cause of the fatalities.

50

APPROACHING UNALAKLEET, WE crested a rise and met an oncoming dog team driven by a native musher. I gee'd Silver and Duran over to the right – like ships, dog teams passed port to port – but the opposing leaders cut across and tangled our teams. Hackles rose and growling immediately broke out. The native let loose a few oaths which ripened the air, while I placed my snowhook and raced to the front. The teams were easily separated and we resumed our journeys, but soon I began noticing periodic spots of blood on the trail. Rosco's left rear leg was bright red.

It was not a serious wound but it bled copiously until a rest allowed the cold to thicken and stem the flow. It was a tear caused by a bite. I made a fuss of him and rubbed his chest, thankful that he had not retaliated. Weather, Sickness, and Injury were the three Furies never far from my thoughts, and fights the swiftest agents of the third. 'How's my hero?' By this time the hero had turned upside-down and was gyrating on the spot, oblivious of any wound. How that dog loved to roll!

And so we entered 'where the east wind blows', a motley crew of the sick, the bloodied, the proud and fretful – and six dogs besides. Unalakleet occupied a jut of land with the sea on one side and a river on the other, though it might have been a hundred miles inland for all the signs there were of water. What gave it away were the figures standing over holes in the ground jigging for tomcod. Fish was prominent in the subsistence lifestyle here, too, but as a basic

174

distinction between the two races, the forest and salmon orbit of the Athabascan had given way to the coast and sea mammal orbit of the Eskimo. Lieutenant L. A. Zagoskin of the Imperial Russian Navy first recorded the name of a settlement here, 'Ounalaklik', in 1850 but archaeologists have dated house pits on a nearby beach at between 200 BC and AD 300.

No log cabins here, for the nearest trees were five miles away and spindly at that; the houses were of the same dimensions but built of plywood and weatherboard, painted in greys, blues, greens and reds. This was still the land of spares and they were heaped around each abode as if they were just about to be needed. Otherwise Unalakleet was deep under snow. Heaps were being pushed around by Cats and entire houses were blocked out as they passed. Three wind-powered generators stood at one end of the village as monuments to disrepair. The east wind struck their triple blades and played aeolian tunes.

Unalakleet was *laissez-faire* and enjoyed bingo. A population of 760 lived here, most working at services, government jobs and subsistence, as they did in every village since Tanana. Unalakleet's children were under curfew at night, 10 p.m. before schooldays and 12 p.m. before weekends and holidays. The village policeman enforced it with a warning, followed by fines increasing in five-dollar increments. I heard about this when I went to play bingo.

Judy Katongan called the numbers with faultless fluency and all the right patter: '... legs eleven, number eleven ... all the twos, twenty-two ...', and dozens of faces scanned their cards. One girl was an expert. Not only did she manage to keep tabs on her own six cards, but she frequently pointed out omissions in her neighbour's half dozen. He sat opposite so she had to read his cards upside-down, which she did plugged in and jiving to a Walkman. Money was flowing. One woman bought fifty-dollars' worth of rip-cards at a single fling, and the evening's takings amounted to $900 from about sixty players. Bingo was played five times a week.

Judy Katongan and her husband Victor, known as 'Duke', were friends of friends, on the bush telegraph principle, and had invited me to stay. Judy was from California, and when not calling the numbers, she cooked at the school. Duke was a true-born Unalak-leetan. Sparsely bearded and moustached, he was small and thin and had an air of indestructibility. He spoke softly, in statements which didn't waste a word. He had a reputation as a formidable dog racer and I could imagine him behind a sled, reserved and confident, a carefully-used grin lagging behind a quick humour. On their living room wall was what looked like an ivory tusk, about twelve inches long. Victor said it was an *usik* (my spelling), the penis bone of a walrus. I waited for the smile but none appeared.

My debt of gratitude to all those who befriended me on the trail was immense because they received not only *me*, but also eight dogs, dirty bowls, frozen gear and all the paraphernalia of mushing. To the Katongans I was particularly grateful, because Victor brought back Alf's appetite. He looked him over and thought he had picked up some infection. Probably through a cut in a paw. If we could get Alf to eat, he believed, we would have won.

'Moose, I think,' Victor said.

Alf would not eat moose.

'Caribou heart.'

Alf did not care for caribou heart. Victor smiled and led me to his outside larder. He baby-sat their two children in winter, but in summer he hunted and fished. He opened the larder and I looked in. Here was a food store to rival the variety of horribles that once simmered in a pot on *Sudviking*; here was a zoological collection beyond the wildest dreams of Kaltag's Grade Five. Over the next day we offered it all to Alf.

Victor took it upon himself to administer the menu. I grew despondent each time he came in and shrugged after a new temptation had failed. He had tried frozen salmon, smoked salmon, herring, tomcod, brown bear, walrus and seal — and now beluga had just failed.

An hour later Victor came back grinning.

I leapt up. 'You've done it? He's eaten? You got him to eat? ... WHAT DID HE EAT??

'Chicken noodle soup.'

51

THE FOOD PACKAGES I had sent from Manley and arranged to collect along the trail were working out successfully. The allowance calculated for trail days had been over-generous but the excess was used on rest days and always saw us comfortably through to our next food-drop. Unlike Stuck I experienced no dire occasions when the dogs were out of food and had to be tided over on 'horse oats boiled with tallow candles' or 'even canned, kippered herring from Scotland'.

In Unalakleet I collected three sacks of supplies for the anticipated five-day haul to Elim. I was looking forward to meeting the 'children of Elim' who had sent me such a delightful letter and offered to catch tomcod for Silver and Company. But Elim lay beyond Koyuk, which was separated from Shaktoolik by the stretch of sea ice I had been warned about since Manley: sixty miles of dead flat in the path of the north wind. We began the first leg, forty-two miles to Shaktoolik, with the second heaviest load of the trip.

Snow machines tootled about, and also the odd pickup, for there was a limited road network around villages even though they were cut off from the main road system. Our trail north crossed several roads cleared down to their gravel surface and the sled runners shrieked at the abrasion. Once past the airstrip and cemetery, whose cheek by jowl siting was common (if not significant) in rural Alaska, we took to the hills. A faint smell of wood smoke came from the few houses not using fuel oil, and then smell-less winter took over again. Thereafter noses were mere snorkels and the favourite snack of frostbite.

A cold breeze froze moisture on my eyelashes and caused them to stick together momentarily after each blink. My beard frosted over, my moustache stuck to it, and the realisation came that this was exactly how woolly mammoths would have perished eleven thousand years earlier. The previous day I had come across an advertisement in one of the many mail-order catalogues which proliferate in Bush Alaska. 'Moustache Antifreeze Spray'. I had laughed at it as being something gimcrack and only for *haute coiffure* trappers. Now my scorn seemed misplaced and the idea eminently sensible. It quite possibly would have prevented my discomfort (and saved a species of elephant).

We were alone on the trail now, as Dick had rested only one day in Unalakleet and then pressed on, deciding that his dogs would make it back to Kotzebue after all. We ran through hills parallel to the coast and traversed ridges overlooking sparse timberland. By now the treeline had dropped to only a few hundred feet above sealevel and although some ribbons of thick growth darkened the view, forests were obviously becoming lean and precious. Once we ran out of snow on a ridge which the wind had stripped to grass but the sled continued to run smoothly. When the views opened up to our left we glimpsed the white expanse of Norton Sound. It looked rough travelling, and any naïve image of a solidified millpond was contradicted by the contortions of jostled ice: upheavals, steps, fissures and lumps as-near-as-dammit resembling rush hour traffic.

After twelve miles we descended to shore-level and came to a group of huts and fish racks, a corrugated iron building and a scattering of rusty machinery. This was Egavik, a summer camp where Duke and others came for hunting and fishing. The bits of machinery were the remains of a processing plant, another brainwave of missionary and educator Sheldon Jackson. His introduction of reindeer was ingenious, and to a large degree successful.

Jackson was anxious to find an alternative occupation for Eskimo communities which were totally dependent on hunting. Reindeer, domesticated caribou, were farmed in other parts of the Arctic and provided food, clothing and transport, and Jackson pressed for their introduction to Alaska. As usual he pushed against the dead weight of an uninterested government and, as usual, he raised the money privately and got on with the job. In 1892 he shipped over 171 reindeer from Siberia, as well as a few Siberians to teach the locals what to do. The Siberians went down less well than the reindeer because of traditional hostility between the two Eskimo groups, and were replaced by Lapps two years later. By 1902 the federal government had seen the wisdom of the plan and paid for another

1,280 animals to be brought over. Russia subsequently banned further exports.

The Eskimos of the Seward Peninsula were not farmers by nature, but their reindeer flourished and by 1914 totalled 60,000. Herds remained relatively small and provided additional subsistence means for many families. The commercial potential of large-scale farming was seen by a white family called Lomen, and after 1914 they began buying up more and more herds. Soon the Lomen Company dominated the industry. Finding a market for the meat was always the problem but the Lomens went to great lengths to promote their product, and even sent reindeer down to the lower states to pull sleds at Christmas. During the peak years 1927–30 they sold 50,000 carcasses. Then came the Depression, hostility from meat producers in the south and finally, in 1937, the compulsory purchase of all white-owned reindeer by the government, who felt Eskimo herders were suffering from the competition. Whatever the rights or wrongs of the Lomen empire, with its disappearance went much of the infrastructure and promotion of the industry. Egalik's processing plant closed in 1948, and by 1951 there were only 6,500 animals left. A minor revival has increased the numbers and the Seward Peninsula now holds about 16,000 reindeer in a dozen herds, all under Eskimo management.

After Egavik we climbed more mountains and then negotiated a sharp descent to what I imagined was a beach. Cluttered with slabs of ice, it made a gentle curve into the distance and formed the southern edge of a low peninsula. If the sea were to rise sixty feet, the peninsula would disappear and Cape Denbigh would become an island at the far end. In summer the area was mostly marshland, and in winter, great windows of glare ice. Their colours varied from wine bottle green, through jade to Caribbean blue, but I would have gladly exchanged the prettiness for a practical sledding surface. These windows came frequently and extended for up to a hundred yards; the dogs scrabbled pathetically for a grip and were further hindered by the sled which drifted ineluctably sideways in the wind. It was light by Shaktoolik standards and therefore a good breeze by normal measures. It met no resistance on this peninsula except an occasional musher. Fourteen miles later we reached Shaktoolik.

Few visitors find anything kind to say about Shaktoolik because it is a resort for storms. It is one of those places you find hard to

179

believe exist but, once convinced, you thank God they do. It just suddenly appears when you think you must be miles off course, small and rectilinear and black in a barren view of white. Old Shaktoolik is the first black line, but it was abandoned in 1967 as it was too prone to the ravages of the sea. New Shaktoolik lies two miles further on and runs along the rise of the beach, though with no apparent advantage over the sea. It has a single street with standard frame houses on either side and when we arrived, snow filled it to the rooftops. A passage had been cut along the centre, just wide enough to allow two snow machines to pass. Each house had a passage cut to its door, or else made use of channels blasted by the wind.

Duke had given me the name of an elderly friend, Franklin Paniptchuk. He invited me to stay in a manner which conveyed no enthusiasm. I indicated the empty, doorless shed he owned behind his house and stressed I would happily sleep there. His face remained expressionless and he said, quietly, 'That is not Eskimo culture'. He watched as I prepared the dogs' food and settled them in for the night. No spruce boughs for miles, and a chilling breeze for thin-coated dogs. I found some waste cardboard nearby and used this to line the hollows I dug for them. I built small banks of snow for additional shelter. Franklin continued to watch. His face gave nothing away but I guessed from his eyes that what I was doing was also not Eskimo culture. He saw through me at once, that I mollycoddled my dogs and wouldn't have had the heart to kill a whale.

Franklin's house was kept hot, though this was not immediately apparent to a visitor who entered the hall and stepped through a pile of snow six feet long. Each time it was cleared the wind pushed in a new one, and the occupants now accepted it as an inconvenience between the living room door and the chest freezer. Unlike the houses in the Interior, many on the coast appeared to have running water and full plumbing systems. A combined kitchen-living room, well-furnished and decorated with religious images, took up half the interior. It was a modestly-sized home, and this said all the more for Franklin's hospitality. His wife was visiting friends and his eight children, or grandchildren, were playing basketball. The standard shelf of trophies about to avalanche in a corner testified to the athletic prowess of the average native family, or the generosity of their sports organisers.

Franklin was small and broad, with a sulk which I was frightened my arrival had caused. Sometimes he exercised a tinder dry sense of humour which made his jowls shake, but laughter seemed an effort. He was a fisherman and a hunter – the bountiful waters off Shaktoolik were the reason the settlement existed. It was a short fishing season, he said. They could start around 10 June but there was still much ice about then. By mid-July only an odd lump was encountered and by mid-October freeze-up began. He didn't talk much. The old hunter watched while I prepared my supper, self-consciously resuscitating a packet of soup.

I didn't get to know Franklin well, but his bearing impressed me. I liked his pride. He seemed to have things worked out, a balance between the old and new, between hunting seals and cooking them in a microwave. Only his radio bothered me. It was tuned to a religious station and played in the background. A male voice was preaching, sometimes shouting, on a repetitive theme. It was an angry attack. '... *How can you expect to get to the Kingdom of the Lord unless you nail your mortal flesh to the cross?* CRUCIFY IT. *When you crucify it, it's dead. Only when your mortal flesh is dead can your spirit conquer ...*'

Franklin talked Iditarod. I asked what he thought of the race.

'They make it easy on themselves. And I feel sometimes it's a rich white man's race. Too much money for us. But I like it. I like Libby and Joe and Susan and Herbie. I got good friends there. They all stay with me.'

We talked dogs, weather and my journey. Then he said: 'You hear about Cape Denbigh? They found old Eskimo village there. Iyatayet, it's called. Twelve mile from here. Eight thousand years old, they say. You hear about land bridge? All this was once land bridge. You could walk to Siberia, they say.'

'... DO IT. NAIL IT. *You wanna get to the Kingdom of the Lord* THEN NAIL YOUR MORTAL FLESH TO THE CROSS OF CALVARY ...'

My mind was trying to follow two lines of thought. I couldn't concentrate on what Franklin was saying with this tirade in the background. I wondered what sort of man the preacher was. As he sat before a microphone screaming inane verbiage across the frozen land, did he imagine families gathered before their radios in little villages such as Shaktoolik? And when his frenzy was finished did his wife ask 'Had a hard day at work, dear?' when he arrived home? And how did he climb down from that pitch of emotion? Boil an egg and watch *Miami Vice*? Or did he pore over his Bible, his eyes burning into the night, searching for another nifty little line with which to scourge the tundra?

52

'WHAT DID YOU see on your way from Unalakleet?' Franklin asked.
  I had to think hard. 'Nothing,' I replied. 'Just ravens.'
  'Yea,' he laughed. 'Ravens, that's all you ever see.'
  'Did there used to be more wildlife to be seen?'
  'No, ravens, that's all we ever saw.'
  'What'll I see on the way to Koyuk?'
  He laughed again. 'Nothing. Not even ravens.'

53

HE SPOKE YUPIK, wore Eskimo clothes, chewed his boots the way the Malemut and Kaviagmut did, and lived with them for four years. They called him 'The Man Who Buys Good-For-Nothing Things'. Once he sat for hours in a leaking canoe and became so paralysed with cold he had to be hauled ashore, stripped of his clothes and warmed before a fire. While thawing he caught sight of a *Freisga semipaluata* and immediately set off stalking it, forgetting his condition. His native companions watched in awe as this naked white man pranced across the muskeg in pursuit of a small bird. He caught butterflies with his hat and took the first photographs of Alaskan Eskimos. He sketched, recorded exhaustively and was fascinated by everything around him. But above all he bought old implements, clothes, amulets, masks — anything that might be of interest to the

182

Smithsonian Institution. At twenty-seven he contracted tuberculosis, which plagued him for the rest of his life. His monograph, *The Eskimo About Bering Sea*, remains a classic.

Between the years 1877 and 1881 Edward W. Nelson assembled the world's finest and largest collection of Eskimo ethnographica, even though at the time he was ostensibly employed by the Army Signal Corps to make weather observations. He amassed 10,000 artefacts, 2,000 bird skins, 1,500 eggs, 370 mammal pelts and skulls, besides fish, flowers and insects. He also collected legends.

It was the time when there were no people on the earth. For four days the first man lay coiled up in the pod of a beach pea. On the fifth, he burst forth, falling to the ground, and stood up, a full grown man. Feeling unpleasant, he stooped and drank from a pool of water, then felt better. Looking up, he saw a dark object approaching with a waving motion until it stopped just in front of him. It was a raven. Raven stared intently at Man, raised one wing and pushed up its beak, like a mask, to the top of its head, and changed immediately into a man. Still staring and cocking its head from side to side for a better view, Raven said at last: 'What are you? Whence did you come? I have never seen the likes of you.' And Raven looked at Man, surprised to see that this stranger was so much like himself in shape.

Then Raven told Man to walk a few steps, again marvelling: 'Whence did you come?' To this the Man replied: 'I came from the pea-pod,' pointing to the plant nearby. 'Ah,' exclaimed Raven. 'I made that vine, but did not know anything would come from it.' Then Raven asked Man if he had eaten anything, to which Man replied he had taken soft stuff into him at a pool. 'Well,' said Raven, 'you drank some water. Now wait for me here.'

He drew down the mask over his face, changing again into a bird, and flew far up into the sky, where he disappeared. Again Man waited four days, when the Raven returned, bringing four berries in his claws. Pushing up his mask, Raven became a man again and held out two salmonberries and two heathberries, saying 'Here is what I have made for you. Eat them.' Then Raven led Man to a creek where he took clay and formed two mountain sheep, which Man thought were very pretty. Telling Man to close his eyes, Raven drew down his mask and waved his wings four times over the images, which became endowed with life and bounded away. When Man saw the sheep moving away, full of life, he cried out in pleasure. Next Raven formed two other animals of clay, but because they were not fully dry when they were given life, they remained brown and white. Thus originated the tame reindeer. Raven told Man they would be very scarce. In the same way a pair of wild reindeer, or caribou, were made, being permitted to dry and turn white only on their bellies before being given life. These, Raven said, would be more common, and people could kill many of them.

'You will be very lonely by yourself,' said Raven. 'I will make you a companion.' Going to a more distant spot and looking now and again at Man, he made an image very much like him, fastening a lot of fine water grass on the back of its head. After the clay dried, he waved his wings over it as before, and a beautiful young woman arose and stood beside Man. 'There,' cried Raven, 'is a companion for you.'

In this way, Raven continued for several days making birds, fishes, and animals, showing them to Man and explaining their uses. After a while Woman gave birth to a child, and Raven showed Man how to feed and care for it. As soon as it was born, Raven and Man took it to a creek, rubbed it all over with clay, and then returned. Next morning the child was running about, pulling up grass and plants Raven had made, and on the third day it became a full-grown man.

After this, Raven thought that if he did not create something to make men afraid they would destroy everything he had made to inhabit the earth. So he went to the creek, where he formed a bear and gave it life, jumping to one side quickly as the bear stood up and looked about fiercely. He then told Man to avoid the bear or he would be torn to pieces. Raven then made different kinds of seals and explained their names and habits. He taught Man to make rawhide lines from sealskin, and snares for deer, but cautioned him to wait until the deer were abundant before snaring any of them.

Soon a girl was born to the Woman who was told she should marry her brother in order that the earth would be peopled more rapidly ...

Fitzhugh and Kaplan, *Inua* (Adapted from *Raven Myth*, Nelson 1899)

54

THROUGH THE BERING Sea Eskimos I could trace the origins of man, the animals he hunted and his companion-to-be, dog, back to ingenious Raven. Another no less fanciful or plausible explanation is the one held by contemporary anthropologists: that inchoate man and woman, scaley-bellied and reptilian, crawled out of an African swamp to start a new life in the trees. Sparsely littered with evidence as this theory is, it nevertheless yields results more consistent than any other, and I chose to follow it. I felt a need to glance back in time to see the relationship between primitive man and *Tomarctus*, the progenitor of dogs, their migration east along the trails of woolly mammoth, steppe bison, wild horse and caribou, and their arrival in Alaska.

Shaktoolik stood at the centre of the story. For it was here – or, more specifically, in Beringia, the massive causeway once uniting Siberia and Alaska but now submerged and forming the bed of the Bering and Chukchi Seas – that everything came together. In Beringia the whole zoological cavalcade out of Africa laid eyes on the tip of an unknown continent. It was uninhabited except at one point, the intersection of two myths, where a dark stranger appeared, and said, 'What are you? Whence did you come? I have never seen the likes of you . . .'

Ten million years ago, when mastodons and sabre-tooth tigers were at large below, man and dogs shared the same tree. We were Miocene Ape, I'm told, and they were *Miacis*, a climbing carnivore. We shared our tree reluctantly. By one million years ago we had come down to earth, our brain size had increased dramatically and we began walking upright; the transition from ape to hominid to *homo erectus*. Still defenceless when cornered, we listened in dread for the man-eaters' approach. *Miacis* had descended with us and developed into the ground-based predator *Cynodictis*, who had subsequently diverged into the dog-like *Cynodesmus* and the progenitors of bears, seals, cats and racoons. *Cynodesmus* sloughed off hyenas and what was left became *Tomarctus*, some genetic agglomeration of jackal, wolf, fox and dog waiting to subdivide. Rooted somewhere in this menagerie – in *Cynodesmus*, would be my guess – was the reason why Alf's howl sent a shiver down my vertebrae.

By two hundred thousand years ago we, *homo sapiens*, were wiser and armed with our phenomenal new skill, the ability to produce fire. We had already wandered as far as the edge of modern-day China. By then mastodons had evolved into mammoths. They grew woollier as the Ice Ages ran their course and were able to survive in regions too hostile for our new baby, Neanderthal Man. Our way east was blocked by an expanse of steppe-taiga, a plain whose dryness resulted in limited glaciation but whose bleak surface gave us no cover for the hunt and no protection against the severity of the fourth and last Ice Age. Quite why we wanted to penetrate the taiga remains a mystery to scientists, but not to me. In effect, we were already carrying our flag towards Everest. Yet before we could venture towards Beringia, we had to wait until forty thousand years ago when we suddenly and inexplicably metamorphosed into fully-modern man, *homo sapiens sapiens*, the dangerously clever creature we have remained ever since. Never far away were wolf and dog, as yet one and the same or an inseparable duo.

Beringia is believed to have been exposed twice. Each occasion was the result of a great freeze which turned so much water into ice that the surface of the sea dropped between 280 and 330 feet below today's level, leaving Beringia as a dry plain. The popular reference to it as the 'Bering Sea Land Bridge' is misleading, for it was no narrow walkway but a land mass 900 miles wide with a greater area than Alaska as defined now. A cold, wind-ravaged place, it nevertheless contained a supportive habitat with alder, dwarf birch (isolated evidence suggests even cottonwood and aspens) and enough plant life to support musk oxen, woolly mammoths and awesome steppe bison with coats almost three feet deep. Beringia was exposed – that is, the bridge was 'open' – between about seventy-five and forty-five thousand years ago, and for a second time between twenty-five and fourteen thousand years ago. The sea then rose, covering the archaeological secrets of many lost millennia, and reached its present level about eight thousand years ago.

We now enter the area of more serious contention and will limit ourselves to a few contemporary facts. Before Beringia first appeared, the Americas were inhabited by a wide assortment of creatures, but the complete absence of biological and fossil evidence indicates that man was not among them. There is as yet no proof to suggest that he came with the first 'bridge' traffic of animals. Sea-going voyages are a comparatively modern development and the possibility of his arrival having been by boat is regarded as unlikely. The oldest archaeological site in the Americas is found at Old Crow (close to the Alaska–Canada border at its northern end) and is dated to probably twelve thousand (but maybe fifteen thousand) years ago. Siberia, even less known to archaeologists than Alaska, has produced no verification of a site dateable earlier than eighteen thousand years ago. But one of its sites holds a record unique in the north. At Ushki Lake on the Kamchatka Peninsula a settlement was uncovered, and in the layer corresponding to its use eleven thousand years ago archaeologists found the first evidence of a domesticated dog. Its body had been carefully buried.

We can only surmise that wolves and man had been frequent neighbours; that some wolves – perhaps the smaller, more trusting and less aggressive ones – came closer and began living around man's camps to glean pickings from his kills; that man began to toss them scraps and even found advantage in having them around as watch-wolves; that in time they became pets and, through culling and selective breeding, eventually became *Canis familiaris*: good old short-toothed, bent-tailed, totally dependent dog.

By eleven thousand years ago man, and presumably his dog, was unquestionably established on Alaska's Seward Peninsula. The first Americans, Paleo-Indians, either split into two groups or came at different times in two separate migrations. However the divide came about, the result was that linguistically and culturally the tribes diverged into two distinct entities. One group developed a forest-hunting culture and spread to the rest of the Americas, while the other created a culture based on the pursuit of sea mammals and spread over the Arctic to Greenland. In twentieth-century Alaska the scions of the first group are, principally, the Athabascan Indians of the Interior (though it is believed they came *back* to live in Alaska after a migration south); the scions of the second, the Aleuts and Eskimos of the western and northern coasts.

Paleo-Indian was inseparable from Paleo-dog. It took a long time, however, for man to realise that this, his first success at domestication, could help transport his kills and clutter. For centuries he pulled his own sled – and as often made women pull it – before contriving the means for his dogs to take over. This change may have happened first in northern Eurasia, but no earlier than AD 500 in Alaska. The hard evidence panders little to our ingenuity, for the oldest proof of dog-traction in this region goes back only three centuries. Dogs may have been used as pack animals earlier than this, and they hauled the travois of plains Indians before the advent of the horse, but all we can say with certainty is that driving dog-pulled sleds was common practice by the time Vitus Bering arrived.

By then, 1741, the native peoples had proliferated throughout the Americas, and more than twenty distinct breeds of *Canis familiaris* had evolved. Today only two of those aboriginal breeds remain. The little Tahltan bear dogs had their fate sealed just over a decade ago when the owner of the last female had the dog spayed in the belief that there 'surely' had to be others? There were none, just a few males. Only the Chihuahua and the Eskimo sled dog have survived since the first white man made his landfall.

When I tucked my dogs into bed that night in Shaktoolik, it seemed the very least I could do to improve our record.

55

'WILL IT BE easy to follow the trail to Koyuk?' I asked. This was the big day. The long ice crossing. It was here that Libby Riddles set out in a storm and made her break in the 1985 Iditarod.

'Trees don't grow on the ocean, right? Well, follow the trees.'

Franklin's answer didn't make much sense to me but I nodded cheerfully. A stiff breeze rummaged through my sled looking for loose bags as I packed. I had doubts about setting off into it but my decision was made by Franklin's stolid pronouncement: 'Good weather'. I wasn't convinced. It was Franklin who had advised Libby that the storm wasn't too bad. I decided to go as far as the north shore of the peninsula where there was an isolated shelter hut and make a decision there. Franklin returned my parting wave.

The trail was marked with wooden tripods for the twelve miles across this flat neck of land. It was here that Leonhard Seppala met the seventeenth serum runner, Harry Ivanoff, and took custody of the precious cargo, immediately turning about and heading back towards Nome. To our left, ten miles away, the Reindeer Hills formed the extremity of the headland and at one end were the archaeological sites Franklin had mentioned. Certain flint tools, burins, found at these sites were the first of their kind in the American Arctic to evidence an advance in technology – the Denbigh Flint Culture.

By the time Shaktoolik was a few miles behind us the breeze had halved. I looked back to the thin line of roofs which seemed to attract the wind, and shook my head in disbelief again. The village occupied a void. Even its herd of 300 reindeer had deserted. Franklin said the herdsman had shot fifteen wolves this winter. As wolf pelts were currently fetching $400 each, Eskimo farmers were better off using their herds as bait. No reindeer were in sight. 'Nothing, not even ravens,' he had said, but there *were* ravens. A pair came from behind and caught us unawares with their liquid, gurgling calls. All the dogs turned round. The ravens tumbled and glided low over us, deliberately following the line of dogs. No wonder they, *tu-lu'-kau-gûk*, were at the centre of native mythology, with their curiously intelligent eyes, their precocious behaviour, their blackness when all around was white.

They seemed to delight in teasing the dogs, and a game ensued. It lasted off and on for over twenty miles. The ravens would flop down on the trail 300 yards ahead of us and peck at Iditarod leftovers. The dogs would throw themselves into the chase and the ravens would let them approach to within fifty yards and then leisurely hop, hop, hop and take to the air. I was reminded of a passage in John McPhee's *Coming into the Country* (1978).

> He and the others would now and again see a lone raven, flying over the flat tundra. It would fly on and on, close to the ground. Below the raven, almost always, was a running fox. Mile upon mile, the fox stayed under the raven. If the raven sped up a bit and settled to the ground, the fox then stalked the raven. When the fox sprang for the capture, the raven − at the last moment − would jump into the air, and fly on across the tundra, with the fox running below. The relationship was apparently static, a ritual equilibrium, a possible pantomime. One day, such a pair came flying and running ... The raven set down. The fox went into its assassin creep − one carefully crafted step after another − and then made a sudden dash. The raven jumped into the air. After a short flight, it came down, and was again stalked and rushed by the fox. Again it made a short flight, and settled down ... The fox renewed its subtle glide, this historically futile contest with the raven's eye. Once more came the move, the rush, the leap. The fox caught the raven, ate it on the spot, and left a pile of black feathers on the ground.

'What d'you think, you guys?' They were panting after another chase and I wished the ravens would go away. We didn't need any lures or any lessons in perseverance today. I was asking the dogs what they thought of the conditions. The wind was light and bitter but Norton Bay weather didn't come any better than this. After weeks of dreading this stretch, it was going to be a cruise. We passed the shelter cabin on Island Point and struck out into the bay. Somewhere to our right was a place on the shore where mastodon tusks could be found after summer storms. Franklin's cousin had come across a tusk ten feet and two inches in length and he had sold it at the then rate of fifty dollars a pound. ('We can sell old ivory. Only new ivory has laws and we must work on it, carving or scrimshaw.')

Ahead of us was Bald Head, a lump named by Captain Cook while surveying the region in 1778. In former times when winters were colder and the sea ice thicker, dog drivers saved many miles by travelling straight to it. Our trail kept closer to the shore. 'Trees don't grow on the ocean, right? ...' For forty-seven miles the surface of the sea was marked every hundred yards by a line of pine saplings which had been stripped of all but the feathery branches at the top and deployed by Iditarod trail-markers. In a blizzard they would be lost but on a sunny day such as ours they stood out for miles. Each summer they would float away and each year they would be replaced.

The dogs padded across a tabletop of ice, the opposite of the wild surface we had seen the previous day. The sun hit them obliquely and their shadow sides remained frosted for hours. Ice beards formed on their faces, and the front runners required belly covers against the constant chill. However, boredom was their main complaint. The hills to our right were low whalebacks and almost invisible at dog-level, the ones in front never seemed to get any larger, and there was little else on which they could focus their attention. The ravens came and went. Otherwise there was only me. Every so often a dog would turn to see what I was doing. As I was staring at them, we stared at each other, exchanging long glances. Then I began singing to them, as I had read of antarctic mushers doing this to lift their dogs' spirits on long monotonous hauls. My song didn't last long. It was obvious my dogs preferred monotony and low spirits. So I swapped my feet on the runners and turned round to face the way we had come, crouched down in the wind shadow of the sled bag, tied myself to the handlebars and dozed for a mile or two while catching some sun. One of the beauties of mushing is that its autopilot is the most sophisticated system in the world. It was not uncommon for Eskimos to climb into their sled furs and go to sleep on trails their dogs knew well, waking up when the motion stopped to find themselves at home.

We reached Koyuk early in the evening. Its blue fuel-storage tanks had been visible for some time, and gradually its houses had grown out of a wooded patch of hillside. I had been given a name to contact here, but decided not to risk imposing myself on another stranger. I would sleep rough ('siwash' in gold-rush terminology) beside my sled. While preparing to do this beside a fish rack with six intact seals lying frozen at its base, I was approached by a youth on a snow machine. His father had sent him to see if I wanted a place to sleep. Scarcely five minutes had passed since my arrival.

In keeping with all settlements of Eskimo founding, Koyuk was sited for its proximity to good fishing and hunting. Then gold and coal were found to the north and at the turn of the century it became a supply point for miners, and a depot for the extracted coal awaiting shipment to Nome. Tests for oil had proved positive in Norton Bay, I was told, but development had been abandoned in deference to hunting and fishing interests which still provided the mainstay of the village economy. Koyuk was alcoholically 'dry', a factor which appeared to have a bearing on its firefighters. They were sent as far afield as Idaho and California and had an excellent reputation, unlike their counterparts in Unalakleet and Shaktoolik who were notorious for quenching their thirsts before their fires.

Ken Tewey liked dogs. He said anyone who ran dogs was welcome at his home. He had twelve himself and they cost eighty dollars a week to feed. Commercial dog food sold for twice its Fairbanks price here, as did most commodities. A small lighter could freight in supplies from Nome in summer, but it was expensive. The cheapest snow machine cost $4,250 delivered to Koyuk. A replacement track cost $700. Petrol sold for $2.15 per gallon. Ken believed people soon wouldn't be able to afford snow machines any more and would *have* to go back to dogs. He said this with relish because he was trying to preserve some of 'the old way'. 'Kids have it soft now. My kids won't haul water without a snow machine or three-wheeler. They don't walk any more,' he complained. Only he and his cousin kept dogs — other than odd pets — in a village of 200 people.

Ken was about fifty-five but his round wind-furrowed face looked older. He wore large, dark-tinted glasses and walked with a cumbersome gait. He was of average height and with a bulk which disguised the brawn of a carpenter's, hunter's and fisherman's life. Divorced fifteen years earlier he had since raised his five children on his own. His house was kept spotless and seemed twice as large as the one of my previous host. Franklin, it transpired, was his cousin and Franklin's wife was his aunt.

'I got a twenny-eight-foot boat but a permit only three days a week. Fish 'n' Game don't like natives. They tell us we can't hunt, but we just ignore them. We always lived here. We never killed off what we hunt, an' they come an' tell us how much to take. We don't go tell them how to live.' He talked fast and with little intonation. Words were clipped, sentences seemed to run uphill and hit a wall. Native speech forced me to listen hard at first, and so it took time to appreciate its finer qualities, a meaty directness and stark sincerity.

We sat talking in a kitchen expansive enough to take a beluga broadside. Ken smoked incessantly and seemed to want to talk. I asked why it was I saw so few teenagers about the villages.

'Huh!' he exclaimed. 'Why don't anybody see them? They've turned into night people – sleep all day, party all night. Kids don't have no respect now, not for elders, not for parents, not for strangers.' He pointed at his small granddaughter who was playfully hitting my leg. 'In my day we have to wait at the door until they call us in to meet a stranger. Eskimo culture is going out.'

In his day, he recalled, the Covenanter Church was full on Sundays. No one worked on the Sabbath. He remembered women making raincoats from the intestines of bowhead whales, and men stretching walrus stomachs over wooden frames for ceremonial drums. His mother had been widowed young and had raised her five children on her own. They had worn Salvation Army clothes, but once he had been given a new pair of overalls. They were such a treasure he had only worn them on Sundays, until a relative had told him he would soon grow out of them – after that he had worn them every day. Drums, Sabbaths, whale-gut raincoats and Salvation Army overalls – he sketched a vivid picture of the pattern of change. In general, a change for the worse, he believed, and the Settlement Act had accelerated the deterioration of family and village bonds with its sudden influx of money and squabbles.

Ken went to the fridge and brought out a bowl of 'Eskimo ice cream', *akutug*. He made it from seal oil, caribou or reindeer fat, sugar and water, all fluffed up into a sorbet and served in a sea of berries. Seal oil is an acquired taste and I hadn't fully acquired it by then, but I was working hard at it. *Akutug* was said to provide blizzard-proof warmth.

'In summer it gets real hot here. Ninety-two degrees sometimes. Too hot, we get headaches. We like −30° better. We need lots of ice cream at −30°.' He smoked and talked late into the night. Finally he asked:

'Would you like an Eskimo name? When you have an Eskimo name, you become one of us.'

I felt deeply honoured. 'I'd love one.'

He wrote down my new name. Arpiq. 'It means "salmonberry". I give it to you because your face is the same colour.'

'What colour are salmonberries?'

He pointed to some of the berries in the remaining *akutug*. They were bright orange.

The next morning my sunburn was still glowing as I set off for Elim. I had only gone fifty yards when I heard my new name.

'ARPIQ!' Ken yelled. I plunged down the brake and stopped. 'There's many Eskimo girls between here and Nome. Maybe you'll be lucky. It's leap year. In leap years Eskimo girls go out and get the men. ...'

56

If the mind releases its fiduciary grip on time, does not dole it out in a fretful way like a valued commodity but regards it as undifferentiated, like the flatness of the landscape, it is possible to transcend distance – to travel very far without anxiety, to not be defeated by the great reach of the land. If one is dressed well and carrying a little food, and has the means to secure more food and to construct a shelter, the mind is that much more free to work with the senses in an appreciation of the country.

Barry Lopez, *Arctic Dreams*

57

ARPIQ KNEW THIS journey was ruining him. He doubted whether he could enjoy travelling – the actual going – ever again if it had to be by means other than dogs. They heard things he could never hear and sensed things far beyond his atrophied powers of perception.

For these reasons they became an extension of his awareness and led him to probe a relationship with his surroundings on a level he could not rationalise. They touched something primitive and biologically distant in him. Call it instinct if you will, it remained dim and undefined. They linked him to the subconscious land.

Arpiq was at last releasing his grip on time, shedding anxiety and letting his senses have free rein. He would have felt less at ease had he known that bad weather was brewing up ahead, but that was still four days away, beyond White Mountain.

Between Koyuk and Elim, sastrugi, long wind-blown furrows of snow with a Russian name, caused the sled to buck and dive and for a while I felt seasick. I passed an old reindeer-herding corral at Kwik and looked for the possible location of a cabin, with fish bladder window panes, which Ed Jesson had visited when cycling by in 1900. There were several old cabins visible on the coastline which might have been the one, but the deserted shacks on a spit of land, Moses Point, were the modern constructions of a fish camp.

At the junction of the spit with the mainland were three identical houses, two storeys high and of a style so alien to north Alaska they might have been a Hollywood set. The Eskimos had to observe blackout regulations in this region during the Second World War and the information they were given left them in fear of a Japanese, and even a German, invasion. Moses Point had served as an Air Force camp then, and more recently as a Federal Aviation Authority weather station and navigational beacon. Now it was an empty Hollywood set with snow ramps up to the first-floor windows. Nine miles further on, past a handsome series of crags and cliffs topped with pines, we came to an obsolete sign pointing to the right: 'Elim welcomes the Iditarod.'

Two buttresses of rock marked the ends of a slightly bent beach and an opening in both hills and forest. A loose assembly of frame houses and log cabins covered the opening and ran uphill until trees took over. It was exactly the sort of place one would hope to find at the source of a welcoming letter. I drove up to the largest building in sight. Word of my arrival went about in no time.

'Ah, it's a boy after all,' said Tracy Deane, the teacher of grades three, four and five at Aniguiin School. She was sprightly and extremely pretty, with dark wavy hair. She addressed her first remark to a pupil, Marvin Takak, and then turned to me. 'Glad to see you

194

made it. We've had a long debate as to whether Alastair was a boy's or a girl's name.'

I had to laugh. 'Well, I'm glad I didn't arrive in my kilt.'

The children were allowed out of school to look at my dogs, who sat up nervously as nineteen pairs of hands appeared and fussed over them. Within minutes they had divided them out among themselves and given them 'favourite ratings'. Silver and Nanook drew the most points. When I was led into the school I discovered that ratings were the current vogue. Wallcharts showed favourite ratings, and nine was the maximum score. Bugs Bunny was a runaway nine in cartoons, and Cherries (6) won convincingly over the only other fruit rival, Bananas (3).

Animals: Seal, 9; Dog, 9; Ape, 6; Mouse, 4; Frog, 1. Food: Pizza, 9; Tacos, 2; Hamburger, Turkey, Spaghetti and French Fries, all 1. Guns: Pistol, 5; Pellet Gun, 4; 30 06, 3; .22, 2; Shotgun, 1; Gatling, 0.

'They really know their guns, don't they?' I commented.

'Yes, they're into hunting and fishing. Incidentally, I'm afraid we didn't manage to get any tomcod. We went out once, but nothing was doing. We had hoped to go again but now we're into cat tests.'

'Thanks for trying but I sent meat here just in case. What on earth are cat tests?'

'California Assessment Tests. They're designed to help teachers spot problem learners and judge the level a child is at. They're considered quite important, and kids get very worked up about them. They have to do them tomorrow, so we're having an easy day today. How about telling the kids about Scotland now? Every day they've been asking when you were going to arrive.'

The Loch Ness Monsters met their match, or distant cousins, in Elim. A strange sea creature was sometimes seen near here. One of the closest sightings had taken place thirty years earlier when the late husband of one of the teachers at Aniguiin School was out hunting with a friend. It was she who told me the story. The men were in a boat off Bald Head during break-up, which was seemingly the most common time of year for sightings. She had no doubt about the factuality of her husband's account and described a bulky creature with a long neck, two or three humps and armour-plating similar to that of a rhinoceros. At the time it was trying to climb onto the ice shelf but it kept breaking though and falling back into the water. The two men advanced to within rifle range and fired a shot, but this produced no reaction. Eventually the creature gave up and swam away. Alaska had other strange animals, the children added, living in the state's largest body of fresh water, Lake Iliamna.

Aniguiin School took its name from the Eskimo assistant of a Swedish missionary. The missionary, of the strict Covenanter Church (an offshoot of the Lutherans), founded Elim in 1914 on what was then a federal reindeer reserve. For some unknown reason, Elim was a pocket of Yupik-speakers in an Inupiaq region.

'You can tell a white man founded this community,' Tracy said later, when we sat over supper with her husband and another teacher, 'because it's in a beautiful situation. Eskimos would have gone for a more practical one, like Shaktoolik's, closer to good hunting.' The hunting was a sore point among the village whites. One teacher was a keen amateur taxidermist. He only took enough game for his hobby, ate the contents and stuffed the remains. This didn't seem in any way extravagant in a population of 250, but the native council had recently voted to restrict the six whites to fishing activities only. The move was symptomatic of a growing trend in Alaska, demonstrations of strength to highlight the 'ours' and 'theirs' positions defined by ANCSA. ('Around Lake Iliamna whites are charged $25 per night for camping rough in native-owned wilderness.')

We were eating roast caribou (I didn't ask where it had come from) and grey crunchy cubes which I did ask about – pickled beluga skin. Tracy's husband was a hobby pilot who had spotted the first pod of beluga from the air and alerted the village hunters. Pickled beluga skin, *muktuk*, is extremely palatable. If you close your eyes while tucking in, it is indistinguishable from twenty feet of raw cabbage.

'D'you know where I'd go if I were you?' Tracy suddenly said, and her remarks extended my journey. 'Little Diomede. I've always wanted to go there. Last week we had a visit from the Eye Doctor – that's what he's always called – who flies about the villages. He'd just been to Diomede and said it was wonderful. And you mustn't leave here without visiting our hot springs. They're only eight miles away.' She sighed. 'And all I've got to look forward to are CAT tests ...'

California Assessment Tests were standard throughout the USA, she explained, and were a prime example of government departments failing to appreciate the diversity of cultures within the country. Many children in rural Alaska had never seen a bus or a pedestrian crossing. Schools tried to run holiday trips Outside to let these children see city life and experience things like rides in buses and elevators, but costs were restrictive. Television helped by showing how others lived but usually presented a distorted image, and once these distortions had been accepted they were hard to correct. CATs were obligatory, and so Eskimo and Indian children had their intelligence assessed on problems woven around Californian concepts, around red and green traffic lights they had never seen and around 'traffic flows per hour' they could barely imagine in villages which might not have a single car.

In this respect little had changed in fifty years, when measured against the school situation in Hudson Stuck's time.

> The thing is a vain, artificial attempt to impose a whole body of ideas, notions, standards of comparison, metaphors, similes, and sentiments upon a race to which, in great measure, they ... [are] foreign and unintelligible. Here were girls reading in a textbook of so-called physiology, and, as it happened, the lesson that day was on the evils of tight lacing! The reading of that book, I was informed, is imposed by special United States statute, and the teacher must make a separate report that so much of it has been duly gone through each month before the salary can be drawn. Yet none of those girls ever saw a corset or ever will. One is reminded of the dear old lady who used to visit the jails and distribute tracts on *The Evils of Keeping Bad Company*.

58

THE BERING SEA Eskimos looked into the night sky and saw the Milky Way as Raven's snowshoe tracks left behind on a walk across the universe. They saw the aurora borealis as the disturbances made by boy spirits kicking and tossing a walrus skull about space. As I wallowed in a hot creek one evening and looked up, Raven's tracks were clear and a vigorous football match was in progress.

Everything about Elim enchanted me. The keys of its multi-million dollar school were handed to me with instructions to come and go as I pleased, and the ride to the hot springs was another peak in my love of mushing. The trail ran up and down mountain trails so steep I had to descend on roughlocked runners. It spiralled through forest I had not expected to find and over a windswept plateau with great fangs of rock protruding. In sheltered dells it sparkled and tossed up puffs of sequins in our wake. At the far end was a cabin with five feet of snow on its roof and a stove which threw out too much heat and required the cabin door to be left open. The hot springs were only a hundred yards away and when the feeding chores were done I went for a long soak.

It was a piquant sensation to be skinny-dipping in an arctic winter with bubbles *blorping* around me. Above my bath the aurora was an arc of electric green. Delicate, parallel lines rippled along its length, sometimes curling over like breaking waves, tumbling free and fading. The Northern Lights (and their southern counterparts, the aurora australis) were theoretically produced by streams of charged electrons and protons hitting particles of gas in the upper atmosphere, but I never cared much for such killjoy opinions. In Finnish they were *revontulet*, 'the foxy fire', and to Aberdonians 'the heavenly dancers'. They had such vitality, and a hell-bent disregard for distance and space. I lay there thinking of the remaining journey ahead. One hundred and twenty-three miles to Nome.

The following day I headed for White Mountain. On the way I passed over the ridge where Martin Buser had been pinned down for twelve hours by a blizzard. I went through Golovin, which was pronounced GOLO-vin rather than GO-lovin' (as Arpiq had hoped, this being a leap year). The name was of Russian origin, Golovnin, and the settlement was one of many devastated by the flu epidemic of 1918. In Golovin I visited the community office and saw signs such as 'Coffee, 10¢ – pay if you can' and a poster depicting a pair of feet with a name tag on a big toe. 'If you think suicide is the solution, you're dead wrong.'

And I hurried on to White Mountain.

59

'TONIGHT WE'RE HAVING Caesar Salad, Duck à l'Orange, Chocolate Mousse and Louisiana Brown Muffins.'

These were among the first words spoken to me in White Mountain. The fare didn't sound typically Alaskan (apart from the mousse), which one might have expected considering White Mountain Lodge was a village corporation enterprise, but it was irresistible to a hungry musher. And what more appropriate colour of duck?

White Mountain was reached suddenly after a twist in the Fish River, said to be one of the finest angling rivers in Alaska. Its position was similar to that of Elim, but it overlooked a river instead of the sea. The 'Mountain' was five hundred feet high and I assumed 'White' referred to its summer colour, because in winter every other mountain above latitude 64°N could be described the same way. The setting was beautiful, and I was always taken with the Eskimos' exuberant use of paint.

I had no sooner picketed my dogs on old Iditarod straw when the (white) manager of White Mountain Lodge stopped his snow machine and invited me to a pre-season special. For that week only, he explained, the Lodge's two new chefs were practising for the summer run of guests. Each day they were trying out a different menu and twelve dining room places were on offer at ten dollars a head. They were serving promptly at six-thirty. That happened to be in forty minutes, so I walked directly off the trail and into the dining room. It was the first and only time I ate before feeding my dogs.

The Lodge was a new chalet-style building set high above the river and it revelled in spectacular views west to dozens of other white mountains. Eleven diners were already seated in a room of varnished pine. I slipped quickly into the vacant place, thankful for the chance to hide my bunny boots, if not the rest of my wretched wardrobe. My companions were a lively bunch of teachers and maintenance technicians.

The menu was cooked, announced and served by the two chefs; a native woman (tall and very broad) and man (short and very thin) who were both in their thirties and wore full whites, including cylindrical hats. Their smiles packed in so much fun they were worth at least nine dollars fifty of the price.

First we were offered iced tea or hot coffee, and the Louisiana Muffins appeared. Caesar Salad was an oily assembly of lettuce which resembled dock leaves, adorned with some slices of boiled egg and a shaving of fish. Duck à l'Orange came on a huge plate and the contents were so small and spread about that they looked like a winter nativity scene. I thought this was just the vegetable selection and the duck would arrive separately, but the slivers of 'mushroom' were the duck. However, I appreciated the necessity for feeding twelve out of one bird, as birds were out of season. I hadn't seen a duck since Wyoming. Chocolate Mousse was also out of season, a partially tanned cream-colour.

It was delicious. I heartily recommend White Mountain Lodge. A musher straight off the trail may find the portions modest but the memory of a quality meal is worth many miles – and if the same two chefs are on, dinner is an absolute snip at fifty cents.

60

THE TRAIL HAD turned inland to reach White Mountain and here it offered a choice. To reach the mining district of Council, twenty miles away, a musher followed the Fish River and headed north. To reach Nome, seventy-seven miles away, the westbound traveller was led back to the coast. The 'modern' Iditarod trail did not head for the sea directly but stayed inland and swung round to the coast at Topkok Head. The last of the Seward Peninsula's trees were on this route and they stood ranked by size, a downward projection from the tallest at White Mountain, through the lesser and sparser to nothing at Mile 15.

The 'old' Iditarod trail did not visit White Mountain but branched off at Golovin, hopped over a headland and reached the coast long before Topkok Head. It passed a mining community at Bluff, on Daniels Creek (a name I was to hear mentioned later), and it was here that Stuck once came across an enterprise of wondrous ingenuity. Miners had sunk an 'ice shaft' to the seabed through twelve feet of water. They had hollowed out a hole in the surface ice and stopped when there was only a thin skin remaining before reaching the water. Overnight frost would build up new ice underneath, allowing them to excavate several inches deeper, and again they would stop before breaking through. In this way they had reached the bottom inside a cylindrical wall of ice. 'They had a curious chute, like a ship's ventilator, to catch the wind and funnel cold air down the shaft' to prevent it from thawing.

Topkok Hill was another nasty Iditaspot, a sharp climb followed by a long exposed summit. A cold wind drove straight into our faces and maintained a moving blanket of snow close to the ground. Fortunately the sky was clear and the visibility good. A musher I'd met in Galena, Gary Guy, had got caught here in the previous year's Iditarod. He and a fellow racer were beset by 30 to 50 knot winds for two days. The temperature was −20°F which equated to an extreme of −90°F in terms of wind-chill. They had cocooned themselves in their sleeping bags in the lee of their sleds. Their dogs survived with no protection, for the wind blew away any snow that might have built up to afford some insulation. Gary was unable to feed them during the ordeal. On the third day conditions improved and they made it to a shelter cabin, spent several hours cooking and eating and then carried on to Nome.

Half-way across the top we passed this shelter cabin, and found it transformed into an ice sculpture. It was an A-frame hut with a wedge of snow at one end, the entrance end. The wedge was too steep to climb without a struggle and the only way into the hut was through an eighteen-inch hole scraped through the top of the wedge. We drove on, over a surface striated by furrows, and came to the end of Topkok, the drop down to sea-level. The view showed a clear coast for a couple of miles and then the world ended in a whiteout. Our run of good weather was coming to an end just fifty miles from home.

When we entered the storm it was hard to tell whether snow was actually falling, or just being whipped up by the wind. The trail ran along a raised beach strewn with logs and stumps but was regularly marked by tall tripods. The wind was bitterly cold and it came knifing in from right to left. It forced a way into every gap in my clothing and found zips no obstacle at all. I stopped to put belly covers on the dogs. The warmth evaporated from my hands in seconds and my fingers turned clumsy and muddling. At first visibility stayed at a hundred yards, which was the minimum to see the markers; then it began falling.

Even with my parka hood narrowed to a slit the wind penetrated and forced me to turn my head and squint through the hairs of the ruff. It was worse for the dogs. Their eyes watered and knuckles of ice built up around the lids. Every fifteen minutes I had to remove these by pulling gently and thawing the side frozen to their fur with what warmth was in my fingers. After a couple of miles of this the sled struck an end of driftwood. There was a splitting sound and the handlebars went loose. I called the dogs to a halt.

A crosspiece bracing the handlebars had cracked and was no longer giving any support. The damage was not severe but it affected my control of the sled and I feared that a sudden wrench would break the handlebars completely. The twenty minutes it took to lash a temporary repair, with frequent stops to warm my hands, felt like hours.

Visibility was fluctuating between fifty and eighty yards, though there were moments when Duran and Rosco in lead were barely discernible. I had to stop frequently to look for tripods, sometimes leaving the dogs and walking ahead on foot. Then Duran decided he wanted to run with the wind behind him and kept pulling off to the left. When I gee'd the leaders over Rosco would respond for a while but gradually Duran would pull him aside. I replaced them with Silver and Alf.

The wind had transformed Alf into a peculiar shape. He was completely flat on one side and all billowing hairiness on the other. But he was no good either. I swapped him with Sensor. Sensor was a timid dog and usually went wherever Silver indicated. For several hundred yards he endured the discomfort, but then began pulling back. Silver turned and snapped at him – her usual form of discipline when a companion was disputing her control – but Sensor was more intimidated by the wind. I stopped yet again, added an extra section of gangline and put Silver in single lead. I felt nervous about giving the command to go, for this was my last resort.

'All right. GEE, GEE.'

In retrospect, I suppose, it was only a small manoeuvre, and perhaps my predicament wasn't as serious as I imagined at the time, but I will never forget the way that dog immediately turned into the wind. She flattened her ears and headed into the blast without any hesitation. The snow continued to fly and ice still formed around the dogs' eyes, and still Silver gee'd and hawed on a single word and we wove a zigzag course along the elusive line of markers. It is easy to become maudlin about dogs and I daresay every musher has a shared moment treasured above all others. This is mine, this is how I see Silver yet, leading us through a whiteout on the last leg to Nome.

Fifteen miles later we emerged from the blizzard as suddenly as we had entered it. The wind dropped by half and visibility ahead returned to normal. At the foot of hills a mile to our right was Solomon, which Gunnar Kaasen had overshot while on the Serum Run's final stage. I wasn't surprised, for Solomon was just a straggle of half-buried houses. Once it had been a thriving mining camp, but now only one family lived there during winter. Like Shaktoolik it looked as if it cultivated storms. Kaasen had experienced a bad one on his journey. It was night, the sled had overturned and to his horror he found the package had gone missing. He groped frantically in the dark for several minutes before stumbling across the serum. Then he missed Solomon and the Health Board's message to wait out the storm there.

We rested in the lee of a ghost house and then continued. The wind dropped to a breeze and the day ended in a tranquil sunlit evening. Behind us the storm continued, with a clearly-defined edge. We came to summer huts in increasing numbers and then a road sign appeared: SHARP BEND! And beyond was a road. It caught me by surprise and I felt as if I had just failed my first CAT. A quick look at the map showed it clearly marked. It was the summer road from Council to Nome.

The dogs looked fit for more miles but I wanted to reach Nome the following morning rather than late that night. I stopped beside some driftwood and cooked supper. A low sun softened the land and made it look smooth and gentle but it couldn't con me into thinking my cheeks weren't windburned. Stuck hadn't liked this region. 'A savage, forbidding country, this ... Seward Peninsula, uninhabited and unfit for habitation; a country of naked rock and bare hillside and desolate, barren valley, without amenities of any kind and cursed with a perpetual icy blast.' It was unusual for him to inveigh against the land so strongly, too strongly. I guessed he'd had a worse day than mine.

The dogs' food was ready. They were ignoring the smells and had all turned to face Nome. When I followed their gaze, I saw a dog team approaching. And another. And another. Eight teams in all passed, four of them so close together they appeared as one. I stood mesmerised, realising how few other teams I had seen in 800 miles. Excluding the Iditarod and St Patrick's Day Races, I could recall only seven up to this moment. These turned out to be running the annual Nome–Council–Nome Race. Only four teams finished, and one musher suffered frostbite in the blizzard, which had worsened after we passed through.

After supper I hitched up the dogs once more and set off towards Port Safety in the hope that it might be a more populated community with some shelter. My optimism seemed misplaced until the third to last house, where a figure was standing by the door. Francis Walton beckoned me over. He was an Inupiaq Eskimo, seventy-six years old, whose grandfather had fled Czarist Russia and died in Liverpool.

61

ESKIMOS OCCUPY A larger geographical area than any other ethnic group, a wraparound people and culture covering the top of the world. Inupiaq is the predominant language and despite regional differences, an Eskimo of Thule would be able to converse with Francis Walton of Port Safety. Traditional lifestyles within the group shared many elements in common, with differences developing to suit local conditions. The dome-shaped snowhouse generally assigned to all Eskimos, for example, was a temporary shelter used by the people of northern Canada and was unknown to the Bering Strait Eskimo, whose environment was one of ice and wind rather than house-building snow. (Unlike English, which treats snow as a menace and affords it a meagre vocabulary, Inupiaq has twenty-seven words to distinguish snow according to quality and specific uses.) Edward Nelson's sojourn among the Eskimos between the mouth of the Yukon and Sledge Island (near Nome) revealed a highly sophisticated lifestyle, and one so finely tuned to the means of survival that women even raided the tiny 'winter larders' of voles.

Hunters crafted sleds from driftwood and used the ribs of bowhead whales or segments of walrus tusks for runners. Nets were made through a time-consuming process of scraping and weaving sinew from caribou and beluga. As much as 300 feet of almost unbreakable harpoon line could be obtained from a single bearded seal flipper. An Eskimo possessed a full array of other devices for gaining access to his prey. One such device was the seal scratcher. This was simply a piece of wood with three prongs at the end, and it could be made to mimic exactly the sounds of a seal clearing out its breathing hole in the ice. A hunter would slither towards a resting seal, hiding behind his large mittens, and if spotted he would stop and scratch away at the surface. The seal would soon relax, reassured that what had caught its eye was merely another of its kind at work.

Eskimos brought down birds with the *bolas*, a whirling arrangement of four balls and sinew more commonly associated with South American Indians. The balls were made of wood so they would float in the event of a miss over water. They employed an extraordinary braining trap in which a spiked club was held in sinew and twisted to immense tension. When triggered the club descended and drove the spike into the victim's skull. Some traps were large enough to kill polar bears (*nanook*) but mostly foxes, wolves and wolverines (*kavik*) were taken.

Wolverines were the most reviled pests. They were intelligent and fearless and constantly devoured the contents of traps or stole bait. For use against them, and also wolves, a gruesome trap was devised. A thin strip of baleen plate was sharpened at both ends, soaked until it became pliable and folded into a compact bundle like a concertina. This was wrapped in an oily fish skin and left on the ground. A wolverine gulping it down whole would suffer an agonising death after the fish skin had disintegrated in its stomach.

Life was not all hunting and work. Saunas were a popular form of relaxation and they were usually fired to such temperatures that breathing was only possible through special wood-shaving respirators. At saunas and at home Eskimos washed themselves from tubs of urine, which dissolves grease and is an effective form of soap. Like soap, it requires rinsing for best effect. Urine was also used to tan fur clothing and garments made from salmon skin and the feathered skins of duck and geese.

Eskimos were addicted to tobacco. They obtained it through trade with their Siberian cousins, a warlike bunch who used suits of armour made of walrus-bone slats. Tobacco was regarded as a status symbol, for only the most successful hunters could afford to habitually smoke, or chew 'quids'. Athabascans traded a fungus commonly found on dead birch trees and Eskimos burned this and mixed the ash with finely shredded tobacco. The resulting quid was softened by chewing – the hard initial chew usually being performed by a hunter's wife – and stored for later enjoyment, being then tucked against the cheek and the juices swallowed. Nelson noted that men often removed the quid, rolled it into a ball and stuck it behind their right ear to keep for later.

And Eskimos loved playing games. Children used skipping ropes of plaited grass while adults went for more demanding tests of skill and strength. One game of particular note was observed by Nelson. It went by the name of *tu'-kû-kă-gu'-tă*, or the Battering Ram Game.

This is played by four men in the *kashim* [a large, semi-subterranean building used as a communal 'hall']. Two of the players each takes his partner upon his shoulder, the latter lying face downward with his body stiffened and feet projecting horizontally in front of the man carrying him. In this position the carriers face each other and run one at the other so that the feet of the two men on their shoulders shall come together, trying in this way to upset each other, the defeated pair falling ignominiously to the floor.

62

FRANCIS WALTON BECKONED me over to his cabin entrance, which was sunk below the level of the snow. Against the light of the interior his silhouette was of medium height and portly, and his head showed a glint of spectacles. In the light he was a good looking man with a benign expression, and huge hands. His manner was relaxed and he exuded an air of solid competence.

'If you want to stay here the night, I got plenty room,' was his greeting.

'But you don't even know me . . .'

My remark made no sense to him. 'It don't matter. I got plenty room.'

The cabin contained two large rooms with a half wall dividing them, and a stove in each turned the interior into a sauna. For a time I thought I might need a wood-shaving respirator. The walls were festooned with four rifles, pots and pans, clothes, lanterns, binoculars and other items in a hunting and household miscellany. He showed me a sealskin wallet which was over a hundred years old. It had been sewn with a bone needle and the minute stitching was so precise it might have been done by machine. At the far end of the cabin a shelf held a long row of books and I glanced along their spines while hanging up my harnesses to dry. They were Reader's Digest condensed books, mainly on the subject of war. Francis noticed my interest.

'I'm not very educated,' he said, 'but I like reading.' His voice toned regret, and for a moment we sat in silence with our own thoughts.

The Council Race and my appearance had interrupted his work. He led me outside and then into a lean-to greenhouse where in the long summer days he grew carrots, potatoes and enormous cabbages. In winter the greenhouse was his workshop. He had been out shooting that day and had brought back sixty-seven ptarmigan and a red fox. He had just case-skinned the fox – slitting along the legs and drawing the body out through the mouth so that the fur was turned inside out, and removed relatively intact – and was about to work on the ptarmigan. He would dip each bird in boiling water to make plucking easier. He was sitting on a small sled with ivory runners, carefully sliced from walrus tusks and fitted together to form a near-seamless length. Of all the materials used for runners, he said, ivory was the quietest and this was important when hunting seal on ice.

I'm not very educated . . .

Francis also operated crab pots and last week had caught twelve large kings. He was reluctant to go and check again because his wife would throw a fit at all the game he was bringing in.

'You must be unique in Eskimo history,' I commented. 'A hunter who's too successful.' He chuckled for some time, and then told me a story in which only dates were missing.

Francis was one-quarter Russian. His grandfather, Tetaworph, had come from Siberia. Tetaworph had been involved, or at least implicated, in a plot to assassinate a Czar, and fled to Alaska. He married and then moved south to San Francisco with his wife. Shortly after their son was born Tetaworph was shanghaied and disappeared, and years later his family heard that he was ill in Liverpool. He recovered, but he never returned to America. Whether the means or the will to do so was lacking is not known, only that Tetaworph ended his days on Merseyside.

His widow came north with her son, Francis's father, first to Dawson City and then to Unalakleet, where the boy finally became too much for her and she gave him to the Swedish mission to be raised by the Covenanters. Around this time he changed his surname to the simpler 'Walton'. The young Walton became a guide leading miners to the new strikes on the Seward Peninsula. One of his journeys led him past Daniels Creek, which he noticed had very black sand. While working for a spell in Nome he overheard an old Forty-niner from California telling someone, 'Wherever there's black sand, there's gold.'

Walton set off at once for Daniels Creek with a friend named Hanson, a white man much older than himself. They found gold at Daniels Creek. For some reason Hanson would not stake a claim for himself and refused to stake one for Walton who, being under sixteen, was legally under age. Walton decided that the only person he could really trust to stake a claim was his mother. He knew she was intending to return Outside that winter and he took a boat to St Michael in the hope of intercepting her. But his mother, who had already reached St Michael, suddenly changed her plans and headed north to look for her son in Nome. They crossed at sea.

'My father was always unlucky like that,' Francis added. 'Some time later he got back to Daniels Creek and found the whole area had been staked. It was the custom to keep one plot free for the discoverer of a strike – and Hanson had claimed it.' For a time Walton worked on gold dredges at Council (an important strike immediately prior to the one at Nome) before becoming a teacher. Francis himself had followed the mining rather than the academic lead.

Francis offered me a spring bed which was so comfortable I hardly slept. Siwashing in White Mountain the previous night had actually provided more rest, but cabin mornings were always preferable because I didn't have to pour hot water into my bunny boots. After breakfasting, packing and harnessing my team, I set-to washing the dishes while my host cleaned out the ears of his fox. Dolly Parton was singing to us on the radio, and it wasn't until her song was finished that the strange sounds coming from outside were audible. They were the sounds of dogs fighting. I dashed out of the cabin, knocking over a chair in my haste.

The dogs had been left attached by their necklines only, to allow them freedom to turn around and relax before the day's haul. This had been my normal practice throughout the trip. Now six of the team were bunched together in a frenzy of biting. Silver and Rosco were at the front, keeping out of it. Alf and Sensor were on the fringe in defensive postures but snarling and lunging. One dog was down and the others were attacking it. The growls were fierce and interspersed with yelping. I couldn't work out which dog was down and ran screaming into the thick of them.

It was Duran. He was underneath, on his back and being bitten on all sides. It is not uncommon for dog fights to leave fatalities. When a dog goes down, its cries seem to incite the attackers further and bring in others to add their measure. Only by appearing as a bigger threat can a musher hope to break up what becomes a wild free-for-all, a chance to settle old scores. Still yelling I lashed out with fists and feet. I picked on the dog most likely to have started it and the one attacking the most ferociously – Kavik. I threw him to the ground and pinned him by his throat while undoing his neckline. By then Nanook and Sisco had set on Duran once more and I had to release Kavik and separate them. Francis came to help and dragged Kavik away. Duran was terrified and snapping at anything within reach. He bit my hand several times while I worked above him and held Sensor and Nanook away. There was a lull while we all held our positions, and during this Francis removed Nanook and Sisco.

When I bent down to unhook Duran he seized my hand between his teeth once more and then slowly released it. He was panting heavily, strings of saliva hung around his mouth and his eyes were wide with fear. His fur was tufted, wet from bites and already freezing.

A strip of bloody flesh hung down from a torn ear, and streaks of blood marked his legs and chest.

Back in the cabin Francis and I cleaned Duran's wounds. Fortunately these were not as serious as I feared. The ear was the only bad tear, but it would soon heal and the remaining injuries were punctures. We waited an hour until his fur had dried and he was looking a little better. He was still in low spirits, and I was depressed as well. My trust and confidence in the team had taken a tumble. Eight hundred miles without a fight and suddenly this, twenty-two miles from Nome. I would now have to run Duran up front, at the opposite end from the dogs which had been chiefly involved.

Twenty-two miles to go.

'DAS-VEED-ARN-I-YA,' the cabin radio pronounced, 'goodbye, До свидания.

It was hoped that tourist flights might soon start between Nome and Provideniya in Siberia. Nome, formerly the wildest and greatest of Alaska's gold-rush towns, was having its word-a-day Russian lesson.

63

'NOTHING IN THE world could have caused the building of a city where Nome is built except the thing that caused it: the finding of gold ... It has no harbour or roadstead, no shelter or protection of any kind; it is in as bleak and as exposed a position as a man would find if he should set out to hunt the earth over for ineligible sites.' So wrote Stuck some fifteen years after Nome had been put on the map.

The strike is credited to the so-called 'Three Lucky Swedes' who panned rich colour out of creeks around the Snake River, seventy miles from the nearest tree and below a mountain with a tall rock in the shape of an anvil. The settlement that resulted was called Anvil City until the US postal service, repeatedly confusing the name with others, forced a change. 'Nome', the name of a nearby cape, was grudgingly accepted. The story goes (though it has never been popular among Nomers) that an officer on a British ship surveying the coast in the 1850s scribbled a query against the cape on his chart. Either he had bad handwriting or the cartographer who later examined the chart had poor eyesight, but '? Name' was transcribed as 'C. Nome'. Like Eskimo chewing tobacco, 'Nome' stuck.

The Lucky Swedes had about six months' prospecting experience between them. The youngest, Jafet Lindeberg, was only twenty-four when he was brought over from his native land to oversee an ambitious project: reindeer were to be used to haul food supplies to Dawson City, then in the heyday of the Klondike. Lindeberg was not Swedish but Norwegian and he knew nothing about reindeer; however, he was a Scandinavian and this was all that mattered to the US government who had thought up the scheme. Lindeberg simply wanted to reach the goldfields. He arrived with 500 reindeer whose rapid deaths by starvation caused the project to be abandoned, and freed Lindeberg for prospecting. He met the Two Swedes by chance in Council and they set off west in a flimsy boat. It was said they were not able to tell 'a placer from a potato patch', but years later they left Alaska as millionaires.

Anvil City was troubled from the start because the Swedes, unfamiliar with mining traditions, changed the rules and made it permissible for one person to stake claims on behalf of friends. As more miners heard about the strike and appeared, claim-jumping became rife. The situation deteriorated into virtual anarchy and had one particularly ugly protest not been broken up by half a dozen soldiers, the Swedes would have been stripped of their claims and driven out. Several days later came a second discovery, one which was to have far greater consequences for the township's future. Gold was discovered a matter of yards away, on the beach.

Beach placers were what made Nome's stampede unique. It was called the 'Poor Man's Paradise'. By law claims could not be staked on beaches and so the diggings were open to everyone. In fact, some rights of claim *were* introduced – a circle two-shovel-lengths in diameter, centred on the digger for the duration of uninterrupted work – but these did not detract from the Paradise. If a newcomer found no space, he or she only had to wait for someone to finish their day's work and quickly move in. The scene was then set for the full force of the rush, for the woman who appears in an old sepia print. She stands in a dark, full-length dress which is crimped around her waist and has long sleeves. On her head is a tall bonnet like a Christmas cracker, bound around its middle by a band of ribbon. It descends to touch her shoulders and is cut away at the front to expose her face. She wears gloves and is pitched slightly forwards as if about to curtsey, only she's standing on Nome beach shovelling black sand into a rocker.

The Swedes made their strike in July 1898. By May 1899 Nome had a population of 250 miners. By autumn the same year the population had increased to 3,000, of whom an estimated one third was destitute, and it was only freeze-up which stopped a mass invasion. Nome was icebound for eight months of the year, and was said to have only two seasons: winter and the Fourth of July. The winter of 1899/1900 was hard on the residents of the young town, not only because of the weather but because they knew it was the calm before the storm. Quite how severe the storm would be they didn't know – nor what was happening in the Philippines nor in the rest of the world – until a man cycled into town with news. On 29 March Ed Jesson arrived on his wheel with eyes sore from snowblindness and seven well-thumbed newspapers.

'All trails lead to Nome' was true in 1900. The rush was inspired by the belief that the *sea* was the source of the gold, and accordingly the supply was unlimited. In fact Nome's beach pickings were easy, producing between $80 and $100 in gold per day, but meagre compared with the richness of the inland placers.

Eighteen thousand stampeders arrived in the summer of 1900. They were transported by 162 steamships and seventy sailing vessels which had to anchor out at sea. The roadstead was never closer to shore than one mile because of the shallow water, and sometimes as far away as four miles when the ice was bad. Lighters ferried passengers ashore but they reached Nome totally drenched, or at least with wet feet, because the last few yards always had to be walked. Women rode on the backs of men.

Back in Seattle the word 'Nome' had been the catchpenny of advertisers, and the stampeders arrived with their Nome rockers, Nome cash registers, and Nome Doctor Kits which included 'Trusses for the ruptured ... First Class Suspensories ... Dr Charcot's French Nerve Treatment for nervous people.' And plenty of people were nervous when they laid eyes on Nome.

It was five miles of mud, piles of possessions and densely-packed tents, 'all length and no breadth', crammed between tundra bogs and the sea. It was estimated that in the month of June 15,000 people arrived and brought 6,000 tons of supplies, which were heaped on the beach. Nothing was easy. It took hours to collect a letter at the post office and there were five filing boxes just for the 'Johnsons'. Worst of all was that the Paradise for the Poor Man was over. Nome's sands had been sluiced several times over and the easy gleanings were gone. That June the beach was described as 'the world's longest junkyard' and some of the contraptions which had expired there were awesome; monstrous 'vacuum cleaners' with wooden frames and wire wheels eight feet in diameter, cranked by hand or powered by steam. One of these, The Red Elephant, had cost $30,000, employed a crew of fifteen and, as legend has it, recovered ninety cents' worth of gold.

Gold was still found on the beach that summer and it was reckoned the season's takings had a value of $350,000 (and that between three and six million dollars were spent by those who actually found it and those who had hoped to find it). US census figures registered one third of all Alaskan whites as being in Nome for its one-season stampede. Most were disillusioned and destitute, more became so after the first of four severe storms wrecked part of the city in September, and by the time the ice sealed off Nome a month later, between ten and fifteen thousand people had left. Yet a large population remained.

Boom-time Nome had over a hundred saloons and gambling houses, which – gold be damned – is the true measure of a stampede. Plenty of 'sports' occupied the red-light district, the 'tenderloin', set bang in the centre of the city. When Nome's citizens refused to pay the voluntary taxes invited by their council-elect, a sporting tax was imposed and collected. Nome's prostitutes bailed the city out of insolvency by paying ten dollars a month. Sports of a different nature played pool, faro, panguingue, poker and roulette; and boxers attracted large crowds at fights which sometimes ran to twenty-five rounds.

Gold-rush Nome had a full complement of stores and services. There were dentists, doctors, barbers, paper-hangers, estate agents, photographers, launderers and massage artistes. Nome even had a brewery. Yet the town remained unsightly, unhealthy and unsafe because it lacked three basic requirements – streets, sanitation and justice. People placed shacks and tents wherever they could and they relieved themselves wherever they liked. Glaciers of urine were reported between the saloons during winter and the situation became so serious that the council enforced the use of public latrines. Tickets cost three for twenty-five cents, or ten cents each, and violators of the regulation were arrested and fined. Fears of an epidemic persisted and it was said that the bloody evidence of dysentery could be seen in every latrine.

Few murders occurred but this was the sole consolation for the early Nomers. The rush had brought the usual riff-raff of confidence-tricksters, pickpockets and thugs. Among them were C. B. Heath, 'alias Hobo Kid; general crook, clever poker player, will ... likely be found living with a dance-hall girl by the name of ...', and Bill Doherty, 'general tough, killed a man in Boise ...', and Hank Freize, 'gambler; runs a sure thing game'. Footpads stalked between the dwellings at night mugging whomever they could. Thieves even carried off an entire building on one occasion, though the owner came along in time to recover it. Chloroform gangs were all the rage; they slashed holes in tents when the occupant was sleeping and used a saturated rag at the end of a pole to induce a slumber deep enough for them to steal everything, including the bed. But the most infamous lawbreakers were Judge Noyes and his mentor, Alexander McKenzie.

Noyes was a pusillanimous attorney from Minnesota who drank too much. McKenzie, a North Dakotan with twenty-one years' service as a Republican National Committeeman, befriended him for these weaknesses and used him as a stooge for the plan he master-minded. He used his influence among Washington politicians to have Noyes elected judge of the division of Alaska which included Nome, and he himself formed the Alaska Gold Mining Company. The company's sole investments were two tickets to Nome.

Once there Judge Noyes obeyed all his friend's instructions. The goldfields were still in turmoil over the ownership of claims and whenever a case came before him, Judge Noyes ordered the disputed ground to be placed in the hands of a temporary receiver until the matter was resolved. The receiver's task was simply to hold the property in neutral custody, but the receiver was always the Alaska Gold Mining Company, whose owner worked the mines as if they were his. Noyes never resolved any disputes, but deferred judgement indefinitely; to speed up the whole process of appropriation a firm of lawyers was co-opted to bring ownership of the most valuable

214

mines into dispute. Before he was stopped McKenzie had shipped out $600,000 in gold.

The pair arrived in Nome in July 1900, and had complaints not seeped out and resulted in their arrest and removal on the last boat three months later, it is probable they would have been added to the town's murder statistics. They were tried for nothing more serious than contempt of court. Noyes was fined $1,000 and McKenzie was sentenced to one year in prison. After serving less than four months he was pardoned by President McKinley (later of Denali fame) and released on grounds of pitiful health – a verdict which brought about an immediate cure. To this day the recollection of the affair makes the United States Justice Department shrink into its wig.

The turbulent year of 1900 ended on a happier note for many of the five thousand gold-seekers who stayed through the winter. One of Nome's favourite sons, Tex Rickard, who went on to build Madison Square Garden and become the giant among boxing promoters, threw a Christmas Day party for all those down on their luck. No one was turned away that day and 750 turkeys were bought, cooked and reduced to soup bones.

By 1902 Nome's rush was over and the town had settled down to a quiet life. Its first car arrived in 1905, and it survived its first serious fire the same year. The area yielded increasing quantities of gold, with a value of $7 million in 1907, but Nome's interests had diversified. It had gardens, dairies and electricity, Edna Burmeister topping the dance-hall bill singing 'I Have No Sweetheart But You – To Zither accompaniment', and, more excitingly, the event that was always winter's ultimate entertainment: seeing *who* would be the first visitor into town, *when*, and *how long* the journey from ship to shore would take. The *Nome Nugget* ran a one-page special edition with the answers. In 1907 it was Louis Hank on 1 June in one hour and thirty minutes. And the unique Pupmobile was running.

The Pupmobile was a general term applied to numerous home-made carts with flanged wheels pulled by dogs along a disused railroad. The railroad, built to serve the claims of the Wild Goose Mining Company, was narrow-gauge and incorporated rises and falls along its ninety-mile route. On the downhill sections dogs were allowed to hop on and enjoy the ride. Proficient pupmobile teams learned to adjust their stride to the spacing of the sleepers, to leap aboard before the downhills, and to step down and pull when the freewheeling stopped. (Leonhard Seppala's rig and newly-introduced breed of huskies became known as the 'Siberian Express'.)

Nome's existence was threatened several times in subsequent years, by its most destructive fire in 1934 and by storms in 1913, 1945 and 1974, but the town always pulled itself through and added a few more tales of the extraordinary to its impressive repertoire. The 1913 storm produced one of the most celebrated and macabre. In October of that year a hurricane ravaged the city for three days, blew buildings away and drove waves over roofs and into the tundra. The cemetery was torn up, 'scores of coffins' – to quote the *Nugget* – were unearthed and the contents of some were scattered. One of the coffins floating about intact contained Goldie, a universal sweetheart and queen of the dance-halls who had died a decade earlier. Her coffin was washed up against the door of a cabin belonging to an old prospector who returned after the storm to find it there. When he saw the name 'Goldie' on top he couldn't resist looking inside. He prised the lid open, stared and sank back with a sigh.

'Ah, Goldie, you're still the best-lookin' gal in town.'

64

NOME, NOW A city of 3,700 people and one parking meter, came into view on the thirty-second morning of our journey from Manley. Beyond an avenue of telephone posts which lent the coastal flats their third dimension, beyond a defunct gold dredge marooned on the tundra ice, bunched compactly together on the horizon, were the fuel tanks, radio masts and coloured wooden houses of our 'destination'. I looked on the scene with mixed feelings, torn between the elation of a safe arrival and the anticlimax of a premature one. Even with that morning's dog fight still fresh in my mind Nome was coming several hundred miles too soon; it had never been a *real* destination, merely an excuse for driving a dog team.

My dogs seemed unaware of the significance of what lay ahead. To them the glimpse of Nome represented another few days' lolling about on the longest trek of their lives, and they looked keen enough for a bid on the Pole. Duran had recovered his spirits within a few miles, although he looked nervous whenever we stopped. We stopped several times before my camera indicated the temperature was in the film-breaking minus thirties, and thereafter we kept moving into a breeze which made snow snakes wriggle over the trail.

Since leaving Port Safety the trail had stayed on the sea ice for several miles until it had rounded the cape, '? Name', whose rocks had been quarried for the storm-proof breakwater recently built above Nome's golden beach. Once round the cape the trail rose onto tundra and followed the telephone poles to the horizon. We passed deserted fish camps, and dog lots whose occupants erupted into excited barking. Swanberg's old dredge, one of forty-four in the vicinity of the city, was followed by a cemetery of gold-rush machinery from stamper batteries to Red Elephants. Then we reached Nome by-pass and had to skirt the city. Dogs were not allowed within the city limits and, as if to enforce this regulation, the streets were kept clear of snow. An exception was made during March, when the situation was reversed. Nomers endorsed the sentiments of a note found in 1983 in an abandoned sled on Front Street, penned by an unknown hand and called 'The Nome Iditarodda'.

> BE happy amid the snowdrifts and the wind-chill factors and remember what peace there may be in warm boots. ▲ As far as possible be on good terms with your neighbours and their dogs and know who your friends are. ▲ You are a denizen of the great city of Nome and therefore conduct yourself hospitably for March is the Month of Iditarod. ▲ Respect the signs of nature, preserve the Alaskan environment, recycle your memories and watch out for polar bears, be they in animal or human form. ▲ When you see the mushers mush, mush with them. ▲ Eat of the muktuk, the seal oil and the smoked fish and taste the flesh of walrus, the moose and the moosquito. ▲ Enjoy yourself and may the best man, or woman, win.

But the Iditarod was over and dogs, mushers and snow were no longer allowed in Nome. With the help of a hand-drawn map I made my way between the houses of the city and the dog lots of the tundra, turned inland towards Anvil Mountain for a mile and came to the suburb of Icy View. Architect Jim Dory and partner Suz were expecting me. Theirs were yet more names that had been given to me through Alaska's brotherhood of mushers, and I had written to them asking if I might use their mailbox as my final pickup point.

They had responded in such a welcoming manner that my request might have involved no more than holding onto a postcard, instead of three sacks of dog food, two bales of straw, a box of odds and ends and air cargo boxes (for dogs) weighing over a hundred pounds.

Jim was jacking up his house when I arrived. He used a standard car jack and cranked away until his spirit level indicated the building was sitting evenly, and then he inserted pieces of wood between the base and the supporting legs. Architects face special problems in regions such as this where permafrost and earth tremors make subsidence inevitable. Buildings are designed around the need to minimise contact with the unstable ground, avoiding unnecessary corners which require extra supports. Piles are one method of support, but they are expensive to install and have to be sunk to a depth three times that measured between the surface and the start of the permafrost. The cheapest and most common method of building a house is to lay a plastic sheet on the site, cover it with several feet of gravel, lay 'floating' blocks on top and build a house on legs to stand on these blocks. The blocks gradually sink, but it is a simple matter to jack up and relevel a square or rectangular house on four legs, and this usually has to be done twice a year.

Jim and Suz were in their early thirties and kept a similar number of dogs on a crust of ice outside their floating house. The ice avoided the house but built up around it, so that during the early stages of winter the dogs and their boxes had to be regularly dug out and moved upwards, and then during the thaw they sank seven feet and returned to earth. Life in Nome seemed to be all about staying out of the wind and on the level.

'Don't you miss trees here?' I asked.

'We're used to it,' Suz replied, 'but I always miss them at Christmas. Last Christmas I was getting ready to decorate the plant' − she nodded towards her six-foot Dieffenbachia − 'when a friend flew in a pine tree from Council. It was a real treat.'

Over the next few days we drove our dogs on visits to friends and met some participants in the annual contests of Beard Growing and Outhouse Decorating, the Memorial Day Polar Bear Swim and the Labor Day Bathtub Race (first prize − a fur-lined honey bucket). I was very taken with life in Nome and soon understood why Nomers had a predilection for bizarre contests.

Nome's population, forty per cent white, was a redoubt of gritty individualists and an inspiration to me. I had met their type all along my route, and I had usually met them twice; once as medics, lawyers, pilots, counsellors, teachers, mechanics, fishermen, or trappers, and again, when they were a decade younger, as snapshots in their photograph albums. In Kodacolour they were identical, dressed in casual clothes, wearing their hair long and matching the images of the hippy era. In this they were indistinguishable from the black-and-white and sepia characters of the gold-rush era, thus underscoring a trait found throughout Alaska history – residents of the Bush have always been alternative-lifestylers, whether by tradition as natives or by choice as whites. Nome held a concentration of those who felt themselves inheritors of the pioneering gene, of the spirit which won the west and the north. Front Street had been paved only in the 1970s and even then against strong protest; it was felt that what had been good enough in 1900 would be good enough in 2000.

Front Street was the only flaw in an otherwise delightfully run-down town centre. It looked too spruce to fit the surrounds, a half-hearted compromise between the pragmatists who had wanted the buildings modern and the way paved, and the 'unpaved' lobby who had ended up with soulless pieces of mock history ideal only for the selling of souvenirs. It had wooden blocks of offices, false-fronted gift shops, a couple of Pepsi and Pizza signs, a Disneyesque polar bear above the door of 'Janatorial Supplies' and a signpost pointing to 'Moscow 4,376 miles' and 'London 4,052'. Dirt-blasted snow filled the gaps between buildings. In summer the snow would be replaced by the sound of waves.

The parking meter stood *inside* the office of the *Nome Nugget*, though formerly it had been on the sidewalk outside. The city council had erected it to spite Albro Gregory, the then editor, who had written a scathing editorial when the proposal to install meters in Nome was being discussed. Albro discovered it one morning when he arrived for work, and immediately penned another acerbic attack. Nome's only meter never did accept coins, though plenty were offered, and it was unable to survive snowploughs or louts leaning on it.

The *Nome Nugget*, Alaska's oldest newspaper, employed a staff of seven and, according to its banner, was 'published daily except for Monday, Tuesday, Wednesday, Friday, Saturday and Sunday'. Nearby, parked out of meter range up a side alley, was the spruce-log arch wheeled out each year to mark the end of the Iditarod, and a statue to Roald Amundsen commemorating his 1926 'Rome to Nome' voyage in the dirigible *Norge*, the world's first transpolar flight. (The air ship was blown seventy miles further and actually landed at Teller.)

Nome's true character was to be found in its side-streets, some of which had survived the onslaughts of fires, storms and pragmatists. Here were the tumble-down houses I had expected, cars buried under deep drifts – a sight only a musher could enjoy – and other surprises: a rocking horse and a snow machine side-by-side, a building marked 'Nome Pubic School' because some footpad had stolen an 'l', Wink's Plumbing Service sporting the raw jingle 'Don't stink, call Wink', and the Twin Dragon Chinese Restaurant which looked old and derelict enough to have sold chow mein to Ed Jesson. In a dramatic reversal of Nome's vital statistics there were now more churches (thirteen) than saloons (nine), crime was down and drunks may have been physically down, but numerically were about the same or possibly even up. At midday, one lay inert across the step of a liquor store.

And on the beach was the world's largest Red Elephant, a successful one and a sign that Nome was still a major producer of gold. Compared to other strikes Nome ranked equal to the Klondike in terms of output, each with a total yield of around eleven million ounces. Fairbanks produced twice as much as Nome. The Californian Strike yielded five times the quantity of all Alaskan goldfields combined. South Africa currently produces in one year almost as much as the combined output of Alaska and the Yukon Territory over eighty years.

The modern Red Elephant was called Bima (a Malaysian goddess of fortune), a converted tin-mining dredge with fourteen decks and a capability of working the seabed 150 feet below the surface. Bima had only been in Nome for two years and was spending the current winter behind a bulwark of snow sixty feet high, which had been built at the insistence of the insurers against the threat of winter storms which had never materialised. The cost of bulldozing that massive defence was estimated at $250,000 and now it would have to melt away before its captive could be released.

Between mid-June and November Bima would work non-stop and raise 11,000 tons of seabed every twenty-four hours. It had an endless chain of 137 steel buckets, each with a thirty-ton capacity, which emptied gravel and sand into its innards. Gold was digested and waste material ejected. The previous season it had worked a mile offshore in twenty feet of water, hoping to find the gold pushed out by former glaciers. In five months it had recovered 36,000 ounces of gold, and two walruses. One of them, named Big Wally, was immediately caught again after his first release and it was suspected that Big Wally was enjoying 'riding the buckets'. He was taken twenty miles away before being set free. The other walrus was indignant at having been hoisted off the bottom and had to be cautiously herded back to the sea one bucket at a time.

Onshore or offshore, the problem, always, was staying on the level.

Meanwhile, Jim and Suz offered to look after my dogs during my forthcoming excursion to Little Diomede, and a chance meeting introduced me to Donna.

65

DONNA'S SON WAS now seventeen but she had seen little of him because he had been taken into custody as a baby and then adopted by a Mexican family. Her mother had succumbed to a mental illness and both her brothers were in prison, one of them serving a twenty-five year sentence in Kansas. Joe had got caught up in gangs and drug dealing in Anchorage, she said, and she showed me pencil drawings he had done of his two children. He had had to sketch them from memory because Kansas was too far from Alaska for family visits.

Donna Mary was thirty-five, a Yupiq Eskimo from the Yukon delta. For years she had been an alcoholic and a heavy pot-smoker but now her only addiction was chewing tobacco. ('My mother started me on it. I'll never forgive her. I've tried to stop but can't.') She worked for Alcoholics Anonymous and the Regional Health Board. Most of the time she toured schools lecturing on alcohol and drug abuse.

'There *is* hope,' Donna stressed, 'and I'll tell you why. Because I'm here. Because I came back. I know what it's like to touch bottom.'

She pulled back her sleeves and revealed the scars of her suicide attempts. In her innocence she had made the cuts too high.

The children Donna worked with were ordinary village kids and there wasn't one who was not affected by a family alcohol or drug problem.

Even on Little Diomede, I asked? Everywhere, she repeated.

Diomede was dry but the villagers came to Nome for their binges. The island had a bad drug problem. You could buy anything on the streets here, she explained. The scale of the problem had only recently been exposed and admitted. *A People in Peril* had aroused indignation in natives but it had hit home. Now, sometimes, she could see encouraging signs of change.

Donna was small and slight, her somewhat plain face dominated by a large pair of glasses which seemed precariously supported. Her black hair fell straight to her shoulders. At times she looked prim. Her facial expressions registered only extremes, with a sad, dismal look being normal and an occasional flash of smile being the alternative. Her voice was dulled to a bored tone as if excitement had been bleached out, a seen-it-all, done-it-all modulation which sometimes rose in defence or attack. Two years earlier she had undergone an operation for breast cancer and although later tests showed it had been successful, she didn't expect to live longer than another ten years. The rest of her life was to be devoted to fighting alcohol and drugs.

Donna flashed a smile and pressed something into my hand. It was a little beluga, made of ivory. 'You did understand, didn't you? About hope?'

66

THE DIOMEDE ISLANDS are situated exactly in the middle of the Bering Strait where it narrows to a width of less than sixty miles. They stand at the intersection of two divides; on a horizontal axis they mark the boundary of the Chukchi Sea and the Arctic Ocean to the north, and the Bering Sea and the Pacific Ocean to the south; on a vertical axis they straddle the boundary drawn up by the United States–Russia Convention of 1867 which separates east and west.

Little Diomede Island is two miles long, one and a half miles wide, one thousand feet high, and American. It has a flat top and steep, boulder-covered sides. Big Diomede Island is four times larger, the same height, similar in shape, and Russian. They are 2.7 miles apart. Little Diomede has a population of 124 and its only village, Inalik, is sited on the west side of the island. The houses look out over the sea and over the International Date Line to their big neighbour, to tomorrow, to a solitary building at the base of a gully. They know they are being watched. Big Diomede, or Ratmanov, no longer has a native population. It serves as a military base, and the solitary building is the most conspicuous of several observation posts.

In 1728 Vitus Bering came upon these islands on the festival of Saint Diomede, for whom he named them, but he found no cause for celebration. Fog obscured his view and he sailed south, having been deprived of his first glimpse of the Alaskan mainland. History gives the islands scant mention after this. The Russians renamed them the Gvozdev Islands. Appleton's *Guide-Book to Alaska and the NW Coast*, published in 1899, boldly declares that 'telegraph cables and railway bridges have been planned to connect the continents at this point'.

In 1948, at the time the Iron Curtain rose far to the West, travel was banned between the two islands. Eskimos paid little attention to this until 1954 when forty Little Diomeders went over for a quick visit, and disappeared for four months. The Soviet authorities held them in a work camp to show that the ban would now be enforced.

After this incident all communication between the two communities ceased. The Big Diomede villagers were removed to the Siberian mainland, housed in blocks of flats and given reindeer to herd. Friends and relatives split by this arbitrary political line had no news of each other until 7 August 1987, when a thirty-year-old Californian girl broke the ice.

67

LYNNE COX GAVE up her ambition of becoming an Olympic swimmer at an early age when she realised the competitive distances were too short to suit her style. She turned towards ultra-distance feats on quirky waterways. She became the first person to swim the Strait of Magellan, around Cape Horn, and in-and-about the Aleutian Islands; the first woman to swim New Zealand's Cook Strait; and, in two successive years, she was the record-holder for the English Channel. She swims in a standard bathing suit and cap and uses no grease or any other protection against the cold. In attempting to swim the Bering Strait between the Diomedes, Cox faced immersion for two to three hours in water at around 40°F. Water this cold is generally considered to offer a survival time of between three and ten minutes.

Her ability to withstand cold has baffled the medical researchers monitoring her metabolism during swims. Her natural insulation and pre-swim acclimatisation are thought to be key factors. Cox is five feet six inches tall, weighs 180 pounds and has a body temperature half a degree lower than normal. She starts a swim by entering the water gradually. The first stage of hypothermia, a loss of sensation at the extremities, occurs as normal but thereafter her condition deteriorates slowly and she experiences no sudden reduction in body core temperature. Her Diomede swim was to be a first not only for the location, but also for endurance in waters so cold.

Two years of negotiation with the Soviet government preceded the attempt and permission was not granted until a few hours before she planned to enter the water. Two *umiaks*, traditional skin boats, accompanied her, carrying a doctor, a cardiologist, an expert on frostbite, eight Little Diomeders and seven other people.

It was a misty day with visibility dropping to 200 yards but Cox completed the distance in two and a half hours. She could have made the crossing in a shorter time but the current carried her away from a landing spot with a charcoal stove and reception tent erected on the Soviet shore. She covered extra distance to arrive at the appropriate place. Then the first official visitor to Big Diomede since 1948 was welcomed and popped into a heat bag. Waiters served tea, smoked salmon, bread and cakes, and under the supervision of a medical specialist from Moscow, Cox's body temperature was restored to normal within an hour.

More important than the athletic achievement was the attendance of Margaret Guchich and Zoya Ivanova, two Siberian Eskimos formerly of Big Diomede. They had been flown in from their homes in the reindeer region of Chukotkan Lawrentia. By two-way radio they talked to the villagers of Little Diomede and caught up on four decades of lost news.

Within sight of this event, nailed to the store in the heart of Diomede village, was a sign in cyrillic script. МИР. The letters were six feet tall. PEACE.

68

LITTLE DIOMEDE HAS one telephone and its number is 8001. I called from Nome and spoke to a teacher, John Hewson, who invited me to stay at his house and added that any fresh vegetables I brought would be welcome to stay as well. 'You're not thinking of mushing here, are you? . . .' he asked. My original thought had been to mush to Cape Prince of Wales which was only twenty-three miles from Diomede, but local opinion dissuaded me. It was said to be a particularly exposed and treacherous stretch of coastline. I denied any intention of mushing. '. . . Oh good! In that case the vegetables should get through.'

Planes can only fly to Little Diomede in winter, when a landing strip is provided by the frozen sea. The exact site varies each year depending on the suitability of the ice, and a one-way fare from Nome costs $75. There is no boat service and access in summer must be by helicopter, which costs $200 for the same journey. With summer travel expensive, winter visits unpopular and no official guest accommodation, the island sees few strangers. Those who do make it, I was told, are either members of the media or weirdos of the type I heard about in Nulato. One of these called himself Amigo.

Amigo was of Mexican origin and lived in California before he made his winter migration to Diomede in 1987. Diomeders always watch newcomers closely when they emerge from the plane, and they were suspicious when Amigo reached land and then said he had dropped something on the ice. He returned to the runway, which was further out than normal that year, and began running towards Big Diomede. Some Diomeders gave chase on snow machines but turned back when he crossed into Soviet territory. He reached some cliffs and began climbing them, but soon became stuck. Through binoculars they watched guards close in from several sides, and then darkness fell.

Amigo was returned fourteen days later, after diplomatic exchanges. He was delivered by a Soviet helicopter which made no attempt to conceal a cameraman filming the village, and was collected by a plane sent from Juneau. He said he had been treated well. After spending several days in a guardhouse he had been blindfolded and taken to the Siberian mainland. There he was questioned, and women brought him treats such as chocolate.

Such incidents angered the Diomeders, who were anxious to avoid confrontation and hasten the day when visits to their Soviet relatives would be allowed.

So, when I stepped off the plane at Little Diomede, I was being watched from all sides.

Bering Strait did not willingly give itself up to ice, and a bulldozer had had to clear a landing area in a battlefield of pressure ridges. If our twin-engined Navajo had overshot the runway we would have been stopped by the village dump, a tall pile of plastic bags destined to thaw into the sea. Some distance beyond, a lone figure hunched over a fishing hole was occasionally consumed by swirls of wind-whipped snow. All the plane's eight seats had been taken, the seventh passenger occupying the co-pilot's position, and we tumbled out onto the Arctic Ocean amid a gathering of Diomeders on snow machines and three-wheelers. With my arms weighed down by vegetables I was unable to stop a box of cargo from sailing off down the runway. And they said it was a calm day.

Diomede's houses had once been semi-underground structures, pits surrounded by stone walls, covered with driftwood and sods, and entered by a short tunnel. In the late fifties and sixties these were replaced by one-storey box-like dwellings with two or three small rooms. The houses were clustered together on land so steep many were built out on stilts on their seaward sides. One man's doorstep was virtually another man's roof. Five healthy strides took one from door to door. No machines rode the paths of this tiered village, which occupied an area roughly two hundred yards along and a hundred yards up. Above the houses the island's thousand-foot boulder fields swept skywards. The rest of the island was too precipitous for building, and it appeared that the dislocation of a single rock at sea level would bring about the entire island's collapse.

Diomede's school was a large sectional building connected by covered walkways, set above the community at one end. The last Molly Hootch school to be built in Alaska, it was believed to have been the most costly. I made my way up to it, passing the old barge which served as a helipad in summer, and past the storage tanks, the launderette and the wellhouse where water was bought for ten cents a gallon. Above me on a path to the right was the community meeting spot where a group always gathered to discuss events, kill time and watch for weirdos. My path made a turn between six *umiaks*. They rested upside-down on racks and resembled dug-outs, with room for a dozen crew. They had driftwood ribs and were made of walrus skins sewn together. The school door opened into another world, one hundred degrees warmer, where children were watching a computer screen and a notice-board displayed a score of lyrical names: Soolooks, Oquilluks, Tocktoos, Teayoumiks and Paniptchuks, and Maude Moses, Clara Ione, Carla Kakoona, Tina Bekoolook, Tom Sagoonick, Aaron Mute, Dusty Gillespie, Angel Tom and Kimberley Alaska.

I found John in the gymnasium with some of the older pupils. They were practising for an inter-school sports contest on the lines of the Eskimo–Indian Olympics which took place each July in Fairbanks. All the disciplines were traditional, and because of the size of the meeting houses in which they were formerly contested, their aim was to test strength and endurance in a confined area. (These Olympics had a winter equivalent which featured such events as a 1,500 metre snowshoe race.) The Sitting Jump required a person to kneel with toes straight out behind and, in a single movement, to leap for distance. In the One-Footed Kick, contestants had to leap, kick a suspended ball, and land, using the same leg throughout. The ball was subsequently raised until it was too high for all but the winner. The Arm Reach worked along similar lines, only athletes had to reach up for the ball while balanced in the posture of a one-armed press-up. Press-ups also formed the basis of the Seal Hop, the human seals bouncing along on their knuckles for the greatest distance. I looked around for the Battering Ram Game which Nelson had observed a century earlier, but its day was past. Its effects were still being duplicated, however, in this roomful of boys and girls kicking, reaching, Stick Pulling, Ear Pulling, Wrist Hauling and Scissor Jumping. No wonder the survivors were able to kill whales.

'Welcome to Diomede,' said John, slightly breathless after the Toe Kick, which required a long leap onto a stick lying on the ground. The stick had to be neatly nudged out of the way, with both toes, while landing. Despite a heavy midriff John was apparently quite a Toe Kicker. He was in his late thirties, bearded, enthusiastic and forceful. He wiped his brow and replaced his glasses. 'ALL RIGHT, YOU GUYS! That'll do for today.'

He led me outside to the teachers' quarters, through a cut in a snowbank and up a grid catwalk to the next tier of the village. A thieving wind tugged at me and my vegetables. 'We're kinda lucky here. We've got central heating and plumbing. The rest of the village cook on Colemans with Blazo, and in the real cold their homes never get warm. Not enough snow to insulate against the wind.' Behind the house five polar bear skins were draped over a rack. Above them, where the boulder field suddenly turned steeper, was a collection of crosses.

'Is that the graveyard up there?'

'That's it. There's not much you can do here. Just pile a lot of rocks on top.'

I was introduced to John's wife, Pat, who was also a teacher, and to their eight-year-old son, the only white boy on the island. When sitting, Andrew was the same size as a walrus skull and tusks which were propped up in a corner. The tusks were three feet long and curved in perfect symmetry to touch at their tips. John and Pat had been on Diomede for three years and planned to stay on for a few more.

'It's an unusual life here but there's all the normal problems. The island's been dry for ten years but booze gets brought in and people head off to Nome to hit the bottle. I could name several kids whose brains have been fried with drugs, and we got family feuds ... but then, who hasn't? We're like anywhere else, no better, no worse.'

He reiterated the remarks teachers had made all along my journey, how there were times when teaching in Alaska was a soul-destroying occupation, how teachers went back to villages where they had taught and found their former pupils were now wife-beaters and drinkers. Their teaching had changed nothing and the feeling of failure was immense. 'If we judge these kids by Outside standards, then few are going to be successful. I think the emphasis has to change from an academic curriculum to one concentrating on creating technological and manual skills. But above all I see our job as teaching them good values. It's hard because the role models in their families are so poor. The hope is in changing a generation to create a better generation.'

'Reading is a particular problem we've found here,' Pat added. 'Some kids are five grades below what they should be. Reading has never been a popular activity and is not encouraged. And televisions run all day in this village.' She explained that Diomede's only telephone was at the cable television office. When a call came in for an islander the television operator was able to interrupt a programme and announce 'Phone call for Joe Nassuk', and the message came over every set. So people kept their televisions on all day for fear of missing a message.

Despite the influence of television it seemed to me that with their old understanding of how to live in this environment coupled with modern technology, people were surely better equipped than ever for life on Diomede. 'When technology breaks down here, do the islanders easily slip back into their former self-sufficiency?'

John shook his head. 'Not really. The older people obviously cope better, but no one finds it easy to do without things they've got used to. And attitudes definitely change.' He cited the case of a fire a few years ago. Once the shout of 'FIRE!' would have had everyone rushing to help. On this occasion the fire was in the generating plant and electricity was cut off as a result. No electricity, no siren. When the shout of 'FIRE!' went up, no one moved. No one believed it, because the siren hadn't gone off.

'If you want to hear about the changes here, you should go and visit the Little Sisters,' Pat suggested. 'And old Albert. He tells great stories.'

69

'IF YOU WANT to hear my stories, you got to pay twenty thousand dollars.'

'Twenty thousand! . . .'

'Yep. Then you can go write a book and get your money back.'

Albert was frail and gaunt. He was seventy and had a thin moustache, and gaps in an assortment of yellow and silver teeth. He left it up to the listener to work out if he was joking or not; neither expression nor tone gave anything away. He was lying on his bed recovering from flu.

His fee was quickly forgotten. Albert said he was one of perhaps only three islanders who could trim an oil lamp. This used to be a woman's work and it took a lot of practice to learn the technique and keep a lamp burning smoothly. They used seal oil and wicks of moss picked from Diomede's rocks. Lamps provided heat and also the only source of light, for pit houses never had windows. Many evenings were spent around the lamp telling stories.

He explained that long ago it was believed that when an animal died its *inua* — spirit — assumed the form of an unborn creature of the same or similar species. The same was true of man, and it was possible for a man's *inua* to enter an animal or an animal's to enter a man. No one could ever be sure of a creature's real identity, and inappropriate behaviour could easily cause offence or attract bad luck. A hunter had to observe strict rituals and treat all animals with respect so that they would return and provide him with food.

'A Little Diomede hunter and his wife lived over there,' he began, pointing to the north end of the island where there had once been another settlement. 'They had no children but one day the hunter returned with a small polar bear' — he held his hands twelve inches apart — 'and told his wife this would be their child. They raised it and it grew very large. One day it walked to Big Diomede and was killed by the people there. The hunter was so angry he went to pay back his son's death. He hid by a path on Big Diomede and killed six or seven men, the first to come along. Then he went to fish for blue cod over there' — he waved a hand towards the southern end of Big Diomede — 'because it was good fishing there. But Big Diomede hunters surrounded him and he was shot with arrows, so much the body couldn't lie flat on the ice. People from Little Diomede heard of this and came to return the body to his widow. She carefully plucked out all the arrows sticking from him but there were bits of arrows left inside. So she rubbed him with seal oil and this drew out the bits and he came back to life ...'

He paused.

'What happened next?'

'I'm not telling you unless you give me twenty thousand dollars.'

70

CHARLES EUGENE FOUCAULD, who died in a crudely-built hermitage near the summit of Mount Assekrem in the Algerian Sahara, was a French aristocrat from a wealthy family. Born in Strasbourg in 1858, he joined the army and was part of a force sent to Algeria in 1881 to suppress an uprising. The country captivated him. He led exploratory expeditions, made a study of oases, and was profoundly affected by the Muslims' devotion to daily worship. Gradually he developed a yearning for a simple, aesthetic life.

In 1890 Foucauld went to Syria and became a Trappist monk. The severity of monastic life did not impress him, and after seven years he still found it too rich. The simple life of Jesus was his goal, and he moved on to an anchoritic existence in Nazareth. Somewhat against his will but influenced by others, he joined the priesthood in 1901. Yet North Africa still ran in his veins. Le père de Foucauld was one of the first French civilians to enter Algeria after its subjugation. He built a hermitage near a disused fort of the French Foreign Legion and led a life of prayer and study among the Tuaregs. In 1916 a group of rebels became suspicious of his motives and believed he might be hoarding arms. They found none, but a sixteen-year-old youth panicked and shot him.

A book written about Foucauld's life inspired the founding of an organisation to continue his work as a passive missionary. The Little Brothers of Jesus were founded in Algeria in 1933, and six years later their counterparts, the Little Sisters, came into being. They live in small groups in communities outside or at the lowest end of money economies, occupying ordinary dwellings and supporting themselves by manual labour. Theirs is a policy of non-interference. By leading quiet, ordinary lives and maintaining a Christian presence in a community, they hope an acceptance of their beliefs will spread.

It is the opposite approach to shouting into a microphone.

71

EVERYONE CALLED THEM simply the Little Sisters. They lived in a modest hut which was entered by a door set above ground level and small enough to exclude some of the gale which intruded on its opening. It was a single step from the main path into their hall. They responded to my knock with smiles and an immediate invitation to tea, in a way which would have persuaded the hundredth visitor of the day that he was a unique event. A few minutes later Father Jakobsen arrived. I had met him on the plane and learned that he was a Jesuit priest, based in Nome but with responsibilities in many outlying villages. A jovial, sympathetic man whom I'm sure Stuck would have liked, he took off his boots because both Father Jakobsen and the ceiling were six feet four inches high.

The Little Sisters were in their late fifties and before coming to the Arctic they had trained at Touggourt in the Sahara. L. S. Nobuko was from Japan but she had lived on Diomede since 1956. She was petite and reserved. Recently, Japanese television had invited her back to Tokyo for an interview – from Touggourt to Diomede to Tokyo, a more bizarre journey could scarcely be imagined – and she'd found the experience 'interesting', but her life was here on Diomede. L. S. Damiene displayed the same gentleness but was more outgoing by nature. She had come to Diomede a few years after her companion, and still spoke with a strong accent of her native Alsace-Lorraine.

'Try some of these cakes,' L. S. Nobuko said. 'We make them with murre eggs. They have a fishy flavour, but we like them.' She passed them round. A frying pan of polar bear meat was quietly sizzling on the cooker.

'Do you hunt polar bears as well as murre eggs?' I asked.

The question was not well timed, and L. S. Damiene choked on her cake. 'No,' she laughed, 'we are given presents of meat and sometimes we trade fish or other things for it. I think twelve bears have been taken this winter. One was shot here in town on Christmas morning from the porch of a hunter's house.'

Only natives could hunt polar bear and although there was no restriction on numbers, pelts could not be sold unless they had been made into clothes or showed signs of traditional workmanship. The polar bear was still the most respected of Eskimo game despite the advantage given to hunters by snow machines and more effective rifles. Trying to decide which applications of progress should be permitted to hunters and which were unfair was a controversial issue in the Arctic. The celebrated Eskimo blanket toss – sending a hunter as high as twenty feet into the air on a skin 'trampoline', which was the original way of searching for game on a flat landscape – was unquestionably outmoded, but was using spotter planes to hunt for whales taking things too far the other way? My three companions proffered no opinion, for they had found their peace among these hunters, and comment was restricted to some of the curious marriages between old and new, such as walrus-skin boats with Yamaha outboards.

Father Jakobsen turned the conversation to a technological advance of a different nature. He had heard that telephones were going to be installed in Diomede homes.

'Yes, it's been talked about but I don't know if it'll happen. I rather hope not, personally. I'm afraid people will stop visiting each other.'

The Little Sisters had seen many changes over the years. The best of them was the building of the school, which had kept the older schoolchildren on the island, the gymnasium providing an excellent meeting hall. Yet the school had brought other problems. As elsewhere, the children now acquired little experience of town or city life and the world beyond Diomede became more intimidating. Most youngsters enjoyed the hunting life here but didn't see how it could offer them a future. Diomede's housing shortage was acute, with little space for expansion. Marriage prospects appeared gloomy, and were further aggravated by the closeness of family blood lines and a surplus of males.

'Not many young people marry now,' Father Jakobsen explained. 'A side-effect of the welfare payments is that they offer quite a financial incentive against marriage. The elders don't approve of the young people living together, but they've had to accept it. They call it having a "play-wife" or "play-husband".'

Although the traditional view of marriage had changed, other customs were maintained, such as the passing on of a Christian name to perpetuate the memory of the original holder. Eskimo names were also given, but more as nicknames, and they were usually thought up later in life when a child had displayed a peculiar characteristic.

'Do you know Moses?' Father asked. 'He's a marvellous character. You should go and speak to him. He's a fine ivory carver.'

Ivory carving was experiencing a boom, but native dances were on the decline. Both sexes danced and sang, but only men beat drums. These were made of walrus intestine and shaped like a large tambourine without the jingles. Each drum was flapped like a fan and its underside made to strike a curved stick. The stick could be adjusted so that both wooden frame and skin sounded simultaneously. Dances involved slow precise movements and were enactments of stories. Women maintained a sitting posture while 'dancing' with their upper bodies. The elders still knew the movements well and the previous year two women had performed the Eagle dance, which had not been rehearsed for five years; their synchronisation had been faultless.

The young were not learning these dances except in vague form, under John and Pat's guidance. Eskimo teaching methods had always been blunt and harsh, making fun of mistakes and tending towards humiliation as a means of arousing determination in the pupil. Children were now less prepared to accept such treatment and preferred not knowing to the indignity of learning. I asked if it was the same with the language. It was Father Jakobsen who replied.

'Unfortunately, yes. I think the youngest fluent speaker of Inupiaq is thirty-seven. Now the young only learn words when working in the *umiaks*, as all the boat jargon is in Inupiaq. I'd like to try and copy the example of the Nelson Islanders. They're managing to bring about a small Yupik revival. They have a lay minister who leads prayers and hymns in Yupik, and the Catholic Father there wears vestments which mix Christian motifs with elements of native custom. My problem is that so little has been translated into Inupiaq. People here often say to me, "We look to Nelson Island to know who we are". I'd like them to say that of Diomede.'

Murre cakes merged into avocados, polar bear and blueberry pie. Father Jakobsen was unable to stay as he had to prepare for a quintuple baptism. His visits were infrequent and most religious duties had to be delayed and then performed in multiples. The avocados, the Little Sisters explained, were a treat, a present from Father Jakobsen, the bear had been cooked for the usual five hours, and the blueberries had been picked on the mainland near Teller. We had no sooner finished our meal than a man began walking about the village ringing a handbell.

'Church. Are you coming?'

It was only a matter of two minutes' walk but one had to be careful for it was easy to stray from the path and end up on someone's roof. The church conformed to the standard building style, a wooden cuboid jutting out from the hillside and held level by stilts – the terrain and elements tolerated no other architecture. Its windows yielded the finest view of any place of worship in Christendom, of that madly sculptured sea and the buttresses of Big Diomede. About twenty villagers attended.

Although he had plenty of headroom, Father Jakobsen conducted the service in his socks. He talked at length on the responsibilities of parents, how the little life in their hands needed their sustenance, their care, their love; how their child depended on them for a healthy development and instruction in good values. He expanded this into the importance of leading an exemplary life ... and then hesitated. From the solemn faces before him, he realised he might be striking too stern a note. He beamed generously and back-pedalled. 'It's a *wonderful*, awesome task.'

A lesson followed, read by a teenager wearing a T-shirt advertising 'Canada's LABATTE'S BEER/BIÈRE'. Then Father Jakobsen continued, reading the standard baptismal introduction: 'These white garments we wear ...'. It was tricky. The five mothers and children up front were wearing everyday clothes. No one was wearing white. Father Jakobsen broke off and explained that sometimes the recipients were dressed in white, for white symbolised purity, innocence, new life, happiness ... He checked himself. Tricky again. He didn't want to emphasise any colour distinctions. He beamed afresh. 'This white garment I wear ...'

I found in his performance an extraordinary display of sensitivity. There was no hint of condescension in his attitude. He was a compassionate mediator, aware that his tools were not wholly appropriate for the job. I changed places there and then from white to native, and tried to see the situation from the other side. I wondered how the white world would have reacted if Jesus had been born black, or an Eskimo? Would it have so readily identified with Him and His cause? I admired all the more such people as were around me then for having been able to accommodate a hero from another country, culture and race.

Water was sprinkled, some of the babies cried, and a blast of wind rearranged the snowscape.

72

'GOING FISHING, HUH?' Moses Milligrock asked.

'Yes. Thought I'd have a shot.' He watched me go down to an area about one hundred yards offshore where I had seen other figures fishing the previous day. The Little Sisters had lent me a line with three feathered hooks and an eight-foot pole with a chisel point –

they called it a 'toothpick'. I thought I would pay them back for the meal with a basket of blue cod. When I reached the fishing area there was no sign of where the previous fishing holes had been. Everything had been refrozen and rearranged. I set to work chipping out my own hole.

After strenuous exertions I had dug a hole wide enough for a good-sized cod and four feet deep, and convinced myself I must have chosen a spot with an iceberg underneath. Another trial dig elsewhere produced the same results. I was perishing. For three days the community windsock had not fallen below the horizontal and polar bear skins had shuffled endless jigs below their racks. I gave up.

Moses happened by. 'How many fish you catch?'

'I've been out there an hour. I haven't even found the water yet.'

He told me to keep digging. I tried again and discovered the Bering Sea at four and a half feet. My hole filled up to within four inches of the top. Bailing out bits of ice was the worst part. I lowered my lures, jiggled them about, and within half an hour had landed six bullheads. It seemed to be a bad year for blue cod. Bullheads were covered in gorgeous blotches and stripes and had butterfly wings, but they were mostly mouth. Big ones were kept for eating, but tiddlers were used for crab bait. I threw mine back and went to talk to Moses about whales.

He had an enormous pot belly which forced him to sit back from his work bench. A vice clamped a miniature kayak whose cockpit he was smoothing off with a hack-saw. Half an Eskimo, holding a harpoon, sat nearby ready to be glued into place, polished, and sold for fifty dollars. Moses was about sixty and had an Eskimo's traditional propensity for a quick jibe.

'I think you're the worst fisherman Diomede has had.'

'But I caught six bullheads.'

'Pah! Women's work. I wouldn't trust you with a harpoon.'

'No, I wouldn't either. Do you use harpoons much nowadays?'

'We use them for walrus but usually we shoot them first. Harpoon stops them from sinking. We harpoon whale if we can, but we haven't killed one here for a long time. Maybe this year, though. This year Wales have a quota for two and they give us one.' He said it was dangerous work. Few Eskimos know how to swim. They never have a chance of learning and, furthermore, swimming is pointless when

237

can survive more than briefly in such cold water. They still use *umiaks* because they are manoeuvrable, seaworthy and light enough to be lifted over ice. They are made with female walrus skins because these shrink more tightly around the frame than male ones. Skins are scraped, allowed to dry for weeks to let the hair fall out, soaked for three days and then sewn over a wooden frame. In the old days driftwood would have been used for the frame. The great danger in the past arose when *umiaks* were blown far out to sea, because if the skins were not dried, after two days they stretched and detached from the frame. Nowadays the skins are covered in pitch. They have to be replaced every two years.

There is food to be found in every season, and Moses ran through the hunter's calendar. In spring, seals (bearded and ringed) and beluga appear in the weakening sea ice. After breakup, grey and bowhead whales migrate past, sieving the plankton-rich waters of the strait, and walrus head north to their breeding grounds. Summer brings sea-birds by the million – puffins, fulmars, guillemots (murres), auklets, cormorants, geese and ducks – and they nest on the Diomedes. Winter is a leaner time, when only polar bears approach, occasionally, and the predominantly hunting Little Diomeders turn to fishing, 'woman's work', and pull up king crabs, bullheads and, supposedly, blue cod.

'Do you feel threatened by the Russians on Big Diomede?'

'No, we don't think about them much any more. Anyhow, we got National Guard here.' He allowed himself a chuckle. The National Guard was seen more as an afternoon with pay than a defence force. But he remembered that incident in 1954 when forty Little Diomeders disappeared and how they returned 'lookin' kinda skinny, as if they hadn't eat.' Before that, visits between the two islands had been frequent. The successes of hunts were shared. Little Diomeders went over to pick two types of edible greens and four roots which were not found on their island.

No, he didn't feel intimidated by Russia, but abused by both Russia and his own country. He repeated what I had heard often on Diomede, that Washington didn't know anything about this island and didn't care. Washington and Moscow were both alien places. Just names. The Diomede Eskimos had never fought a war, they said. They had never done anyone any harm. Then why, they asked, had their islands been split and why had they been the ones to suffer? Resentment remained but the three great Eskimo traits – patience, acceptance and adaptability – had prevailed.

'Phone call for Moses Milligrock', the television announced. Moses held up the ivory paddler, turned it against the light and put it down. 'Phone call,' he said, and hurried out.

I met him again, shortly before leaving, and he spoke as if something had been troubling him. 'Maybe you only see problems here. Maybe you say bad things about us. You don't know what it is like to ride *umiak* after whale, to see the ice go and the birds come. You don't know about bear or seal. You cannot know, and I'm sorry.'

The Navajo took to the air and made a sweep round the island. Humpbacked clouds sat on Little Diomede's top and sagged into its gullies. The village looked like flotsam thrown up by a storm, and yet defiant among the rocks stacked up around it. Then we were over the sea ice, cracked and darkly opaque along the edges where it was fragmenting into open water. And finally over land again. It was too fast; I couldn't adjust to seeing everything rush past underneath.

Finally we approached Cape Rodney and I saw sled tracks on the tundra flats. I couldn't take my eyes off them. They were the signs I had been following for six months, for 2,000 miles. I wondered where they led to, and felt defeated. They taunted me, so many miles left untravelled and so much of Alaska left unseen. And I felt cheated because this moment should have been a beginning. I had discovered dogs, myself, and a nomad's life.

Spring was coming and, with it, an overwhelming sense of loss.

73

'ALASKA – THE LAST frontier.'

The words appeared together with monotonous – almost obligatory – regularity, as if the one was incomplete without the others, as if the state had a double-barrelled name.

This was the image portrayed in the state song, bandied about in the tourist brochures, in the advertisements of those with Alaskana to sell, on the banner head of *Alaska* magazine. The image was cherished because this state crept into an individual's consciousness and became personal, it still *appeared* so vast and empty that simply being in it instilled a feeling of uniqueness.

The expression irked me. It betrayed an ocean mentality, an assumption of immensity in which one could do, and had a right to do, what the hell one liked. It was the cant phrase of newcomers who knew no better and of exploiters who had yet to start or still to finish. You heard it in the Lower 48, and you heard it in Alaskan cities. You heard it from those who gazed through double-glazing and willed themselves into the stature of pioneers, and from those who saw in Alaska's wilderness a venal feature, another consumer-friendly slogan, another estate agent's asterisk.

You never heard it from those who knew the place. You never heard 'the Last Frontier' mentioned in Bush Alaska.

Old attitudes persist. The desire to know the land remains the desire to exploit it. Before Oil, Alaska was always bigger than the boom; After Oil, the imbalance seems to have swung the other way.

'In a country in which the future of an entire landscape is at stake,' wrote Lopez, referring to the Arctic and sub-Arctic, 'the racial, social, and intellectual barriers remain. The good minds still do not find each other often enough.'

74

WITH THE DOGS brought to a halt, I listened to their rhythmic panting. Strong at first, the sounds slowed, coalesced and faded.

Ice lay heaped in disorder to our left and formed a wall along the shore. Sledge Island rode the horizon and mimicked our profile as we rested on Cape Rodney. Around us willows raised their harried growth through the snow. They made sallies across the tundra flats until they reached hogback hills to our right and disappeared. The world seemed at one, an alliance of whiteness, silence and the light of a shrouded sun. It embraced us too, as a part of the scene now rather than as a foreign intrusion. And in such moments of quiet, when communication is deepest, I saw most clearly the interplay of forces which bonded together myself, eight dogs and the great land.

Alf was sitting testing the air. It carried the salty tang of breakup. Kavik lay sprawled in his chaise-longue pose, waiting for his chest to be rubbed. Nanook was dozing, using Sisco as a pillow. Sensor and Duran were curled up, and Rosco was rolling. How he loved to roll!

The eighth dog was still on her feet. She stood with her face to the sun and her eyes closed. I only had to say the word and she would take us anywhere.

EPILOGUE

Seven of my team flew back with me from Nome to Fairbanks and were then delivered to various destinations.

Of the four dogs lent to me by Joee Redington:

SILVER stayed in Nome. She now leads a recreational team, and is scheduled to have pups soon. I sold her (on Joee's behalf) to the Suz mentioned in the text, and could not have left her in better hands.

ALF returned to Manley and became a pup trainer. As I write he is preparing to run this year's Iditarod as a command leader of the poodle team.

SENSOR returned to Manley and joined Joee's squad of sprint racers. Subsequently he was sold to a musher on the Kuskokwim river.

DURAN was sold soon after his return to Manley. He went to California to participate in freight-racing (distance events in which sleds are loaded with fifty pounds per dog).

ROSCO, NANOOK, SISCO and KAVIK – the four dogs I owned – I gave back to their original owner in North Pole. He was missing them as much as I am now.

APPENDIX

	Equipment	Quantity
Tent	(Blacks G. C. 'Major'; no poles, 8 pegs)	1
Sleeping bag	(Mountain Equipment, 'Redline')	1
Insulating mat	('Therma-rest' – caribou skin is better)	1
Tarpaulin	(= groundsheet, plastic)	1
Rucksack	(Karrimor; adapted to clip to sled)	1
Rucksack	(small day pack)	1
Carry-all	(yachting bag type)	1
Space blanket		1
Bow saw	(21")	1
Spare saw blade		1
Axe	(small)	1
Cooker	(Coleman double burner)	1
Fuel can (full)	(1 US gal., plastic)	1
Cooking pot and lid	(16 qrt, for mixing dog food)	1
Cooking pot	(5 gal. can, for melting snow)	1
Saucepan	(1 qrt, 1 for my food, 1 dog dipper)	2
Mess tin and lid	(1 qrt)	1
Hot pan tongs		1
Spoon		1
Swiss Army knife	(inc. tin opener, tweezers, scissors)	1
Large knife	(sheath, attached to sled)	1
Thermos	(1 litre, unbreakable)	1
'Cooler'	(Coleman; 16 quart, plus special lid)	1
Mapcase		1
Maps		
Compass		1
Whistle		1
Sewing kit	(dental floss for thread)	1
Headlamp		1
Spare torch		1
Batteries		20–30

Hot pads		20
Tarpaper		
Matches	(waterproofed – kept in several places)	lots
Candles		lots
Nylon cord	(1/8th inch)	30 yds
More cord		25 yds
Parachute cord		50 yds
Elastic rope	(1/8th inch)	4 ft
Wire	(1 mm)	8 ft
Duct tape		6 yds
Tools	(straight s'driver, Phillips s'driver, spanners to fit all bolt sizes, 1/2" and 1/4" fids, pliers, large eye darning needle)	
Spare bolts and screws	(all sizes), and snaps	lots
Camera gear	(body, battery pack, 28–70 mm, 70–210 mm, flash, accessories, film)	
Diary/writing gear		
Money		
Passport		
Toothbrush/paste		
Glacier goggles		1 pr
My first aid	(lipsalve, sunblock, vaseline, elastoplast, lint)	
Dogs' first aid	Vetrap bandages	2
	Tetracycline (gen. antibiotic)	50 pills
	Bio-sol M (diarrhoea)	50
	Corticosteroid (for injection, used in conjunction with antibiotics)	10 mls
	Syringes and needles	8
	10 cc syringe (for force drinking)	1
	Electrolyte powder (for dehydration)	1 pkt
	Asprins (Advil)	150
	Foot ointment (pink)	1 jar
	Foot ointment (yellow-green)	1 jar
Dog bowls	(aluminium)	8
Dog bootees		100
Dog belly jackets		4
Spare harnesses		2
Spare harness webbing		4 ft
Spare tuglines	(ready made up)	2
Spare necklines	(ready made up)	4
Spare gangline	(ready made sections, nylon)	4
Clothes		

Wearing:	Thick socks	1 pr
	Bunny boots and gaiters	1 pr
	Cotton long johns (track suit btms)	1 pr
	Corduroy trousers	1 pr
	Polypropylene (thick) shirt	1
	Thin sleeveless wool pullover	1
	Thin sleeved wool pullover	1
	Thick Icelandic pullover	1
Packed:	Parka (down-filled, wolf ruff)	1
	Mukluks (moose hide, 2 felt liners and felt inner sole)	1 pr
	Fleece overtrousers (army)	1 pr
	Fleece long johns (ex oil rig)	1 pr
	Thin polypropylene vest	1
	Thick shirt (army)	1
	Polo-neck pullover (brown)	1
	U/pants	1 pr
	Spare thick wool socks	1 pr
	Spare thick wool socks (kept 'dry' for mukluks)	2 prs
	Thin polypropylene socks	2 prs
	Huge sheepskin over mittens	1 pr
	Goretex Mittens (Mountain Equipment)	1 pr
	Thick fleece gloves (polarfleece)	1 pr
	Work gloves	4 prs
	Thin polypropylene glove liners	2 prs
	Wool glove liners	3 prs
	Thin surgical rubber gloves	3 prs
	Wool balaclavas (nylon inner lining)	2
	Nose/headband (nylon inner lining)	1
	Scarf	1
	Poncho (for rain)	1
	Face cloth (to act as towel)	1

GLOSSARY

Aleut	a native of the Aleutian Islands
ANCSA	Alaska Native Claims Settlement Act
Athabascan	(also Athapascan) an Indian of the Alaskan Interior
berm	ledge, bank or mound
cheechako	tenderfoot, greenhorn (used by Hudson's Bay Company traders)
colour	mining term for particles of gold
dock	weed (*Rumex*) with large coarse leaves
flume	artificial channel for water
Haida	a coastal Indian of South-east Alaska
Inupiaq	language of northern Eskimos
kicker	outboard engine (boats)
logan bread	loaf made with flour, eggs, kelp, dried fruit, nuts, sunflower seeds, peanut oil, honey and molasses
mukluks	knee-high boots, made of sealskin or moose hide and bound on with thongs. They are lightweight and warm (and, if sealskin, also waterproof)
muskeg	flattish region of marsh or swampland
Okies	the inhabitants of Oklahoma. Many Okies and Texans (sometimes lumped together as Oklatexans) migrated to Alaska to work on the oil pipeline
placer	superficial deposit from which gold can be washed
rocker	apparatus, only one step more advanced than the prospector's pan, for washing gold out of small quantities of paydirt

246

set	arrangement of bait and trap
slough	backwater, marshland creek
sluicebox	trough for separating gold from sand and gravel
snow machine	snowmobile, snowgo, skido
Tlingit	a coastal Indian of South-east Alaska
travois	pair of trailing poles, to which luggage was lashed, dragged from the saddle and used as a 'trailer' by certain North American Indians
Yupik	language of southern Eskimos